Look Your Best with Excel 4 for Windows™

Rick Winter
Grant Tonkin
Cheryl Brumbaugh
Patty Winter

que

Look Your Best with Excel 4 for Windows™

Copyright © 1992 by Que® Corporation.

Library of Congress Catalog No.: 92-060683

ISBN: 1-56529-930-6

95 94 93 92   4 3 2

Interpretation of the printing code: the rightmost double-digit number is the year of the book's printing; the rightmost single-digit number, the number of the book's printing. For example, a printing code of 92-1 shows that the first printing of the book occurred in 1992.

Screen reproductions in this book were created using Collage Plus from Inner Media, Inc., Hollis, NH.

Look Your Best with Excel 4 for Windows is based on Excel 4.0 for Windows.

Publisher: Lloyd J. Short

Associate Publisher: Rick Ranucci

Product Development Manager: Thomas H. Bennett

Book Designers: Scott Cook and Michele Laseau

Production Analyst: Mary Beth Wakefield

Graphic Imaging Specialist: Dennis Sheehan

Production Team: Claudia Bell, Paula Carroll, Michelle Cleary, Brook Farling, Joy Dean Lee, Laurie Lee, Jay Lesandrini, Caroline Roop, Linda Seifert, Sandra Shay, Lisa Wilson, Phil Worthington, Christine Young

Dedications

I would like to thank my new son, Danny, who has been a joy, an inspiration, and a cause of the need for the money.

　　—Rick Winter

A very special thanks to Marilyn, whose support and encouragement make anything possible.

　　—Grant Tonkin

I'd like dedicate this book to my father. He introduced me to computers and, in particular, to spreadsheets. He has been my mentor and computer confidant. Thanks, Dad!

　　—Cheryl Brumbaugh

A big wonderful thanks to my daughter, Molly, whose patience and support have been incredible.

　　—Patty Winter

Credits

Product Director
Joyce J. Nielsen

Production Editor
Fran Blauw

Editors
Diana Moore
Anne Owen

Editorial Assistant
Melissa Keegan

Senior Acquisitions Editor
Chris Katsaropoulos

Technical Editor
Donald A. Buchanan, a Microsoft Excel consulting partner whose consulting business, based in Burbank, California, specializes in custom applications development using Microsoft Excel.

Composed in 1Stone Serif and MCPdigital by Que Corporation.

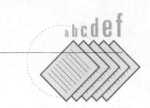

About the Authors

Rick Winter is a senior partner at PRW Computer Services. He has trained more than 1,500 adults on personal computers. He is the coauthor of *Q&A QueCards*, published by Que Corporation. He is the revision author of Que's *1-2-3 QuickStart Release 2.3*, *1-2-3 QuickStart Release 2.4*, and *1-2-3 QuickStart Release 3.1*. Mr. Winter is also the revision author of *MicroRef Quick Reference Guide to Lotus 1-2-3 Release 3.0* and *MicroRef Quick Reference Guide to Lotus 1-2-3 Release 2.2*. He is the revision script writer of Video Professor *Lotus 1-2-3 Version 2.2 and 3.0 Level I* and *Lotus 1-2-3 Version 2.2 and 3.0 Level II*, and script writer of Video Professor *Lotus 1-2-3 Version 2.2 and 3.0 Level III*. Other technical editing projects include MicroRef's Q&A and SuperCalc 5 keyboard templates, quick reference guides for WordPerfect 5.0 and dBASE IV, and on-line help for WordPerfect 5.0, Symphony, and DisplayWrite 4.

Grant Tonkin is a computer consultant who lives in Denver, Colorado and works throughout the Rocky Mountain region. He does system design, programming, and teaching. Most of his teaching is done in the private sector, but he has also taught at several universities. He is an owner and instructor at the Training Connection, a full-service PC training center located in Denver.

Cheryl Brumbaugh has worked with spreadsheets since 1976, and learned spreadsheets on Visicalc. After receiving a degree in Elementary Education, she worked four years as a computer specialist. She taught kindergarten through 8th grade. In 1988, she switched careers to work for Random Access, Inc., as a Macintosh computer trainer. Ms. Brumbaugh has trained users in applications from beginning Macintosh to high-end desktop publishing, graphics, and animation packages. She is now the training manager, and Training Access has grown from two training facilities to six facilities in Denver; one facility in Grand Junction, Colorado; and one facility in Phoenix, Arizona. Ms. Brumbaugh enjoys computers—especially computer graphics and computer animation. She is presently working with Macromind Director and its lingo-scripting capabilities.

Patty Winter is a senior partner at PRW Computer Services. She has trained more than 1,000 adults in the art of using personal computers. She is the coauthor of Que Corporation's *Q&A QueCards*. She established and is President of Colorado Q&A User Group. Ms. Winter is also very active in her daughter Molly's life.

Trademark Acknowledgments

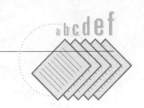

Que Corporation has made every effort to supply trademark information about company names, products, and services mentioned in this book. Trademarks indicated below were derived from various sources. Que Corporation cannot attest to the accuracy of this information.

Ami Professional is a trademark of SAMNA Corporation.

AutoCAD is a registered trademark of Autodesk, Inc.

Bitstream is a registered trademark of Bitstream, Inc.

CorelDRAW! is a trademark of Corel Systems Corporation.

Freelance Plus is a registered trademark of Lotus Development Corporation.

Harvard Graphics is a registered trademark of Software Publishing Corporation.

Helvetica, Times, and Palatino are registered trademarks of Allied Corporation.

HiJaak is a registered trademark of INSET Systems Inc.

HP and LaserJet are registered trademarks of Hewlett-Packard Co.

Microsoft is a registered trademark, and Windows is a trademark of Microsoft Corporation.

Microsoft TrueType is a registered trademark of Apple Computer Corporation.

PC Paintbrush is a registered trademark of ZSoft Corporation.

PostScript is a registered trademark of Adobe Systems Incorporated.

Windows Draw is a trademark of Micrografx, Inc.

WordPerfect is a registered trademark of WordPerfect Corporation.

Trademarks of other products mentioned in this book are held by the companies producing them.

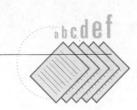

Table of Contents

3 Using Excel To Enter and Edit Text　　　59

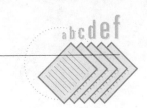

6 Editing and Enhancing Charts 131

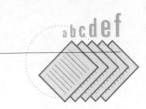

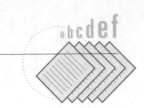

Introduction

If you have been using Excel for some time but want to create more professional-looking output, Look Your Best with Excel 4 for Windows *is for you. This book's unique approach details both the procedures for enhancing your worksheets and a background of why you need to use these procedures.*

Look Your Best with Excel 4 for Windows offers many design suggestions for your projects and provides examples of well-designed and poorly designed documents.

This book covers Microsoft Excel 3 and 4. You also can use this book with the two most recent versions of Microsoft Windows—3.0 and 3.1.

How Is This Book Organized?

The chapters in *Look Your Best with Excel 4 for Windows* give you a background in desktop publishing, show you how to use the desktop-publishing features of Excel, and indicate how to create specific kinds of projects such as reports, forms, and slides.

Part I: An Introduction to Excel and Spreadsheet Publishing

Chapter 1, "Using Excel as a Desktop Publisher," defines desktop publishing with reference to Excel. This chapter summarizes Excel's capabilities, including WYSIWYG, fonts, formats, word processing, charting, and working with other programs. The chapter also is an overview of the types of projects you can create with Excel.

Chapter 2, "Understanding Excel Desktop Publishing Basics," explains terms relevant to publishing with Excel. This chapter includes references to fonts, typefaces, type styles, borders, shadows, colors, line spacing, justification, and page layouts. This chapter explains how to use these elements to create a professional-looking project.

Chapter 3, "Using Excel To Enter and Edit Text," explains the basics of how to use Excel's text and formatting capabilities. This chapter shows how to use Excel's text box; format text; edit data; and use the menus, keyboard, and toolbars.

Chapter 4, "Printing with Excel," covers the basics of printing an Excel document. You learn how to print and how to change the page setup, including page orientation, margins, headers, and footers. You also learn how to use print preview, select a print range, set titles, and set up the printer.

Chapter 5, "Using Excel To Create Charts," discusses what is necessary to create an effective chart. Included is checking for accuracy, determining the message, identifying your audience, determining the presentation's

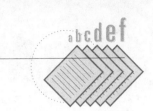

form, and choosing the chart type. This chapter also shows you what you can do with an Excel chart and how to use ChartWizard.

Chapter 6, "Editing and Enhancing Charts," shows you how to modify a chart. This chapter explains the basics of enhancing and annotating charts in Excel. You can add and manipulate text, arrows, lines, shapes, borders, and legends. You also can make the chart three-dimensional. This chapter also discusses design rules for creating good charts.

Part II: Excel Office Applications

Chapter 7, "Enhancing Excel Worksheets," shows you how to make your worksheets look better. The chapter teaches you how to format and highlight the worksheet, add charts, and automate the process of producing desktop-published worksheets.

Chapter 8, "Creating Business Memos, Letters, and Reports," shows you how to use the word processing and formatting capabilities of Excel to create business correspondence. You also learn how to use tables and columnar information in your correspondence. The chapter also tells you how to use the font, border, and pattern row and column capabilities to create templates you can use for memos, letters, and reports.

Chapter 9, "Creating Business Forms," discusses how to design and create business forms. You learn how to use formatting commands such as borders and patterns, how to determine the best layout, and how to use the columnar and row format of Excel.

Part III: Excel Business Presentations and Promotional Pieces

Chapter 10, "Creating Computer, Slide, and Overhead Presentations," shows you what looks good in a slide or overhead transparency. This chapter talks about the amount of text on a slide, choice of fonts, emphasizing text, using charting and clip art, and how to use Excel's automated slide show template.

Chapter 11, "Creating Brochures, Newsletters, and Other Promotional Pieces," shows you how to design and produce promotional pieces and newsletters. This chapter explains how to use the columnar and row format, emphasizes simple design techniques, and demonstrates how to use Excel's formatting capabilities.

Chapter 12, "Importing and Exporting Text and Graphics," explains how Excel works in the Windows environment. This chapter also shows you how to copy and link information and graphics from word processing and graphics programs.

Appendixes

Appendix A, "Glossary of Desktop Publishing Terms," lists the terms you may come across when you are using Excel or other programs for desktop publishing.

Appendix B, "Excel Character Sets," includes characters that are available with the extended character set in Excel as well as characters available with the Symbol font. These characters include foreign letters and currency, scientific symbols, business symbols, and other miscellaneous symbols.

Appendix C, "Excel Toolbars," shows you the Standard, Formatting, Utility, Chart, and Drawing toolbars. Appendix D, "Excel Shortcut Menus," shows you the nine shortcut menus that you can access by clicking the right mouse button on certain items.

Who Should Read This Book?

Look Your Best with Excel 4 for Windows was written for people with a general knowledge of Microsoft Excel or another spreadsheet program. You can use this book if you are entirely new to Excel, or if you are upgrading to Excel 4. You may have extensive experience with the analytical capabilities of Excel, but not much background on how to make your work look professional or how to use the desktop publishing features of Excel. If you only use Excel to create worksheets, *Look Your Best with Excel 4 for Windows* also will show you additional capabilities of what Excel can do. Finally, many of the new features offered in Version 4 relate to desktop publishing.

What Do You Need To Use Excel 4?

The minimum system that Microsoft recommends to run Excel 4 includes the following:

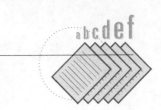

- A computer with ISA (Industry Standard Architecture) such as IBM PC/AT or Micro Channel Architecture (MCA) such as Personal System 2 or compatibles.

- A graphics card compatible with Microsoft Windows 3.0 or later (IBM VGA, EGA, or Hercules).

- At least 2M RAM

- MS-DOS 3.1 or later

- Microsoft Windows 3.0 or later

- Mouse (recommended)

- Printer (optional)

If you are going to use Excel as a desktop publisher, however, you probably will want the following setup:

- Microsoft Excel 4

- Microsoft Word 2.0 with Microsoft Draw

- Microsoft Windows 3.1

- MS-DOS 5.0 or later

- A 386SX or better microprocessor

- At least 5M of RAM

- At least 80M of hard disk space

- Laser or PostScript printer

- Mouse or other output device

- VGA or better graphics card and monitor

Where Can You Find More Help?

You can use Excel's context-sensitive Help feature to answer some of your questions while working with Excel. You also can refer to the appropriate sections of the Excel documentation provided with the Excel program.

Should all else fail, contact your computer dealer or Microsoft Customer Support at 1-206-635-7070. If you want to hear a list of the most-asked questions, call 1-206-635-7071. A list of support numbers for other countries is provided at the beginning of the Microsoft Excel documentation.

For more information on how to use Excel, refer to Que's *Using Excel 4 for Windows*, Special Edition. For more information on how to use Windows, see *Using Windows 3.1*, Special Edition.

What Conventions Are Used in This Book?

A number of text conventions are used in *Look Your Best with Excel 4 for Windows*. This section provides examples of these conventions to help you distinguish among the different elements of Excel.

Special typefaces in *Look Your Best with Excel 4 for Windows* include the following:

Typeface	Meaning
italics	New terms or phrases when they are defined; function and macro command syntax.
boldface	Information you are asked to type, including the character of menu options that you can press to select the command.
`special typeface`	Direct quotations of words that appear on-screen or in a figure; menu command prompts.

Words printed in uppercase include range names (SALES), functions (=SUM), indicators (CAP), and cell references (A1:G5). DOS commands (CHKDSK) and file names (STATUS.WK1) also are presented in uppercase letters.

In most cases, keys are represented as they appear on the keyboard. The arrow keys occasionally are represented by symbols (↑, for example), but more often by name (for example, "the up-arrow key"). The Print Screen key is abbreviated PrtSc, Page Up is PgUp, Insert is Ins, and so on; on your keyboard, these key names may be spelled out or abbreviated differently.

Note that throughout the text, the term *Enter* is used instead of *Return* for the Enter key.

Ctrl+B indicates that you press the Ctrl key and hold it down while you press B. Other key combinations are performed in the same manner. If key combinations aren't indicated with a plus, don't hold down any of the keys; press each key once in the order listed (for example, Alt F).

An Introduction to Excel and Spreadsheet Publishing

I

FINANCIAL HIGHLIGHTS STANDARD INTERNATIONAL CORP.

(Dollars in millions except per share data.)

Year ended December 31,	1993	1992	1991	1990	1989
Sales of products and services	**$456.7**	$352.4	$382.3	$327.1	$270.8
Operating income	**$75.2**	$12.1	$53.8	$46.	$35.5
Net income	**$45.1**	$5.5	$28.3	$23.8	$18.2
Earnings per common share, before extra-ordinary items, assuming full dilution	**$4.01**	$0.54	$2.69	$2.31	$1.91
Average number of common shares, assuming full dilution (000)	**15,249**	13,154	11,276	10,466	9,646
Cash dividends per common share	**$0.95**	$0.72	$0.72	$0.60	$0.53
Depreciation and amortization	**$25.7**	$21.5	$17.2	$13.6	$10.1
Shareholder's equity	**$158.3**	$135.2	$137.6	$115.1	$98.4
Return on shareholders' equity	**35.0%**	5.0%	22.1%	21.9%	21.7%

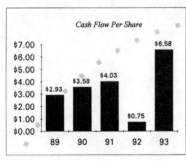

Cash Flow Per Share

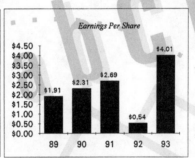

Earnings Per Share

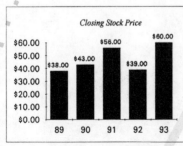

Closing Stock Price

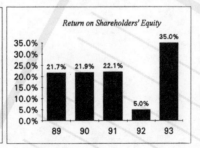

Return on Shareholders' Equity

Includes

1. Using Excel as a Desktop Publisher

2. Understanding Excel Desktop Publishing Basics

3. Using Excel To Enter and Edit Text

4. Printing with Excel

5. Using Excel To Create Charts

6. Editing and Enhancing Charts

1

Using Excel as a Desktop Publisher

The average office desk overflows with memos, reports, letters, and proposals. How are you going to get your customer or manager to look at your work? How are you going to get them to spend time with your proposal instead of competing products in the pile?

The work you do reflects on you. Written products are your calling cards. They last long after your smile, warm handshake, and strong argument. They can determine whether you get that sale, whether your proposal is accepted, and maybe whether you get that promotion.

Content certainly is important, but your audience has many distractions from your presentation. Meetings, deadlines, telephone calls, and other pressures compete. Besides being a good speaker, you need supporting material that stimulates and maintains interest.

Excel for Windows has become more than an analytic tool. Besides creating the numbers, Excel offers you the opportunity to make the numbers and text look more interesting.

Excel provides the tools to create professional-looking output that draws your readers to your content. These tools are the spreadsheet publishing features of Excel.

Defining Spreadsheet Publishing

Spreadsheet publishing goes beyond simply producing output. When you print a nonembellished spreadsheet with one font and no borders or shading, you produce an answer to a question. When you use fonts, borders, shading, and charts, you produce documents that are interesting, stimulating, and something you can be proud of. Most important, your documents will hold your audience's attention.

Until recently, standard printed output was the only option for most work in an office—unless you wanted to send your product to the graphics department or outside professionals. In addition to being expensive, however, this option took a great deal of time and last-minute changes were next to impossible.

Recently, a few factors have come together to give you the opportunity to create quality documents from your desk:

- Hardware prices have dropped dramatically. You now can buy high quality laser printers for less than $2,000.

- Hardware power has increased to meet the requirements generated by adding graphics and publishing capabilities to software. The price of computers has dropped continually while storage space, internal memory, and processing speed have increased greatly.

- Quality software that takes advantage of the capabilities of the hardware has been introduced. Excel is a leader in producing quality output.

To create spreadsheet publishing documents, the software must have the following features:

- Flexibility through a number of different typefaces or fonts

- Capability to format text as bold and italic

- Capability to draw borders and add shading to important parts of the spreadsheet

- A great deal of flexibility with graphics and charts, including the capability to manipulate text, add drawings, intersperse charts and spreadsheet data, and retrieve art from other sources (graphic programs and clip art)

- Good preview capabilities to look at the page layout

Excel has these features and more.

Excel 4 adds features that enhance the publishing aspect of your spreadsheet. These new features include the following:

- Spell checker

- Capability to wrap text in a box or a cell

- Predefined spreadsheet formats

- Step-by-step charting tool

- Automated slide show capability

Enhancing Spreadsheets the Old Way

In the "olden days" not so long ago, you had few options to enhance your spreadsheet. To add lines in the spreadsheet, you could create a repeating label of dashes (-) or equal signs (=) for single or double lines. To create vertical lines, you could use the vertical bar (|) and copy it to a border around the worksheet.

If you wanted to add a chart to the worksheet, you could print a portion of the worksheet, then print your graph, and finally print the remainder of your worksheet again. You often had to go in and out of different programs to print as well. Another alternative was to cut and paste pieces together manually and photocopy the whole thing.

Figure 1.1 shows you the "old" way things were done.

E xcel has a great deal of flexibility to enhance your work.

```
LaserPro Corporation
Balance Sheet
December 31, 1992


Assets                          This Year       Last Year       Change
Current Assets
    Cash                        $247,886        $126,473          96%
    Accounts receivable          863,652         524,570          65%
    Inventory                     88,328          65,508          35%
    Investments                  108,577          31,934         240%
                                ---------       ---------
        Total current assets   $1,308,443        $748,485         75%


Fixed Assets
    Machinery and equipment     $209,906        $158,730          32%
    Vehicles                     429,505         243,793          76%
    Office furniture              50,240          36,406          38%
    (Accumulated depreciation)  (101,098)        (64,394)         57%
                                ---------       ---------
        Total fixed assets      $588,553        $374,535          57%


Total Assets                  $1,896,996      $1,123,020          69%


Liabilities and Shareholders Equity
                                This Year       Last Year       Change
Current Liabilities
    Accounts payable            $426,041        $332,845          28%
    Notes payable                45,327          23,486          93%
    Accrued liabilities          34,614          26,026          33%
    Income taxes payable         88,645          51,840          71%
                                ---------       ---------
        Total current liabilities $594,627      $434,197          37%


Noncurrent Liabilities
    Long-term debt              488,822         349,253          40%
    Deferred federal tax        147,844          92,101          61%
                                ---------       ---------
        Total noncurrent liabilities $636,666   $441,354          44%


Shareholders' Equity
    Common stock                  1,000           1,000           0%
    Retained earnings           664,703         246,469         170%
                                ---------       ---------
        Total shareholders' equity $665,703     $247,469         169%
                                ---------       ---------
Total Liabilities and Equity  $1,896,996      $1,123,020          69%
                                =========       =========
```

Fig. 1.1 Standard output without desktop publishing features.

You had two choices of typefaces—standard and compressed. If you were lucky and had a choice of a few sizes of Helvetica and Times Roman typefaces, you had to figure out different complex printer string characters for each printer.

Using the Capabilities of Excel

Microsoft Excel has been a leader in going from the "old" spreadsheets to a much higher quality and easier-to-create enhanced spreadsheet (see fig. 1.2). The analytical power and capabilities required of a spreadsheet program include formulas, functions, database management, and macro support.

Using Windows with WYSIWYG

Because Excel enables you to work in a graphical environment, such as Windows, you get advantages over a nongraphical environment:

- First, the program is easier to learn and use, especially if you have worked with other Windows products. You choose many of the same menu items as other Windows products, and you click on tools for many procedures.

- Second, what is on-screen is what you get when you print (see figs. 1.3 and 1.4). This feature is termed WYSIWYG or What You See Is What You Get. When you produce spreadsheet publishing documents, this ability to see your changes as you make them adds to the creative process because you get immediate feedback.

Unlike other spreadsheet programs for DOS, the WYSIWYG feature is built into the product. In some programs, you need to flip back and forth between the graphical environment and the spreadsheet environment. In other programs, you use separate menus for the main program and for the WYSIWYG feature.

Previewing Documents

Although your screen shows you how the worksheet will print, there are some limitations. When you change margins or add headers or footers to the document, these changes do not appear on-screen in the normal View mode. Excel has a print preview feature to look at an entire page, including margins, headers, and footers.

Excel is strong analytically, but also enables you to add to that power through excellent desktop publishing features.

Excel's capability to display your changes as you make them adds to the creative process by giving you immediate feedback.

LaserPro Corporation
Balance Sheet
December 31, 1992

Assets			
	This Year	Last Year	Change
Current Assets			
Cash	$247,886	$126,473	96%
Accounts receivable	863,652	524,570	65%
Inventory	88,328	65,508	35%
Investments	108,577	31,934	240%
Total current assets	$1,308,443	$748,485	75%
Fixed Assets			
Machinery and equipment	$209,906	$158,730	32%
Vehicles	429,505	243,793	76%
Office furniture	50,240	36,406	38%
(Accumulated depreciation)	(101,098)	(64,394)	57%
Total fixed assets	$588,553	$374,535	57%
Total Assets	**$1,896,996**	**$1,123,020**	**69%**

Liabilities and Shareholders' Equity			
	This Year	Last Year	Change
Current Liabilities			
Accounts payable	$426,041	$332,845	28%
Notes payable	45,327	23,486	93%
Accrued liabilities	34,614	26,026	33%
Income taxes payable	88,645	51,840	71%
Total current liabilities	$594,627	$434,197	37%
Noncurrent Liabilities			
Long-term debt	$488,822	$349,253	40%
Deferred federal tax	147,844	92,101	61%
Total noncurrent liabilities	$636,666	$441,354	44%
Shareholders' Equity			
Common stock	$1,000	$1,000	0%
Retained earnings	664,703	246,469	170%
Total shareholders' equity	$665,703	$247,469	169%
Total Liabilities and Equity	**$1,896,996**	**$1,123,020**	**69%**

Fig. 1.2 A spreadsheet enhanced with some Excel desktop publishing features.

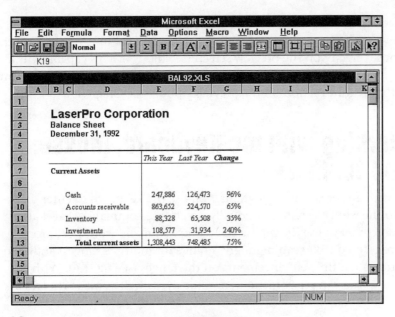

Fig. 1.3   A picture of the screen with WYSIWYG.

LaserPro Corporation
Balance Sheet
December 31, 1992

	This Year	Last Year	Change
Current Assets			
Cash	247,886	126,473	96%
Accounts receivable	863,652	524,570	65%
Inventory	88,328	65,508	35%
Investments	108,577	31,934	240%
Total current assets	1,308,443	748,485	75%

Fig. 1.4   A printout of the same spreadsheet.

Excel's preview feature goes further than merely viewing the page, however. You can change margins and increase column widths with the mouse directly on the preview screen (see fig. 1.5). This capability is a great enhancement for working with spreadsheet publishing documents. For more information on the preview option, see Chapter 4.

Working with the Keyboard, Mouse, and Toolbars

As with all spreadsheet programs, you use the keyboard to enter data into the worksheet and, optionally, to choose commands. Excel also enables you to use the mouse to accomplish many worksheet procedures. You quickly can highlight a range (or multiple ranges) and then perform multiple enhancements on the ranges (see fig. 1.6). With the mouse, you can select menu items quickly, as well as make choices in dialog boxes.

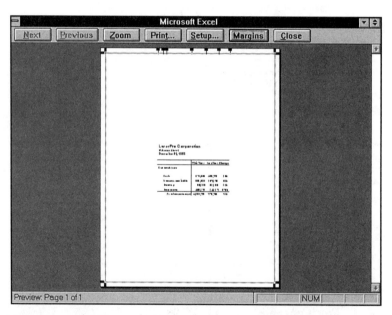

Fig. 1.5 The preview screen showing the margins option.

Toolbars speed up tasks in Excel.

One of the best Excel features for use with the mouse is the addition of toolbars (see fig. 1.7). Each toolbar contains tools, or icons, which perform tasks. Common tasks include making data bold, printing the worksheet, saving the file, aligning text, or creating a chart.

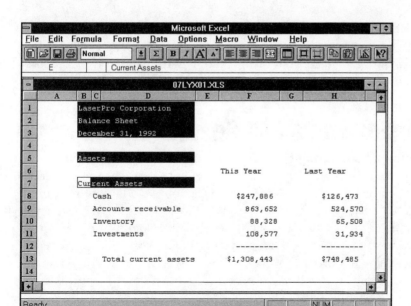

Fig. 1.6 Selecting multiple ranges and performing multiple enhancements on those ranges with Excel.

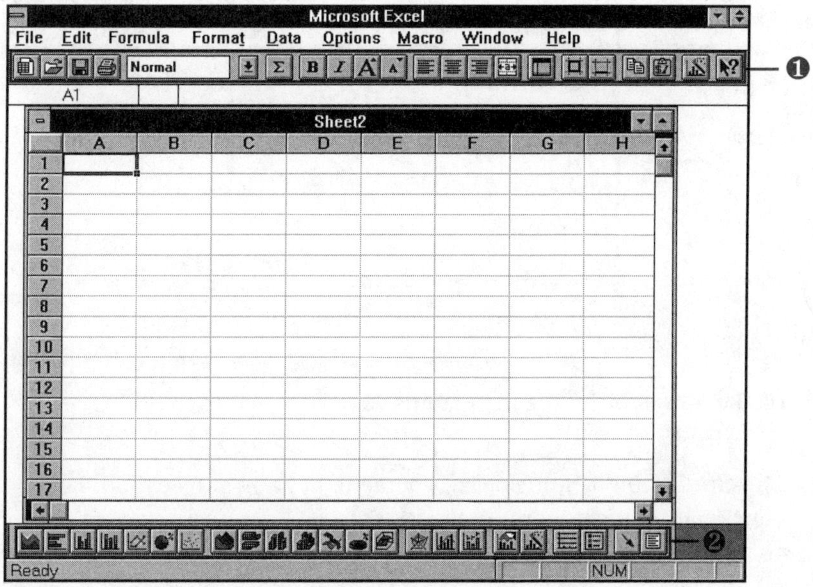

Fig. 1.7 The Standard and Chart toolbars.

❶ Standard toolbar
❷ Chart toolbar

You have several toolbars from which to choose, depending on the work you are doing. In addition to a Standard toolbar, Excel provides a Formatting toolbar, a Drawing toolbar, and a Chart toolbar, which enhance its spreadsheet publishing capabilities. The Chart toolbar appears when you create a chart or select the Options Toolbars option. You also can create your own. For more information on the specific toolbars, see Chapters 3 and 6 and Appendix C.

Using Fonts and Special Characters

In addition to ensuring readability, typefaces and type styles can add balance, consistency, style, and personality to a document.

Without the capability to offer you different typefaces and styles, Excel could not claim that it is a spreadsheet publisher. The proper selection of typefaces adds a great deal to any document. In addition to ensuring readability, typefaces and type styles can add balance, consistency, style, and personality to a document (see fig. 1.8). Not only do you have a variety of typefaces and type styles through Excel, but you also can purchase hundreds of fonts if you have special needs. You gain additional fonts through Microsoft Windows. Windows 3.1 now has TrueType fonts which show on-screen how the font will print. For more information on fonts and type styles, see Chapter 2.

Fonts available on Printer

Sans Serif	Serif	Script
Arial	CG Times	*Script*
Line Printer	Courier	
Modern	Courier New	
Univers	Roman	Σψμβολ
	Times New Roman	(Symbol)

Fig. 1.8 A sample of the many fonts you can use in Excel.

The alphanumeric and special character keys on the keyboard are beneficial for most work; however, they lack many characters needed for creating presentations or special work. Excel has an extended character set and a symbol font that enable you to create bullets, foreign currency and letters, and mathematical symbols (see fig. 1.9). For more information on special characters, see Chapter 2 and Appendix B.

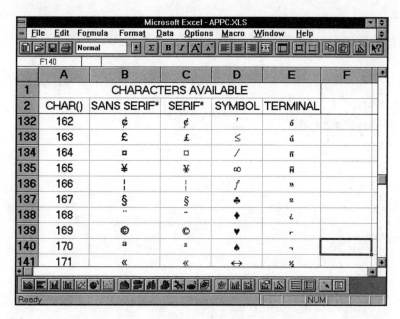

Fig. 1.9 Some of the special characters available in Excel.

One of the problems with fonts (such as Windows 3.0 fonts) is that they sometimes violate the What-You-See-Is-What-You-Get principle. The way the font looks on-screen is not always the same as it prints on paper. Another problem is that fonts often are unique to your printer. If you design a worksheet for one printer, it may not appear the same when printed on a different printer.

Windows 3.1 and Excel 4 address these problems through the addition of TrueType fonts (see fig. 1.10). These fonts, which work for many different printers, enable you to see how your text will look when printed.

Formatting the Worksheet

Fonts alone often are not enough to point out important parts of your worksheet. Patterns and borders draw attention to a specific part of the worksheet. Excel gives you the opportunity to place patterns or shading in cells. It also provides a wide variety of borders to surround or underline cells. Totals, titles, and special data can jump quickly off the page. With the addition of the Drop Shadow tool on the Drawing toolbar, data can stand out even more (see fig. 1.11).

TrueType fonts work for different printers and show on-screen how printed output will look.

Patterns and borders draw attention to specific parts of the worksheet.

TrueType (Windows 3.1) Fonts in Excel	
Arial 12	
Arial 12 Bold	
Arial 12 Italic	
Courier New 12	
Courier New 12 Bold	
Courier New 12 Italic	
Σψμβολ	Symbol 12 pt bold
Times New Roman 12	
Times New Roman 12 Bold	
Times New Roman 12 Italic	

Fig. 1.10 TrueType fonts available with Windows 3.1.

BUFFALO OATS INC.

Sources and Uses of Funds

Sources	
Venture Capital or Bank Loan	205,000
Mortgage Loan	45,000
Owners' Investment	55,000
Total	**305,000**
Uses	
Equipment	130,000
Working Capital	105,000
Inventory	40,000
Reserve for Contingencies	30,000
Total	**305,000**

Fig. 1.11 Using patterns, borders, and a shadow.

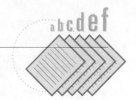

Like most spreadsheet programs, Excel enables you to align or justify text in a cell to the right, to the left, or evenly. But you need to go further for desktop publishing. Excel does by offering the following capabilities:

- Centering data across a number of columns

- Aligning text vertically in a cell (to the top, bottom, or centered in a cell), giving you even more flexibility

- Changing the orientation of text in a cell

- Rotating text in a cell

Figure 1.12 includes several examples of how you can align data with Excel.

Microsoft Excel - ORIENT.XLS

	A	B	C	D	E	F	G	H	I
2		This text is centered over columns B through H							
3		This is			This is			This is	
4		an example			an example			an example	
5		of left			of center			of right	
6		justification			justification			justification	
7		123			123			123	
8									
9				Normal Horizontal Orientation					

B2   This text is centered over columns B through H

Vertical   Ascending Vertical   Descending Vertical

Fig. 1.12 The alignment of data in a worksheet.

This book talks about what looks good with specific fonts, patterns, and shadings, but Excel also has a unique feature called *AutoFormat* (see fig. 1.13). By selecting Format AutoFormat, you can pick from a series of predefined table styles to highlight your data. With a click of the mouse, you can enhance the appearance of an entire range. For more information on formatting the worksheet, see Chapter 3.

rawing tools are available in both versions of Excel, but are placed on different toolbars in versions 3 and 4.

Drawing in the Worksheet

With Excel you also can add lines, arrows, boxes, circles, and other drawings to your worksheet by using the Drawing toolbar (see fig. 1.14). Use drawings to call attention to specific parts of the worksheet.

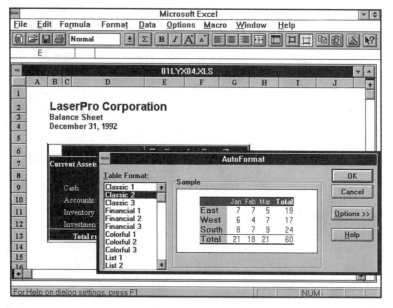

Fig. 1.13 The AutoFormat dialog box.

❶ Drawing toolbar

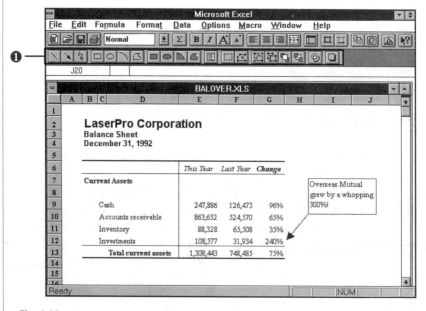

Fig. 1.14 The Drawing toolbar and a worksheet drawing.

Using Excel for Word Processing

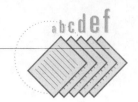

Although it always has been possible to type a letter or memo on a worksheet, Excel has word processing features that enhance its claim to desktop publishing. Through the use of the text box, Excel enables you to highlight a rectangle on the worksheet and then type within that rectangle (see fig. 1.15). The characters will wrap within this text box. For smaller items, you can choose an alignment option for a cell and wrap text within the cell.

After entering text in a text box, you can move that entire box by using the mouse to drag it. You also can change the style of individual words by bolding, underlining, or changing the font. If you want your characters to remain in cells instead of a text box, you can type the characters and then justify them in a range. The characters will be reformatted to fit within the range you select.

Finally, a great word processing feature has arrived with Excel 4. You now can use a spell checker to verify the spelling of your worksheets, charts, or text boxes (see fig. 1.16). For more information on text boxes and spell checking, see Chapter 3.

Text boxes help with titles on charts or spreadsheets.

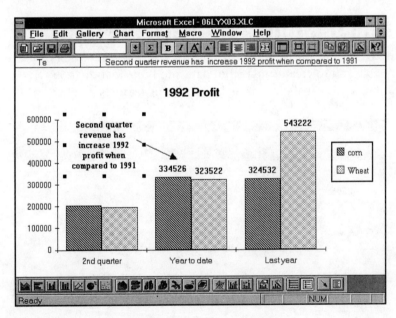

Fig. 1.15 A text box can add an explanation to a chart.

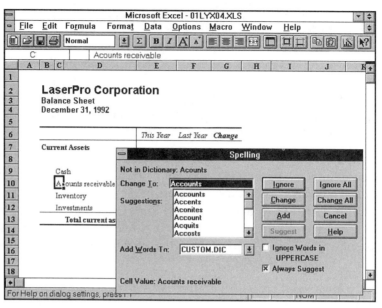

Fig. 1.16 The spell checker.

Using Charting for Analyzing Data

The strength of spreadsheet programs for years has been their capability to enable you to create and record data and then analyze it. Excel maintains this capability through its charting features (see fig. 1.17).

W hen you draw a picture of data, relationships often seem more obvious, enabling you to make better decisions.

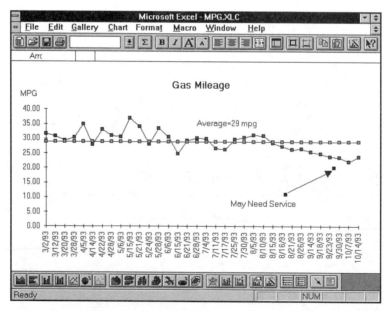

Fig. 1.17 An analytical chart may provide clues for actions.

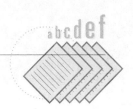

Using Charting with Desktop Publishing

In addition to its analytical purposes, charting can add interest, balance, and contrast to your documents. Moreover, charts often can illustrate quickly an important message—whether the chart is part of a page of data or stands alone as a slide or overhead in a presentation.

Whereas analytical graphics need to show accuracy, presentation graphics need to add the flexibility and enhancements that enable you to manipulate the chart. Excel's charting is an excellent analytical tool, but you can create even more outstanding presentation graphics. Excel offers a wide variety of chart types, including three-dimensional charts. You can change colors, add text, add arrows, and manipulate your chart in a variety of ways.

Excel 4 has an additional feature to make charting easier. The *Chart-Wizard* takes you step by step through the procedures necessary to create a chart. As you go through the process, ChartWizard shows you examples of what the chart will look like and what effect your choices will have on the chart (see fig. 1.18). For more information on graphics and the ChartWizard, see Chapters 5 and 6.

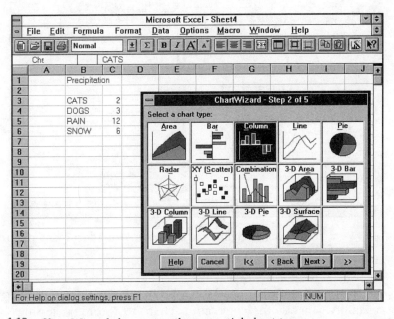

Fig. 1.18 ChartWizard shows you the potential chart types.

Using Other Programs with Excel

I f you have text in a word processor that you want to appear in Excel, you can copy or link the worksheet and word processing document.

Because you are using Excel with Windows, you probably have access to other Windows programs. If you are creating newsletters or manuals, you probably want to use a word processor such as Microsoft Word for Windows, Ami Pro, or WordPerfect for Windows. When you want to create a table in one of those documents using information from your Excel worksheet, you easily can copy the information to the word processor. You even can link the data so that when the worksheet is updated, the corresponding word processing document is updated also (see fig. 1.19). You link applications through Windows' Object Linking and Embedding (OLE) feature. OLE enables you to connect applications in two ways. An *embedded* object includes all the information necessary to make changes to the original document. A *linked* object will change when the original document changes.

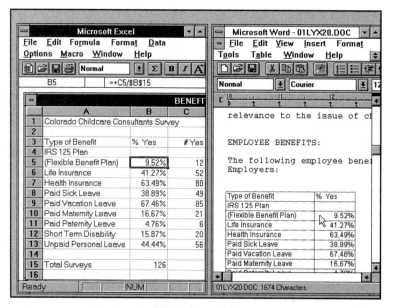

Fig. 1.19 Data from Excel changing in a Microsoft Word document after the two are linked.

Because a large part of what Excel can offer in presentations is its charting capability, you also can copy or link charts to a word processing document.

Finally, if you have other graphics or clip art programs, you can copy or convert images from those programs and use them in Excel worksheets. For more information on working with other programs, see Chapter 12.

Working on Projects with Excel

In addition to providing you with the mechanics to create quality output, this book also shows you how to use Excel's features to create enhanced worksheets, reports, memos, letters, business forms, organizational charts, slide presentations, announcements, promotional pieces, and newsletters.

Enhancing Your Worksheets

Despite all the enhancements to Excel, the backbone of the program is the worksheet. When recording data and analyzing information, you probably do not need to enhance the worksheet at all. When you show or present your work to others, however, you may want to enhance your work to stimulate interest and help the reader focus on specific parts of the worksheet (see fig. 1.20).

Use design principles such as white space, balance, and consistency to give your worksheet a professional look. For more information on how to enhance the design of your worksheet, see Chapter 7.

Creating Memos, Letters, and Reports

If you have a good word processor, you probably will want to use it to create business memos, letters, and reports. If you don't have a word processor or are not comfortable with one, you can use Excel for your word processing. Figure 1.21 shows a report created in Excel.

If you already are using Excel, you easily can create short memos and letters. The use many of graphics and tables in your documents makes an even stronger case for using Excel. Finally, the column and row layout of Excel helps you quickly create tables or plan parts of a large document. For more information on using Excel to create memos, letters, and reports, see Chapter 8.

Creating Business Forms

If you have a choice between using Excel and a word processor for letters and other documents, you probably will choose the word processor. If you are creating forms, however, Excel is your best option. The row and column format and patterns, borders, and font options enable you to create forms that look good and are functional. Excel even can create good organization charts—something very difficult to do with a word processor (see fig. 1.22).

Excel's capabilities help create great-looking forms.

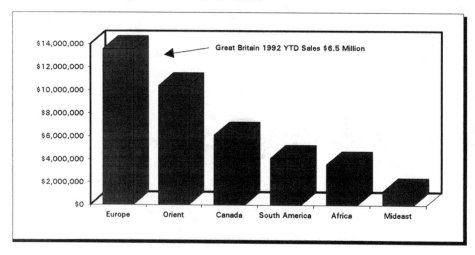

LaserPro Corporation

International Sales

1st, 2nd, and 3rd Quarter 1992 Revenues

Region	$ Sales	Units	% Increase
Europe	$13,574,447	174,143	32%
Orient	$10,370,858	133,045	36%
Canada	$6,116,347	78,465	22%
South America	$4,121,762	52,877	28%
Africa	$3,595,989	46,132	24%
Mideast	$1,246,187	15987	-26%

Fig. 1.20 An enhanced worksheet including a chart as well as data.

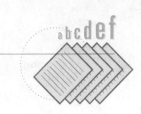

FINANCIAL HIGHLIGHTS   STANDARD INTERNATIONAL CORP.

(Dollars in millions except per share data.)

Year ended December 31,	1993	1992	1991	1990	1989
Sales of products and services	**$456.7**	$352.4	$382.3	$327.1	$270.8
Operating income	**$75.2**	$12.1	$53.8	$46.	$35.5
Net income	**$45.1**	$5.5	$28.3	$23.8	$18.2
Earnings per common share, before extra-ordinary items, assuming full dilution	**$4.01**	$0.54	$2.69	$2.31	$1.91
Average number of common shares, assuming full dilution (000)	**15,249**	13,154	11,276	10,466	9,646
Cash dividends per common share	**$0.95**	$0.72	$0.72	$0.60	$0.53
Depreciation and amortization	**$25.7**	$21.5	$17.2	$13.6	$10.1
Shareholder's equity	**$158.3**	$135.2	$137.6	$115.1	$98.4
Return on shareholders' equity	**35.0%**	5.0%	22.1%	21.9%	21.7%

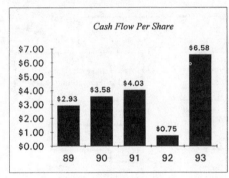

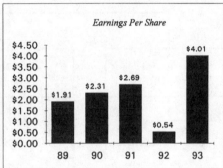

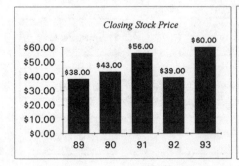

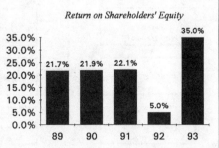

Fig. 1.21   A report created in Excel.

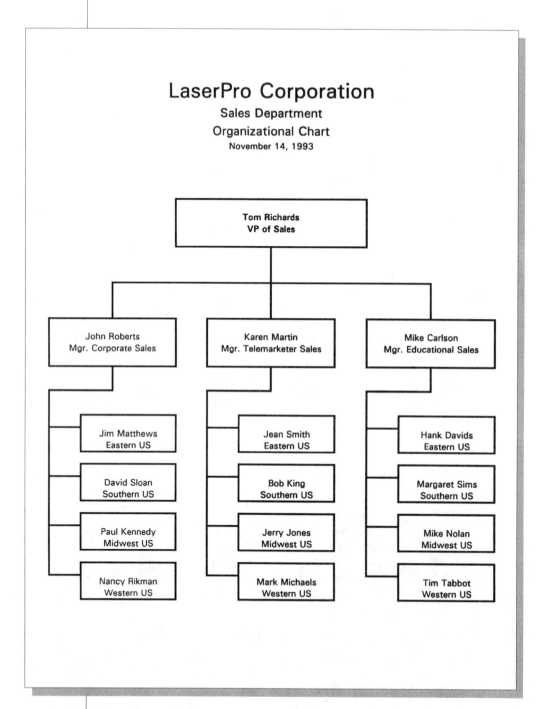

Fig. 1.22 An organization chart created in Excel.

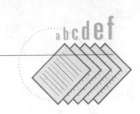

Travel Expense Report								
Dates		**Purpose**						
Date								**Totals**
Airplane/Train/Bus								
Hotel								
Driving Miles @								
Rental - Car								
Meals	Breakfast							
	Lunch							
	Dinner							
Taxi/Tips								
Parking/Tolls								
Phone								
Supplies								
Entertainment								
Daily Totals								

Detail of Entertainment Expenses Above

Date	Place and City	Amount	Guest and Company

Accounting	**Total Expenses**
Received Date _____	Total Paid by Employee _____
Paid Date _____	Less Cash Advance _____
	Total Due Employee _____

Signature _____ Date _____

Signature _____ Date _____

Accounting Copy

Fig. 1.23 A business form created in Excel.

Additionally, your forms may contain data that needs to be calculated, such as taxes and totals (see fig. 1.23). Or, the forms may be attached to a database. As a spreadsheet, Excel provides you with powerful, yet easy, calculation and database capabilities. For more information on using Excel to create business forms, see Chapter 9.

Creating Slide and Overhead Presentations

Because most of your data for a presentation often is located in Excel worksheets, Excel is a logical choice for creating the presentation. Along with its strong charting capabilities, Excel enables you to create text charts (see fig. 1.24). With Excel, you also can change data in the worksheet, thus updating your presentation quickly and easily.

You can create an automated slide presentation directly on your monitor for presentations to a small group. For a larger group, you can attach a projection device to your computer to view the slide presentation on a large video screen. For more information on creating slide and overhead presentations, see Chapter 10.

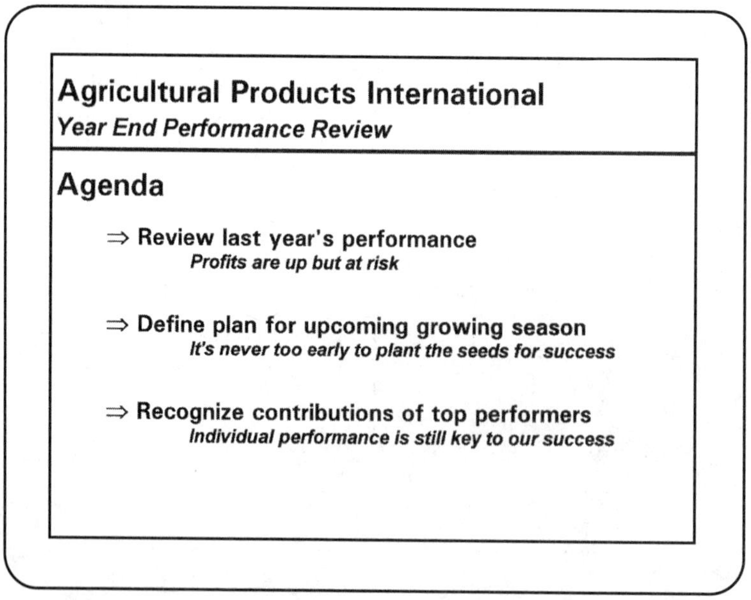

Agricultural Products International
Year End Performance Review

Agenda

⇒ **Review last year's performance**
Profits are up but at risk

⇒ **Define plan for upcoming growing season**
It's never too early to plant the seeds for success

⇒ **Recognize contributions of top performers**
Individual performance is still key to our success

Fig. 1.24   A slide created in Excel.

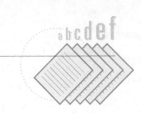

TONKIN & LAMUTH TACKLE
THE FISHING EXPERTS
Your One Stop Shop

Rocky Mountain **Guided** **Fishing Tours**	**The Best** **In Bait and Tackle** **Supplies**
Fly Fishing **Lessons Taught By** **The Best in The Field**	**Topography Maps** **For All Areas** **Of the Rocky Mountains**

15 % Off Sale

Everything in the Store !!

Fig. 1.25 A promotional piece created with Excel.

Creating Brochures, Newsletters, and Other Promotional Pieces

Excel's fonts, borders, and charting capabilities enable you to quickly and easily create brochures, newsletters, and other promotional pieces (see fig. 1.25). The row and column format also works well in planning the layout of a document for balance and content. For more information on creating such documents, see Chapter 11.

Chapter Summary

As you can see, Excel has many capabilities as a desktop publishing program. This book discusses the mechanics of using the desktop features of Excel, as well as how to put those features together to create quality documents and presentations.

The next chapter begins to explain these features by showing you the basics of desktop publishing.

Excel's row and column format helps you plan the layout of a document for balance and content.

2

Understanding Excel Desktop Publishing Basics

Desktop publishing has evolved into a major use of computers. As computer displays and printers continue to deliver higher quality and better performance at lower costs, the price of producing high quality printed output may be within your reach. Many software packages now provide desktop tools for creating printed documents.

In many ways, the advent of desktop publishing has changed the way people work. It has created new categories of businesses that provide and support desktop publishing. With a modest investment in hardware and software, you can produce in your home or office, documents that just a few years ago would have required professional printing services. Many companies are changing the way they work because publishing quality newsletters and professionally printed reports can be achieved quickly and cheaply from within the organization.

Before discovering how you can use Excel as a desktop publisher, you need to understand some basic publishing concepts. The following sections discuss desktop publishing and how its concepts apply to Excel. These sections include the general rules for creating quality reports with desktop publishing.

Understanding Fonts and Typefaces

Typeface refers to the artistic design of a set of characters.

When reading a book or magazine, you probably have noticed that not all printed type looks alike. Most likely you have come across documents that are easy to read and understand. Magazines have design staffs to choose typefaces and design page layouts, but the process is not as mysterious as it may seem. If you're an average spreadsheet user, you can become a desktop publishing wizard by understanding some basic concepts and following a few simple rules.

You can choose from hundreds of typefaces for printing text. Attributes creating the design changes include the following:

- The style of the *serif* (the extensions on letters that give them a distinctive appearance)

- The *text efficiency* (the shape of the letters)

- The *stroke width* and *consistency*

Figure 2.1 shows several commonly used typefaces. The differences in these faces are obvious. Other typefaces, however, may look much more alike.

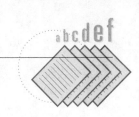

FONTSP.XLS

Fonts available on Printer

Sans Serif	Serif	Script
Arial	CG Times	Script
Line Printer	Courier	
Modern	Courier New	
Univers	Roman	Σψμβολ
	Times New Roman	(Symbol)

Fig. 2.1 Examples of sans serif, serif, and script typefaces.

The term *font* generically is used to describe a combination of typeface, size, style (upright or italic), and weight (regular or bold). *Roman*, for example, is a typeface, and *Roman Italic 10 point* is a font. In practice, most software applications use the terms *font* and *style* differently. A font in Excel is essentially a typeface (such as Courier or Roman). This chapter defines and discusses fonts as they are used in Excel.

As indicated earlier, font style also includes the definition of *style* (upright or italic) and *weight* (regular or bold). When you select a font in Excel, you also select the style (regular, italic, and bold) and a size measured in points—for example, *Roman 12 point*.

Typeface Categories

As described earlier and shown in figure 2.1, typefaces can be grouped into three basic categories: serif, sans serif, and script.

- *Serif* typefaces have serifs—cross strokes or embellishments on the feet and ends of characters. The serifs sometimes appear to connect the letters.

- *Sans serif* typefaces have no serifs. *Sans* is the French word meaning *without*; therefore, sans serif means *without serif*.

- *Script* typefaces resemble script handwriting.

Point Sizes

T ype size or height is measured in units called *points*.

Type size or height is measured in units called *points* (see fig. 2.2). There are 72 points to an inch, so a 72-point typeface is one inch high. The height is measured from the bottom of the lowest *descender* to the top of the tallest *ascender*. The descender is the part of a lowercase character that falls below the line, such as the lower portion of a *p*. The ascender is the stem of a lowercase character that extends above the center of the letter, such as the top extension of an *h* (see fig. 2.3).

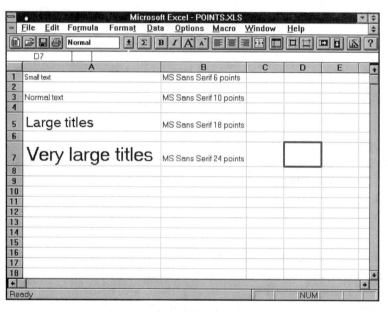

Fig. 2.2   Using larger type for titles and smaller type for notes.

Other terms associated with type are *baseline, cap height,* and *x-height*. Cap height describes the size of capital letters. In figure 2.3, this is the height from the bottom to the top of the C. Baseline describes an imaginary line that is below all caps and splits the descender from the rest of the letter. X-height is the size of the characters from the baseline to the top of all lowercase letters without ascenders.

Serif | Ascender | Point size | Cap height | x-height | Baseline | Descender

Fig. 2.3 Terms associated with type.

To increase or decrease a font size, you can use the Increase Font Size or Decrease Font Size tool located in the center of the toolbar. The large *A* with a triangle facing up is the Increase Font Size tool. The small *a* with a triangle facing down is the Decrease Font Size tool.

MS Sans Serif appears in the Font Name box and is the name of an Excel font (as opposed to a Windows font). MS stands for *Microsoft*.

Proportional and Monospaced Fonts

Traditional spreadsheet fonts resemble the serif type used by typewriters. Spreadsheets often use a *Courier* typeface—a *monospaced* font. Monospacing means there is one width for each letter, with each letter taking up the same amount of space on the line. The default font in Excel depends on which version of Windows you are using and your printer.

In *proportional* fonts, letters are not all the same width. An *m* is substantially wider than an *i* or an *l*. Proportional fonts provide different sizes proportional to the width of each letter or character. Figure 2.4 shows examples of proportional and monospaced fonts.

A monospaced font is more appropriate for spreadsheet applications because it is important that characters in several rows line up over each other. When parsing labels in Excel, for example, you must use a monospaced font. Numbers, however, will line up in columns with proportional or monospaced fonts because every number is allocated a constant line space in each typeface.

Text Attributes

You can use *text attributes* or formats to apply special emphasis to words in titles and headings or in regular text. These attributes include bold-face, underline, italics, and in many programs, strikeout and colors (see fig. 2.5). Excel enables you to apply all these attributes to text.

B ecause the words flow together more smoothly, proportional fonts usually look better on the page and are easier to read.

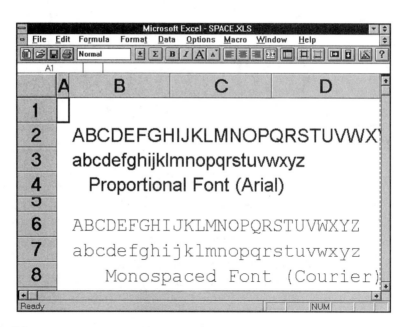

Fig. 2.4   Proportionally spaced and monospaced fonts.

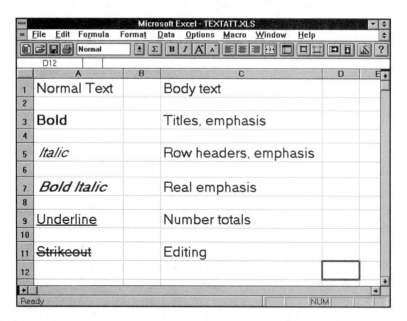

Fig. 2.5   A sample of the available Excel text attributes.

Basic Excel Fonts

The fonts available in Excel depend on your printer, your version of Windows, fonts you have added through Windows, and fonts that come with Excel. When you select Format Font, the Font text box lists the available fonts and Excel shows an example of the font in the Sample text box (see fig. 2.6). Scroll through this list to see what fonts are available for Excel with your printer.

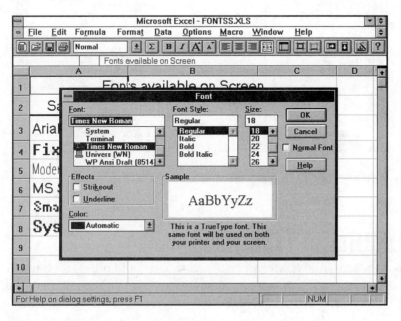

Fig. 2.6 The Font dialog box shows a list of available fonts.

Printer fonts—indicated with a printer icon next to the font name—are internal to the printer. If you highlight a printer font, the note under the sample text box indicates that the font is a printer font and that the closest matching Windows font will be used for the screen. An example of a printer font is Univers, a sans serif font. Univers is available on the Hewlett-Packard LaserJet III.

Some fonts are *screen fonts*, meaning that they are used on the monitor (see fig. 2.7). When you print, Excel attempts to find the closest font available on your printer. Screen fonts are identified by the note that appears below the Sample text box when you highlight a screen font. Some screen fonts indicate the type of resolution within the font name. WP Ansi Draft (VGA), for example, is a screen font for VGA monitors. MS Sans Serif and MS Serif also are screen fonts.

Read the notes below the Sample text box in the Font dialog box to see if the font is a screen font, printer font, or TrueType font.

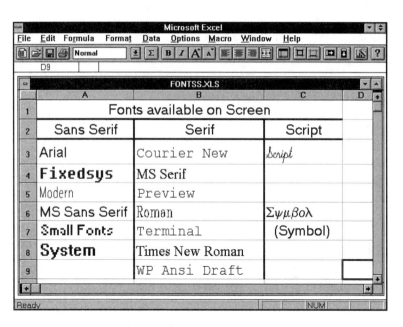

Fig. 2.7 Screen fonts in Excel. Compare this to figure 2.1.

Additional Typefaces

You can add TrueType fonts, printer cartridges, and other soft fonts to your system. *Soft fonts* are fonts that are stored on your computer's hard disk. Adobe and Bitstream are two manufacturers of soft fonts. *Printer cartridges* have fonts stored on a cartridge that fits into a slot in some printers. *TrueType fonts* are described in the next section.

The typefaces included with Excel provide the basic type styles needed for desktop publishing, but you may have valid reasons for increasing your font options. Your company, for example, may have a standard typeface—such as Bitstream Charter—or you may have a reason to use a script font. These additional fonts are easy to install for use with Windows. To install additional fonts, return to the Program Manager and select Control Panel, Printers, Setup, and Fonts.

Windows 3.1 TrueType Fonts

Use TrueType fonts to see what the font will look like on-screen and to have the added flexibility of font scaling.

If you are running Excel under Windows 3.1, one of the major changes in Windows is the addition of TrueType fonts. In the Font text box, these fonts are marked with a TT icon, indicating *TrueType*. These fonts appear on-screen as they will print. As long as you use the same application and print at the same resolution, TrueType fonts look the same from whatever printer you use.

TrueType has an added advantage. You can scale the font to any size you want, even if you have a printer without built-in scalable fonts. The basic TrueType fonts are Arial, Courier New, Symbol, and Times New Roman. For special applications, you can obtain additional TrueType fonts from a font manufacturer.

Simple Rules for Choosing Text Formats

With all the font and style choices available, you may think that making the right choice for your worksheet or document is complicated. The following guidelines can help you create professional quality printed output:

- *Use a serif font (such as Times New Roman or MS Serif) for body text.* The serifs tend to tie the text together, making it easier to read. Most people are accustomed to reading printed text in a serif font because it is the most commonly used.

- *Use a sans serif font (such as Arial or MS Sans Serif) for display text.* Display text is a short text line, such as a title, headline, or sub-head. A sans serif font helps this text stand out from the page, enabling readers to find key information quickly.

- *Use bold for emphasis and to help direct the reader.* Bold stands out to emphasize a word or phrase in a long stretch of text. In table and chart titles, bold text draws attention to the main point of the document. Use it also to distinguish row or title headings from the body of a table.

- *Use italics for subheadings or to indicate a quote or reference.* Italics can help differentiate titles from the body of a table. In a stretch of text, italics often gives the impression of speaking. Use italics also for instructions or when introducing new terminology to distinguish it from other text.

- *Use bold and italics together to make a point stand out.* You also can use this combination in subheadings of charts and tables.

- *Use bold and italic sparingly.* Too much use of bold type makes the page heavy and detracts from the words you really want to emphasize. Italics can be very light and seem to disappear into the page. Because of the increased white space, you can use bold and italics more in tables and charts than in text.

Use a serif font for body text. Use a sans serif font for display text.

- *Use underline for numbers or for one or two capitalized words.* When you use underline with lowercase letters, the descenders (the lower parts of y, p, and j, for example) get lost in the underline. Readers have difficulty recognizing the shape of underlined words and need more time to separate words from the underline. You can replace most underlines with bold or italic. In financial spreadsheets, however, underlines commonly separate data and totals. You can achieve the same effect with borders.

- *Use strikeout to indicate text to be removed.* Strikeout is an editing tool that enables the reader to see text before and after editing.

- *Although you have many available type styles, use them sparingly.* Excessively formatted pages often are called *ransom notes* because they seem to have been pieced together from many different sources. Pick a few text styles and use them consistently to give clarity and continuity to your page.

Understanding Cell Enhancements

To add emphasis or help organize your page, you also can use enhancements other than bold, italics, and underline. Lines, borders, patterns, drop shadows, and colors create interest on the page as well as help direct the reader. These enhancements are discussed in the following sections.

Lines, Borders, and Patterns

Lines can add clarity and organization to the printed page.

When lines surround an area (such as a table), they become borders that draw attention and provide definition for that area. You can use single, double, wide, or dashed border lines in Excel.

Patterns refer to the coloring and design of the background of an area or range of cells. Adding patterns to cells creates shading in the cells. Patterns can range from black (solid) to a light dot pattern to cross hatches. Effective use of patterns can help organize the page and draw attention to relevant regions or gray out irrelevant areas. Figure 2.8 shows how you can use lines and patterns in the worksheet.

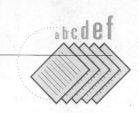

COLLEGE.XLS

College Expenses Model

INSTRUCTIONS

Complete the information in the Family Data and Investment Assumptions sections, then choose
Options Calculate Now to calculate the Payment Schedule.

FAMILY DATA

Children's names		Age now	Age to start college	Years of college	Today's cost of college
Molly		9	18	4	8,000.00
Kylan		8	18	4	8,000.00

INVESTMENT ASSUMPTIONS

College inflation: 8.00%
Investment return: 10.00%

Initial lump-sum payment: *Set to 0 for flat payment schedule.*
Pay in for this many years: 14

PAYMENT SCHEDULE

Date	Children in college		Pay in	Pay out	Accumulated value
1992			6,972.53		6,972.53
1993			6,972.53		14,642.31
1994			6,972.53		23,079.07
1995			6,972.53		32,359.50
1996			6,972.53		42,567.98
1997			6,972.53		53,797.30
1998			6,972.53		66,149.56
1999			6,972.53		79,737.04
2000			6,972.53		94,683.28
2001	Molly's year 1		6,972.53	(17,271.40)	93,852.73
2002	Kylan's year 1, Molly's year 2		6,972.53	(37,306.22)	72,904.31
2003	Kylan's year 2, Molly's year 3		6,972.53	(40,290.72)	46,876.54
2004	Kylan's year 3, Molly's year 4		6,972.53	(43,513.98)	15,022.75
2005	Kylan's year 4		6,972.53	(23,497.55)	

Totals: 97,615.39   161,879.87

Save Monthly: $581.04

Fig. 2.8 A worksheet formatted with lines and patterns. This COLLEGE.XLS
worksheet is available in the \EXCEL\SAMPLES directory.

Drop Shadows

Drop shadows add interest to the page and set off important titles from other text. A drop shadow is a graphic effect that adds depth to a box. This effect places an obscured box behind and slightly offset from the highlighted range (see fig. 2.9). The drop shadow is much thicker than other borders.

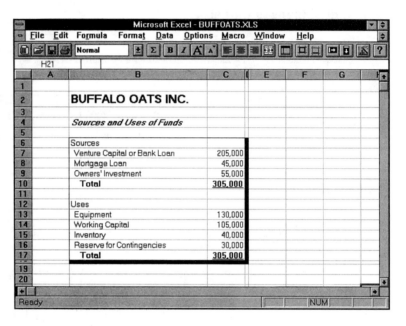

Fig. 2.9 An Excel drop shadow created with Format Row Height 5, Format Column Width .5, and Format Patterns Pattern solid.

You can create a drop shadow with a narrow row, a narrow column, and a solid pattern. Alternatively, you can create a drop shadow by adding a thick border on two adjacent sides of a range and a thin border to the other two sides. You also can create a drop shadow by selecting the last tool on the Drawing toolbar.

Colors

Use color to draw attention to words, phrases, and graphic elements.

Many software programs today support colors for text and backgrounds. Color on-screen can be used for presentations or printed to color printers. Color is printed in different shades of gray on black-and-white printers, offering a wider range of shading options than the light, dark, and solid shading options described earlier.

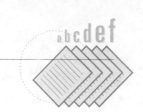

If your output device includes color, you have an exciting range of possibilities to increase interest and enhance communication in your presentation. Use color to draw attention to words, phrases, and graphic elements. Color also can provide orientation to the page similar to the effect of bold, italic, or borders. Output devices that produce color include color printers, plotters, slide imagers, cameras, projection systems from the computer, and the monitor.

Although color is exciting, the incorrect use or overuse of color can distract from your message, decrease the visibility of your page, and create confusion. As with bold and italic, limit your use of color. Many people are *color blind*—usually unable to distinguish red, green, and blue. If you are trying to compare two elements, avoid red, green, and blue combinations. Try to use colors that contrast with each other.

The background should contrast as much as possible with text and graphics. If you have a white background, use dark text. On the other hand, if the background is black (as in slides), use light text. Dark blue on a black background is almost impossible to read, as is yellow on a white background.

You also should be aware that the color on the monitor is not always the same as it will be on your output. Because light reflects off a page instead of shining behind it, printed colors can differ greatly from projected colors. Be sure to test colors for your different output devices.

Color text sets off headlines and subheads and creates a more interesting page. You also can use color for column or row labels to distinguish them from the body of a table. Use color to highlight a series of numbers or specific items you want to draw to the reader's attention.

Some colors have specific meanings. Red, orange, and yellow are warm, vibrant colors, indicating excitement. Red also can suggest a negative picture, however, and should be used with caution, especially with auditors and other financial people. You can use red effectively, however, to indicate financial loss. Use red, orange, and yellow sparingly on small areas of the page.

Blue and violet are cool colors. They are easy on the eye. Use these colors for large areas of the page. Don't forget that black and white are colors themselves. They often provide the most contrast with other colors and work well as text or background.

You can set colors in Excel with the Color option in the Format Font, Border, or Patterns dialog box. When you change the color of the font, the characters in the cells change color. The Color option in the Border dialog box changes the outlines around the cells. In the Patterns dialog

C olor text sets off headlines and subheads and creates a more interesting page.

box, you can change the color of the pattern itself with the Foreground option; you can change the color of the cell behind the pattern or characters with the Background option.

A clever Excel trick is to select Format Patterns Pattern, select a color, select Format Font, and then change the color. This creates a dropped-out text effect, as shown in cell B2 of figure 2.10.

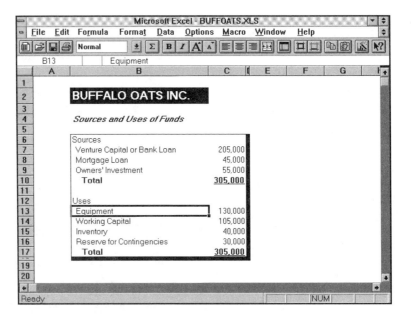

Fig. 2.10   Text dropped out of the background, created with the Format Patterns Pattern and Format Font commands.

Using Line and Character Spacing

The spacing between lines of text is called *leading*. The alignment of characters within a cell or range of cells is called *justification*. Leading and justification are handled automatically by publishing programs, including Excel.

Leading

The standard leading for text is 20 percent. Lines of 10-point type are spaced 12 points apart as measured from the bottom of one line to the bottom of the next. This standard leading is referred to as *10/12 (ten on twelve)*. Excel uses this ratio to space worksheet rows of different font

sizes. Notice that Excel automatically changes the height of rows when you format a cell with a large font. If you change the font to 20 point, Excel spaces the lines 24 points apart.

To adjust the leading in Excel, change the height of the row. Usually there is no need to do this, but occasionally it may be necessary. Multiple-line headlines of a large font, for example, can be tied together with a tighter leading. For special effects, you may want to use *negative leading*—the line or row spacing is smaller than the point size of the font. A 24-point font, for example, could be set in rows of 22 points. Figure 2.11 shows examples of different leading.

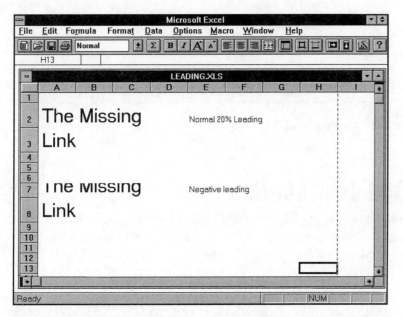

Fig. 2.11   A headline with standard 20 percent leading and one with negative leading.

If you have a large amount of text, you may want to open up the page by increasing leading (see fig. 2.12). When you use sans serif typefaces for body text, you also should increase leading to improve legibility. Generally, increasing leading by 20 percent should improve the appearance, but you may need to try different heights, depending on your document.

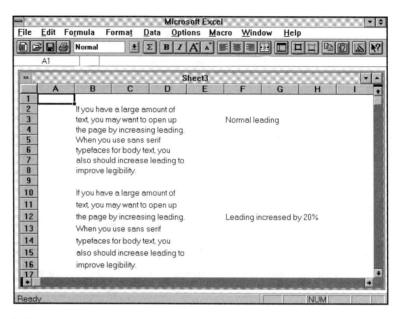

Fig. 2.12 Increasing leading.

Text Justification

Justification refers to the spacing of text for appropriate alignment with page or column margins. Text can be left-justified, right-justified, centered, or centered across a section (see fig. 2.13).

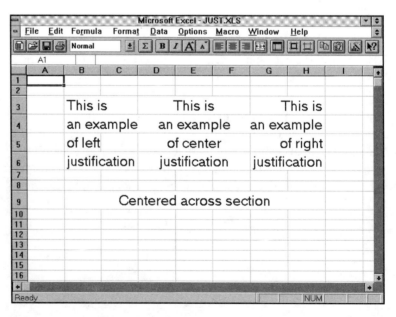

Fig. 2.13 Examples of text justification.

Because English is read from left to right, your audience probably will be accustomed to reading left-justified text. The left-alignment of text provides an easy reference for starting a new line. The right margin can be even-justified or right-justified with ragged, unaligned text.

Be sure to watch for problems with text justification. If you have a long portion of right-justified text, your reader may have difficulty finding the beginning of each line. With left justification, a ragged right margin can result in sudden large differences in text alignment or the appearance of rotated peaks and valleys. Hyphenating words or modifying the line length often can fix the problem. You should apply these steps after editing, however, in order to limit the amount of trial and error.

In Excel, you can justify text by using the Format Alignment command or the tools on the toolbar.

Text Orientation

Excel also gives you the opportunity to change the orientation of text within a cell so that characters are oriented vertically rather than horizontally. The three vertical orientations are horizontal letters stacked on top of each other, vertical letters ascending, and vertical letters descending (see fig. 2.14). Use vertical orientation for special effects in tables or newsletter mastheads.

> If you have a long portion of right-justified text, your reader may have difficulty finding the beginning of each line.

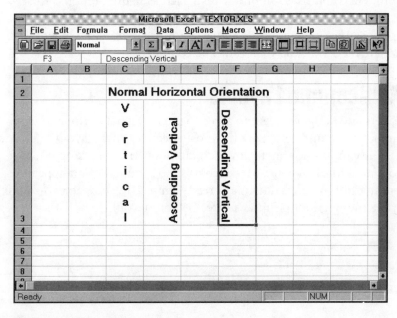

Fig. 2.14 Examples of text orientation.

Organizing the Page

Text and type are only part of creating a formatted worksheet published page. With the flexibility of Excel, creating lively, informative, and professional-looking documents is a straightforward process. Excel provides much of the same flexibility for page layout offered in desktop publishing packages. You can place graphics, such as charts or clip-art files, anywhere on the worksheet and print them exactly as they appear. To achieve the best results, follow a few basic rules for organizing printed pages and use some common sense.

Page Layout Concepts

The first step toward building a document is to picture a clear page layout. You easily can adapt standard page layout formats to the worksheet. The most effective formats divide the page into several columns—a familiar concept to any spreadsheet user.

Standard page layout formats easily are adapted to the column and row structure of the worksheet.

Single Column Formats

Typewritten pages usually are printed in a single column. Most published documents, however, do not use a single-column layout. Even books that may appear to follow a single-column format often use additional columns for nonbody text, such as figure captions. Most magazines use multiple columns of text, often highlighted with callouts, captions, titles, and graphics. Single columns are not used often because they are harder to read than multiple columns.

Multicolumn Layouts

Readers and designers seem to agree that page layouts with an odd number of columns often are the most effective. These layouts give you flexibility in positioning tables and graphics without making the page too symmetrical. When a page layout is too symmetrical, it appears almost artificial and is difficult to read. Figure 2.15 shows a two-column layout and figure 2.16 shows a three-column layout.

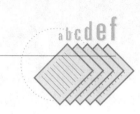

News from the Breadbasket

Agricultural Products Quarterly Newsletter

Sales are up!

This year has been our best yet. Sales are up, and things have never looked better! Let's keep up the good work and keep moving to the future. We've got a lot of potential for success in the years to come. Let's make sure we'll be taking advantage of it.

The most important news is that wheat has finally over- taken corn as our leading product. It shows what a little diversification can really do when you put your mind to it.

I'd like to recognize our key performers this period: Dylan Jones, Richard Pasternak, and Frank Franklin. They've been the key to our second quarter success. Next quarter it could be you! So, let's get out there and sell, sell, sell!

Financial Results

Once again, revenues are higher than ever before. This is the best quarter in our short, but great, history as a company. As you can imagine, there have been a lot of pressures on the harvest and on prices. But we're holding our own and will continue to succeed in the coming years. Thanks again for your continued help and support, and thanks in advance for the next quarter.

Bill

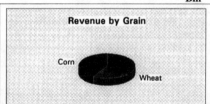

Wheat	Second Quarter	Year to Date	One Year Ago
Bushels	315,160	542,540	412,654
$ per bushel	3.24	3.49	3.31
Revenue	$1,021,118	$1,871,520	$1,365,885
Corn			
Bushels	273,610	457,350	442,674
$ per bushel	2.67	2.81	2.54
Revenue	$730,539	$1,270,734	$1,124,392
Total $	$1,751,657	$3,142,254	$2,490,277

Fig. 2.15 An ineffective two-column layout.

News from the Breadbasket

Agricultural Products Quarterly Newsletter

Sales are up!

This year has been our best yet. Sales are up, and things have never looked better! Let's keep up the good work and keep on going into the future. We've got a lot of potential for success in the years to come. Let's make sure we'll be taking advantage of it.

The most important news is that wheat has finally over-taken corn as our leading product. It shows what a little diversification can really do when you put your mind to it.

I'd like to recognize our key performers this period: Dylan Jones, Richard Pasternak, and Frank Franklin. They've been the key to our success in the second quarter. Next quarter it could be you! So, let's get out there and sell, sell, sell!!

Financial Results

Once again, revenues are higher than ever before. This is the best quarter in our short, but great, history as a company. As you can imagine, there have been a lot of pressures on the harvest and on prices. But we're holding our own and will continue to succeed in the coming years.

In the coming years, we'll have even greater pressures on revenues and expenses, but I have no doubt that

we'll keep growing as we move into the future. Thanks again for your continued help and support, and thanks in advance for the next quarter.

Bill

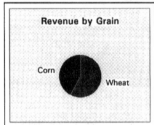

	Second Quarter	Year to Date	One Year Ago
Wheat			
Bushels	315,160	542,540	412,654
$ per bu.	3.24	3.49	3.31
Revenue	$1,021,118	$1,871,520	$1,365,885
Corn			
Bushels	273,610	457,350	442,674
$ per bu.	2.67	2.81	2.54
Revenue	$730,539	$1,270,734	$1,124,392
Total $	**$1,751,657**	**$3,142,254**	**$2,490,277**

Fig. 2.16 An effective three-column layout.

Portrait and Landscape Page Layouts

Excel can print the worksheet in *portrait* or *landscape* orientation. Portrait orientation prints the page vertically (see fig. 2.17), and landscape orientation prints the page horizontally (see fig. 2.18). Although landscape printing looks as though it is printing sideways on the page, it differs from sideways printing. With landscape orientation, each page is formatted individually, and the print will not cross pages. Landscape printing is an internal capability of laser printers and some inkjet printers and is not available on dot-matrix printers. Excel prints only portrait orientation on dot-matrix printers.

When designing the page, consider the print orientation so that your layout corresponds with the dimensions of the page. With a portrait page, your work should utilize the vertical dimensions. You should use landscape pages only when appropriate—such as for wide tables or for some graphics.

D o not use land-
scape orienta-
tion for long lines of
text—the page will be
hard to read.

Charts and Graphics

Charts and graphics add a lot to a printed page. They can break up the text for easier reading, make the page more interesting, and clearly convey important information pictorially. Graphics added with Excel can include a chart or clip-art image. Depending on the column format you choose, you can position graphs and clip art in the text body, off to the side, or even in the middle of the page.

Excel charts can be particularly effective in presenting your worksheets. Replace a worksheet table with graphs that make the page more interesting and clearly communicate the key information.

When adding graphs to a page, place them near their references in the text. Also keep in mind the size of the graphs in relation to their importance and the overall page organization.

Use the ChartWizard tool to create and place graphics in the worksheet. Chapters 5 and 6 contain a complete discussion of the Excel graphics capabilities.

News from the Breadbasket

Agricultural Products Quarterly Newsletter

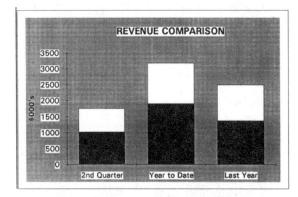

Wheat	Second Quarter	Year to Date	One Year Ago
Bushels	315,160	542,540	412,654
$ per bu.	3.24	3.49	3.31
Revenue	$1,021,118	$1,893,465	$1,365,885
Corn			
Bushels	273,610	457,350	442,674
$ per bu.	2.67	2.81	2.54
Revenue	$730,539	$1,285,154	$1,124,392
Total $	**$1,751,657**	**$3,178,618**	**$2,490,277**

Sales are up!

This year has been our best yet. Sales are up, and things have never looked better! Let's keep up the good work and keep on going into the future.

Financial Results

Once again, revenues are higher than ever before. This is the best quarter in our short, but great, history as a company. As you can imagine, there have been a lot of pressures on the harvest and on prices. But we're holding our own and will continue to succeed in the coming years.

In the coming years, we'll have even greater pressures on revenues and expenses, but I have no doubt that wheat will continue to be one of our biggest money making crops. The demand for bread just won't stop! The most important news is that wheat has finally overtaken corn as our leading product. It shows what a little diversification can really do when you put your mind to it. Let's keep up the good work and keep on going into the future. We've got a lot of potential. We couldn't have done it without you all.

Fig. 2.17   An example of a page printed with portrait orientation.

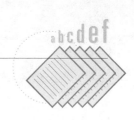

Agricultural Products International

Revenue and Production Summary

Financial Highlights

Revenue for the past year has continued up to expectations. We've seen expected seasonal variations in both availability of grains and price. Because we had planned well, we were able to continue to fill our commitments at the highest available price.

For the first time, revenue from wheat has exceeded corn. There are many reasons for this, but it was not expected. Lower prices for corn has had an impact, but overall the increase comes from higher demand.

Expenses, while not shown here, have been kept in line with inflation and increases in commodity prices. If anything, we're in a better position than ever before. This will be our most profitable year yet.

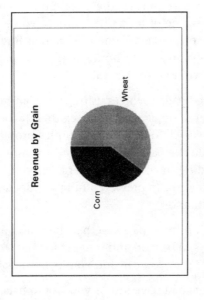

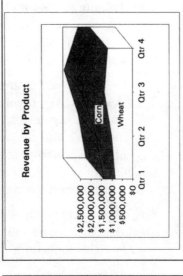

	Second Quarter	Year to Date	One Year Ago
Wheat			
Bushels	315,160	315,160	412,654
$ per bu.	3.24	1.62	3.31
Revenue	$1,021,118	$1,021,118	$1,365,885
Corn			
Bushels	273,610	273,610	442,674
$ per bu.	2.67	1.34	2.54
Revenue	$730,539	$730,539	$1,124,392
Total $	$1,751,657	$1,751,657	$2,490,277

Fig. 2.18 An example of a page printed with landscape orientation.

Creating Balance with the Page Elements

Earlier sections of this chapter discussed the components of a printed page. This section focuses on putting these components together. When designing a page for printing or for a presentation, you want to keep the text, graphics, and any other page elements—such as lined boxes or tables—organized and balanced. Without balance, the page loses its impact and value, and your work is in vain.

Use the preview feature to check the balance of the page.

Creating a well-balanced page involves using your common sense. Designers use a number of quick tests to check their layouts. You can show the page to a few coworkers, who may notice problems you missed. Or you can hold the page upside down or squint. Either method prevents you from reading the content and enables you to focus on the design. With Excel you also can preview a full page document with the File Print Preview command.

You should organize all printed pages so that they can be read easily. The objective of print is to be read and understood, not to use all the available fonts or prove that you can add graphs to the layout.

Balance the components of a page just as you would balance any group of physical objects. Examine the weight of the elements in your layout and position them relative to their weight. Do not put large bold type at the top of a page without something to counter it at the bottom. Heavy graphics often belong at the bottom, rather than at the top of the page.

Chapter Summary

You may not have considered Excel to be a desktop publishing package. And, you may not have thought of yourself as a desktop publisher. With Excel, however, you can produce printed output with desktop publishing quality. This chapter discussed the basic concepts of desktop publishing and how to use these concepts in Excel.

You also learned about typefaces and fonts and the difference between serif and sans serif typefaces. Bold, italics, and underlining draw attention to text as well as borders, patterns, and colors. For special effects, you can change line and character spacing in the form of leading and justification. The layout of the page in columns and the page orientation help make documents easier to read.

The following chapter gives you the basics of entering and editing text in Excel.

Using Excel To Enter and Edit Text

You may not think that a spreadsheet program can meet your requirements for word processing, but Excel 4 offers significant word processing capabilities to spreadsheet users. Excel provides a useful capability for adding, editing, and formatting text in the worksheet. In fact, many spreadsheet users find the text-editing capability of Excel sufficient for all their document processing needs.

You easily can combine text, worksheet tables, and graphics on one page.

The combination of word processing with the Excel spreadsheet and graphics features gives Excel some unique capabilities. Text, worksheet tables, and graphics can be combined easily on one page. Instead of linking to a worksheet table from your desktop publisher, Excel enables you to work in one environment. You can update the worksheet inside the same program without switching applications.

In addition to word processing, document formatting and page layout also are accomplished easily within the Excel worksheet. Because printed pages usually are organized in columns and lines, and spreadsheets are made up of columns and rows, desktop publishing concepts can be applied directly to the worksheet.

Using the Excel Text Box

Using the text box gives you more flexibility when you format the text.

When you enter text in Excel, you can enter the text into one cell and use the Format Font command or the Style Box on the toolbar to modify the text. All the changes affect the entire text. Using the text box gives you more flexibility when you format the text. You can change any part of the text. To change a portion of the text in the text box, select the text you want to change and use any of the formatting tools on the toolbar. You also can use the Format Font or Patterns commands from the menu bar.

Text boxes enable you to type text and use a word-wrap feature common to word processing packages (see fig. 3.1). You also have the flexibility to resize the box and have the text automatically wrapped for you.

Defining and Editing a Text Box

The Utility, Chart, Microsoft Excel 3, and Drawing toolbars display the Text Box tool.

Defining and editing a text box is as simple as locating the Text Box tool, defining the range for the text box, and typing the text. To define a text box, follow these steps:

1. Choose Options Toolbar from the menu bar.

2. Choose one of the toolbars listed that displays the Text Box tool.

   Of the nine toolbars that come with Excel 4, four of them display the Text Box tools: the Utility, Chart, Drawing, and Microsoft Excel 3 toolbars.

3. Click the Text Box tool. The mouse pointer changes to a cross-hair pointer.

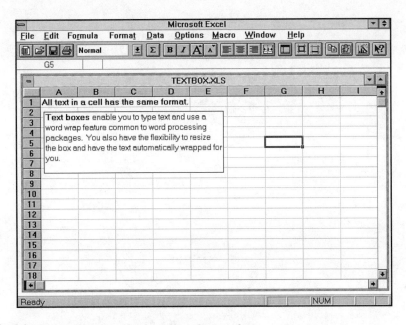

Fig. 3.1 Examples of text in a cell and a text box.

4. Move to the location in which you want the text box to begin.

5. Click and drag the pointer to outline the area for the text box.

6. Release the mouse button.

The text box appears in the worksheet (see fig. 3.2).

7. Begin typing directly into the text box.

8. When you finish entering text, press Esc to exit the text box or click a worksheet cell.

When you want to place a frame around worksheet contents and include text, you can define a text box with a pattern of None on top of the worksheet contents. This action causes the worksheet to show through the text box and include the text you need.

To define a Text Box with a pattern of None, follow these steps:

1. Define the text box around the worksheet contents you want to highlight.

2. Select the Text Box and choose Format Patterns from the menu bar or click the right mouse button to display the shortcut menu and choose Patterns.

The Patterns dialog box appears.

To show the underlying worksheet contents, select None as the fill pattern.

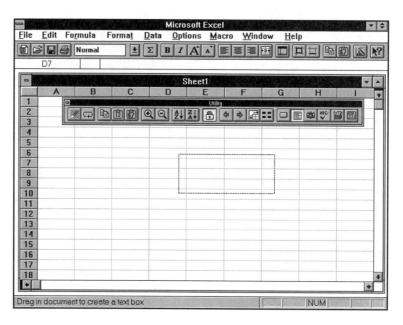

Fig. 3.2 An outline of a text box.

3. In the Fill box, choose None.

4. Choose OK.

The worksheet contents appear in the text box.

After you define a text box and enter text, you can edit the text by double-clicking the text box. When you are in the text box, you can add, delete, and format text.

Ending the Text Line

The text line in the Excel text box, like a word processor, automatically moves to the next line when the text reaches the right margin. To end the line before the right margin of the text box, press Enter.

Rotating Text in a Text Box

You also can rotate text in a text box. After text rotates, select the text to edit, and the text orients itself.

To rotate text in a text box, follow these steps:

1. Type the text you want in the text box.

2. Choose Format Text from the menu bar.

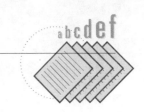

3. Select the type of alignment you want—in this case, vertical alignment.

4. Choose OK.

5. Select the text box again.

The text should orient itself vertically to your specification.

Using the Editing Keys in a Text Box

Special editing keys similar to the keys offered by many word processors are available in the Excel text box. These keys, described in Table 3.1, can speed up navigation in the text range, mark the end of paragraphs, and offer additional editing capabilities.

S pecial editing keys available in the Excel text box offer more editing capabilities.

Table 3.1 The Excel Text Box Editing Keys

Key	Action
← or →	Moves the cursor left or right one character.
↑ or ↓	Moves the cursor up or down one character.
Backspace	Deletes the character to the left of the cursor.
Ctrl+←	Moves the cursor to the beginning of the word to the left.
Ctrl+→	Moves the cursor to the beginning of the word to the right.
Enter	Starts a new line of text.
Del	Erases the character at the cursor.
End	Places the cursor at the end of the current line.
Home	Places the cursor at the beginning of the current line.
Shift	Highlights the text when you press Shift while pressing any of the preceding cursor-movement keys. Useful for Copy, Cut, and Paste or for changing formatting in a text box.
Esc	Exits the text box.
Ctrl+C	Edit Copy.
Ctrl+X	Edit Cut.
Ctrl+V	Edit Paste.
Ins	Switches between insert and overtype editing modes.

Formatting Text

Formatting text in a cell applies to the entire contents of the cell; you cannot format individual characters in a cell. Text input in the Excel text box can have different format attributes throughout.

Wrapping Text in One Cell

You may want to wrap text within a cell on several occasions. You may need to wrap text next to a graph or chart, for example. To wrap text in one cell, follow these steps:

1. Type text into the cell and press Enter.

2. Choose Format Alignment from the menu bar.

3. Choose a Horizontal option, such as Justify.

4. Choose Wrap Text.

5. Choose OK.

Figure 3.3 shows the text wrapping next to a graph.

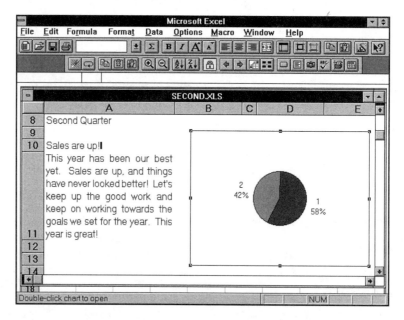

Fig. 3.3 Using the Justify and Wrap text alignment commands.

Using the Toolbars To Format Text

The toolbars provide a quick and easy way to format text. The Standard toolbar includes the Bold, Italic, Increase Font Size, and Decrease Font Size tools.

To apply bold or italics to existing text with the toolbar, follow these steps:

1. Select the range of cells or the characters in a text box to format.

2. Click the Bold and/or Italic tools on the Standard toolbar. The Bold tool is the bold capital *B* next to the Sum tool, and the Italic tool is the slanted *I* next to the Bold tool.

To change the point size of a typeface using the toolbar, follow these steps:

1. Select the range of cells or the characters in a text box to format.

2. Click the Increase Font Size or Decrease Font Size tool on the toolbar. The font increases or decreases in size according to the next available size on the Font Size list. The Increase Font Size tool is a large capital *A* next to the Italic tool on the Standard toolbar. The Decrease Font Size tool is a small capital *A* next to the Increase Font Size tool.

Excel formats the selected cells or characters according to your specifications.

To change the text enhancement *while entering text* in a cell or text box, follow these steps:

1. Click the Bold or Italic tool on the toolbar *before* you type the text. All text typed after this action appears in the format you select.

2. To cancel the format, click the same tool on the toolbar again.

 NOTE You can combine text enhancements by selecting several format commands. To format text in bold and italic, for example, click the appropriate tools on the toolbar before you begin typing the text.

Using the Keyboard To Format Text

The keyboard shortcut keys are Ctrl+B for bold, Ctrl+I for italic, and Ctrl+U for underline.

I f you are doing much formatting, you may want to use the Formatting toolbar, which offers more formatting choices.

When you type text in a text box, you may find it easier to use the keyboard to define bold, italic, or underline. To define these options, select the text to be formatted and press the keyboard shortcut keys: Ctrl+B for bold, Ctrl+I for italic, or Ctrl+U for underline. If you are entering data, press the appropriate keyboard shortcut keys to turn on the enhancement. Press the same keys again to turn off the enhancement.

Using Format Number To Assign Number, Date, and Time Formats

When you enter numbers on a worksheet, you may need to change the way the numbers are displayed. The Format Number command accomplishes this action by displaying a dialog box with different options for formatting numbers. To change the format of numbers, follow these steps:

1. Select the range of cells to be formatted.

2. Choose Format Number from the menu bar.

3. Choose one of the following categories of numbers: Number, Currency, Date, Time, Percentage, Fraction, or Scientific.

4. From the format code list, select the format code for the selected cells.

5. Choose OK.

Fig. 3.4 shows cell contents reformatted using the Format Number command.

Using the Toolbar To Assign Number Formats

If you are working only with numbers that are not dates, times, or fractions, you can assign the number format by using the Formatting toolbar.

To use the Formatting toolbar to assign number formats, follow these steps:

1. Display the Formatting toolbar from the Options Toolbar menu.

2. Select the range of cells to be formatted.

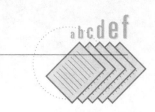

3. Click the number format tool you want to use on the Formatting toolbar. Available number formatting styles on the toolbar include the following: Currency Style, Percent Style, Comma Style, Increase Decimal, and Decrease Decimal.

Fig. 3.4 Reformatting cell contents with the Format Number command.

Aligning Data

When you are creating a presentable worksheet, you may need to align data. You can align data so that it is left aligned, centered, or right aligned. When you are working on an Excel worksheet, you can align data in cells or in a text box.

In Excel, unlike some other spreadsheet programs, you can align values and labels.

Centering Titles

Centering titles is particularly useful when you want to center titles and headlines over a page or table. To center a headline, place the headline text in the far left column of the document. Highlight the range of cells you want to center the text within and click the Center Across Columns tool on the Standard toolbar. This is the eighth tool from the right side of the toolbar, which looks like a lowercase *a* between left and right arrows.

Using the Toolbar To Align Data

When you align data, you can work with a range of cells or a text box. In either case, you first need to select the range to be aligned and choose the correct justification tool on the toolbar. Figure 3.5 shows the different types of alignment in a text box and a range of cells.

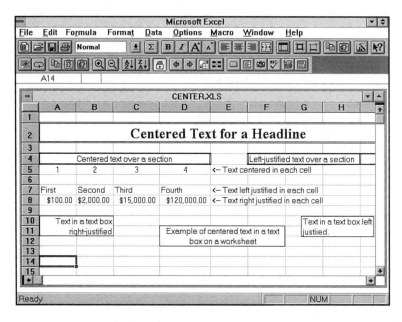

Fig. 3.5   Examples of the different types of alignment.

Using the Format Alignment Command

You can use the Format Alignment command from the menu bar to align text in cells in much the same way you use the toolbar. When you use the Format Alignment command, you need to select the text to be aligned and choose the type of alignment you want to use.

The General alignment option aligns your data according to some general rules. Text is left aligned; numbers, including dates and times, are right aligned. This option is useful if you need to have your worksheet alignment changed back to the defaults.

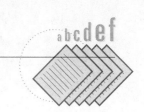

The Left alignment option is the default alignment for text. If you want to left align a number, date, or time format, choose this option.

The Center alignment option enables you to center text within each cell or in a text box.

The Right alignment option is the default alignment for numbers, dates, and times. If you want to right align text in a cell or a text box, choose this option.

The Fill alignment option repeats the data currently in the cell and fills the entire cell with characters. If you need to repeat a character and want to use the asterisk (*) instead of an underline, for example, type the asterisk when in the cell and choose the Fill alignment option. To copy this cell across a range of cells, select the cell and click and drag the handle on the bottom right corner of the cell.

The Wrap Text alignment option works only with cells that contain text. When you choose this option, Excel wraps the text in the cell to fit in that cell alone. If necessary, the row height automatically increases.

Changing Column Widths and Row Heights

You can change the format of your worksheet by increasing or decreasing the column width or the row height of selected columns and rows. You even can have Excel adjust the column width for the best fit. This procedure makes all columns fit the longest cell entry in that column.

To adjust the column width quickly, double-click the line to the right of the letter that is the column header. This action provides the same formatting as choosing the Format Column Width Best Fit command.

To adjust more than one column at a time, select the headings over the columns you want to adjust and double-click the line to the right of one of the columns (see fig. 3.6). This procedure adjusts all the columns selected (see fig. 3.7).

If you manually changed row height or wrapped text in a row, you may want to reset the row height. To adjust the row height quickly to fit the largest font in the row, double-click the line below the row heading. You can adjust more than one row at a time by selecting all the row headings you want and double-clicking one of the lines between the selected rows (see fig. 3.8).

To adjust the column width quickly, double-click the line to the right of the letter that is the column header.

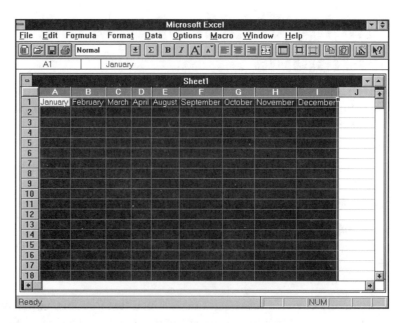

❶ Pointer Double-click

❷ Column header

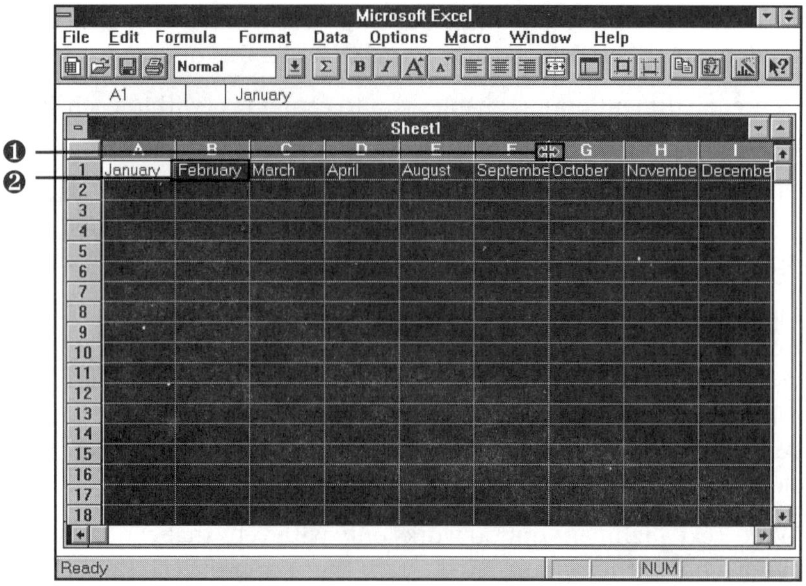

Fig. 3.6 Default column widths selected to be adjusted to best fit.

Fig. 3.7 An example of best fit column width.

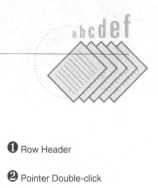

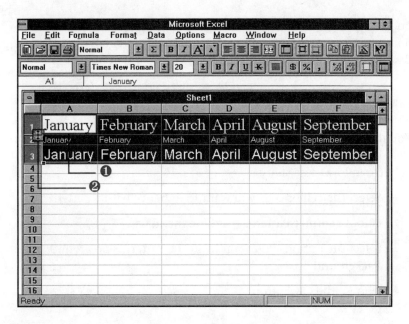

❶ Row Header

❷ Pointer Double-click

Fig. 3.8 An example of best fit row height with different fonts.

Using Borders and Shading

You can enhance your worksheet by using borders and shading. To make one particular part of the worksheet stand out, you can place borders around that part, shade it, or use a combination of borders and shading.

Applying a Border Style

When determining the type of border style to use, keep in mind the impact you are trying to make. A dotted or dashed line will not stand out as much as a double line or heavy line.

To apply a border style, follow these steps:

1. Select the cell or cells you want to enhance.

2. Choose Format Border from the menu bar.

3. Select the options you want.

4. Choose the OK button.

Remember that if two cells share a border and each cell has a different style for the border, only one border style appears. Putting a heavy line on the bottom of a cell, for example, will override a dashed line that is

To make a portion of the worksheet stand out, use borders and shading.

on the top of the cell below it. The order of precedence is from least dominant to most dominant: no line, dotted line, small dash line, long dash line, light line, medium line, heavy line, and double line.

Shading Cells with a Pattern

You may find after adding a border style that your point would be more clear if you shaded certain areas of your worksheet. To shade cells with a pattern, follow these steps:

1. Select the cell or cells you want to enhance with a pattern.

2. Choose Format Patterns from the menu bar.

3. Select the options you want from the Pattern, Foreground, and Background boxes.

4. Choose the OK button.

Using the Toolbar To Add Outlines and Shading

You can add an outline around a selection of cells by selecting the cells and clicking the Outline Border tool on the toolbar. You can add shading by selecting the cells and clicking the Light Shading tool (second from the right on the Formatting toolbar) or the Drop Shadow tool (furthest to the right on the Drawing toolbar).

Editing Data

After you have worked with a new document or worksheet, you may need to edit the data. When you edit data, the Edit menu is very helpful. If you need to copy or move cells or objects, you can select the data, cut or copy it to the Clipboard, and paste it in a new location. With Excel 4, you now have the Cut, Copy, Paste, and Clear options on the Shortcut menu and the Edit menu. Excel 4 also has included a new feature called Drag and Drop. The Drag and Drop feature and the Shortcut menu are discussed in the following sections.

Using Drag and Drop To Move and Copy Data

If you are an experienced Excel user, the new Drag and Drop feature will make cutting and pasting much easier for you. With Excel 4, you now can select the data to be moved and drag it to the new location.

To use Drag and Drop to *move* selected data, follow these steps:

1. Select the range of cells or the object you want to move.

2. Point to the border of the selected area. The mouse pointer becomes an arrow. Drag the selected data to the new location.

3. Release the mouse button

The selected data has been moved to the new location (see fig. 3.9).

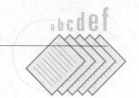

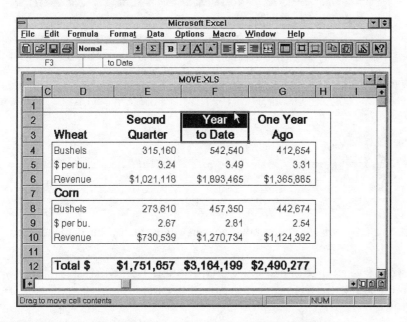

Fig. 3.9 Selected data moved with the Drag and Drop feature.

To use Drag and Drop to *copy* selected data, follow these steps:

1. Select the range of cells or the object you want to copy.

2. Point to the border of the selected area and press Ctrl while you drag the selected data to the new location.

3. Release the mouse button and the Ctrl key.

The new Drag and Drop feature makes cutting and pasting much easier.

Using the Shortcut Menus

The Shortcut menu displays the most common commands you can use for the selected area.

Shortcut menus are a new feature provided with Excel 4. After you select a range of cells or an object, click the right mouse button to display the Shortcut menu. This menu displays the most common commands you can use for the selected area. Most of the choices you have on the Format menu appear when you use the Shortcut menu.

When you select a row header, for example, the commands displayed include the formatting options for the row height (see fig. 3.10).

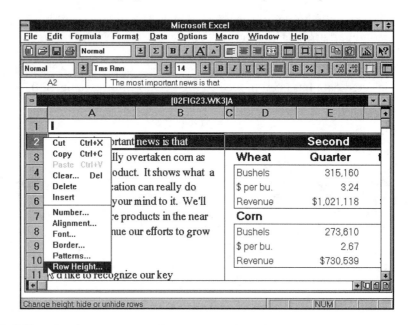

Fig. 3.10 The Shortcut menu that appears when the row header is selected.

If you have a range of cells selected, the Shortcut menu displays the Border and Patterns formatting choices (see fig. 3.11).

Using Spelling Check in a Worksheet

After spending time creating a professional document, it would be unfortunate to leave spelling errors. With the spelling option provided in Excel, you can check the spelling of your entire worksheet by choosing a menu option.

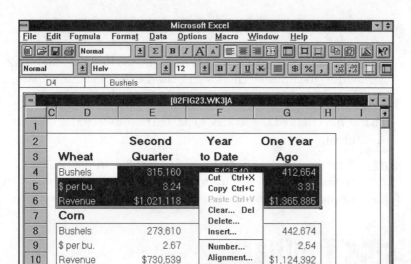

Fig. 3.11 The Shortcut menu that appears when the selected area is a range of cells.

To check spelling, follow these steps:

1. To check the entire worksheet, select a single cell. Microsoft Excel checks all the components of your worksheet: embedded charts, text boxes, buttons, and the contents of individual cells.

2. Choose Options Spelling from the menu bar. Excel begins checking the worksheet or the selected range. When Excel finds a word that is not in the dictionary, it displays a dialog box.

3. To accept the suggested word, click the Change button.

To change all occurrences of the misspelled word, click the Change All button.

To choose a different word displayed in the Suggestions list, select the word and then click the Change button (or double-click the word in the list).

Click the Ignore or Ignore All button if you want to leave the word unchanged for the first occurrence or all occurrences.

Click the Add button if you want to add the word to the custom dictionary.

4. If you were not at the beginning of your worksheet when you started the spell check, Excel prompts you to see if you want to continue checking the document from the beginning. Choose the Yes button to continue checking or choose the No button to stop.

5. When the spell check is complete, Excel displays a message stating that it has checked the requested area. Choose OK to return to the document.

 NOTE You also can use the Spelling tool located on the Utility toolbar. The tool is third from the right end of the toolbar and displays ABC ✓ on the button.

Using Toolbars

Excel's toolbars enable you to select tasks quickly and easily.

Excel 4 includes a Standard toolbar and eight optional toolbars, each containing a related group of tools. These toolbars enable you to select tasks quickly and easily. You have the option to change any of the toolbars or create new toolbars by adding, deleting, or rearranging tools. Tables 3.2 through 3.5 show you the most common toolbars used in desktop publishing with Excel 4. Figures 3.12 through 3.15 show you these toolbars as they appear on-screen.

❶ Standard toolbar

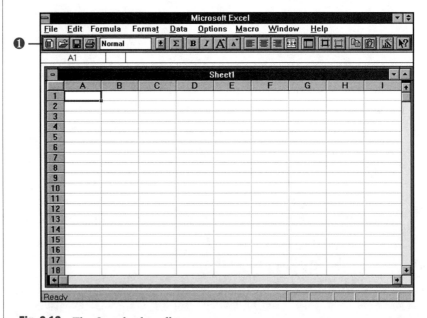

Fig. 3.12 The Standard toolbar.

Table 3.2 The Standard Toolbar

Tool	Name	Description
	New Worksheet	Creates a new worksheet. Clicking this tool is the same as choosing **File** New from the menu bar.
	Open File	Displays the Open dialog box so that you can select an existing file to open.
	Save File	Saves the file you are working on.
	Print	Prints the worksheet you are working on according to the options specified in the Print dialog box.
Normal	Style Box	Enables you to apply a style to the selected cell or cells. You also can define a style based on the current selections.
Σ	AutoSum	Inserts the SUM function into the active cell with a proposed sum range.
B	Bold	Applies the bold enhancement to the selected text in a text box or the text in a selected cell.
I	Italic	Applies the italic enhancement to the selected text in a text box or the text in a selected cell.
A	Increase Font Size	Increases the font size of the selected text to the next size available in the Font size list.
A	Decrease Font Size	Decreases the font size of the selected text to the next smaller size available in the Font size list.
	Left Align	Aligns to the left the contents in a selected text box or cell.
	Center Align	Centers the contents in a selected text box or cell.

continues

Table 3.2   Continued

Tool	Name	Description
	Right Align	Aligns to the right the contents in a selected text box or cell.
	Center Across Columns	Centers the text from one cell across selected columns.
	AutoFormat	Applies the most recently selected table format through the Format menu.
	Outline Border	Adds a border around the outside edges of the selected cells. The same as choosing the Format Border command and using the medium line.
	Bottom Border	Adds a bottom border to the selected cell or cells.
	Copy	Copies the values, formulas, and formats of cells in the leftmost column of the selected range into the remaining selected cells to the right.
	Paste Formats	Copies the values, formulas, and formats of cells in the topmost row of the selected range into the remaining selected cells below.
	ChartWizard	Starts the ChartWizard so that you can edit an embedded chart or chart document or create a new chart.
	Help	Adds a question mark (?) to the mouse pointer. This option enables you to see information about the command or screen region in the status line of the Excel window. If you click the screen region or a command, you bring up context-sensitive help.

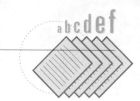

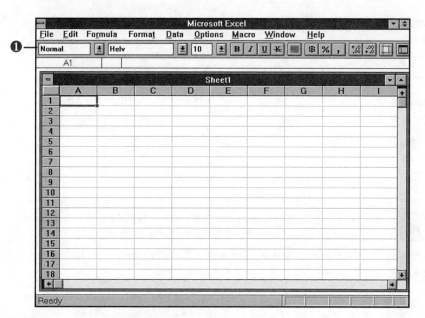

0 Formatting toolbar

Fig. 3.13   The Formatting toolbar.

Table 3.3   The Formatting Toolbar

Tool	Name	Description
 **Normal**	Style Box	Enables you to apply a style to the selected cell or cells. You also can define a style based on the current selections.
Helv	Font Name Box	Lists available fonts and enables you to choose the font you want to apply to the selected data.
10	Font Size Box	Lists available sizes for the font selected. Enables you to change the size of the selected data.
B	Bold	Applies the bold enhancement to the selected text in a text box or the text in a selected cell.
I	Italic	Applies the italic enhancement to the selected text in a text box or the text in a selected cell.
U	Underline	Applies the underline enhancement to the selected text in a text box or the text in a selected cell.

continues

Table 3.3 Continued

Tool	Name	Description
K	Strikeout	Draws a line through the selected text in a text box or the text in a selected cell.
≣	Justify Align	Evenly justifies the contents of a selected text box or cell.
$	Currency Style	Applies the currency style to selected cells.
%	Percent Style	Applies the percent style to selected cells.
,	Comma Style	Applies the comma style to selected cells.
+.0 .00	Increase Decimal	Adds one decimal place to a number format of the selected cells.
.00 +.0	Decrease Decimal	Removes one decimal place from a number format of the selected cells.
▢	Light Shading	Applies a light shading pattern to the selected cells or graphic objects.
▥	Last Table Format	Applies most recently selected table format through the Format menu.

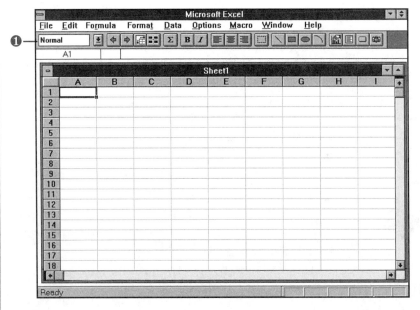

❶ Excel 3 toolbar

Fig. 3.14 The Excel 3 toolbar.

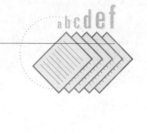

Table 3.4   The Excel 3 Toolbar

Tool	Name	Description
`Normal`	Style Box	Enables you to apply a style to the selected cell or cells. You also can define a style based on the current selections.
	Promote	Raises selected rows or columns to one level higher in an outline.
	Demote	Lowers selected rows or columns to one level lower in an outline.
	Show Outline Symbols	Displays or hides outlining symbols.
	Select Visible Cells	Selects the visible cells on a worksheet. Changes you make affect the visible cells and do not affect the hidden rows or columns. Applies most recently selected format through the Format menu.
Σ	AutoSum	Inserts the SUM function into the active cell with a proposed SUM range.
B	Bold	Applies the bold enhancement to the selected text in a text box or the text in a selected cell.
I	Italic	Applies the italic enhancement to the selected text in a text box or the text in a selected cell.
	Left Align	Aligns the contents in a selected text box or cell to the left.
	Center Align	Centers the contents in a selected text box or cell.
	Right Align	Aligns the contents in a selected text box or cell to the right.
	Selection	Selects one or more graphic objects.
	Line	Draws a straight line.
	Filled Rectangle	Draws a square or rectangle.

continues

Table 3.4 Continued

Tool	Name	Description
	Filled Oval	Draws a circle or oval.
	Arc	Draws part of a circle or an arc.
	Embed Chart	Creates a chart as an embedded object on a worksheet.
	Text Box	Draws a text box where you can type text on a worksheet.
	Button	Draws a button that you can assign to a macro.
	Capture Picture	Creates a picture of a selected range on a chart and pastes the picture as an object on a worksheet or chart. The picture is linked to the source selection.

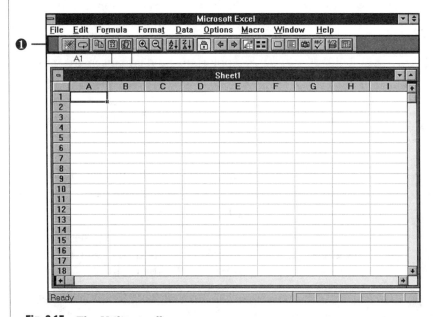

❶ Utility toolbar

Fig. 3.15 The Utility toolbar.

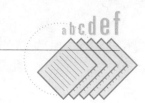

Table 3.5 The Utility Toolbar

Tool	Name	Description
	Undo	Undoes certain commands or deletes the entry you typed last. Same as Edit Undo from the menu bar.
	Repeat	Repeats the last command you chose.
	Copy	Copies the selected cells, characters, or objects to the Clipboard.
	Paste Values	Pastes the values from the cells you have copied to the Clipboard.
	Paste Formats	Pastes the cell formats from the cells you have copied to the Clipboard.
	Zoom In	Enables you to change the scale of the document to the next higher magnification.
	Zoom Out	Enables you to change the scale of the document to the next lower magnification.
	Sort Ascending	Rearranges the rows in your selection in ascending sorted order.
	Sort Descending	Rearranges the rows in your selection in descending sorted order.
	Lock Cell	Locks selected cells and objects from being changed when the document is protected.
	Promote	Raises selected rows or columns to one level higher in an outline.
	Demote	Lowers selected rows or columns to one level lower in an outline.
	Show Outline Symbols	Creates an outline if one does not exist and displays or hides outlining symbols.
	Select Visible Cells	Selects the visible cells on a worksheet so that changes you make affect the visible cells and do not affect the hidden rows or columns.

continues

Table 3.5   Continued

Tool	Name	Description
	Button	Draws a button you can assign to a macro.
	Text Box	Draws a text box where you can type text on a worksheet.
	Capture Picture	Creates a picture of a selected range and pastes the picture as an object on a worksheet or chart. The picture is linked to the source selection.
	Check Spelling	Checks the spelling of the text on worksheets, in macro sheets, charts, graphic objects, or on the formula bar.
	Set Print Area	Defines the area of the active worksheet to print.
	Calculate Now	Calculates all open worksheets, macro sheets, and charts. Calculates the formula in the active formula bar.

For a description of the tools on the Chart toolbar, see Chapter 5. For a description of the tools on the Drawing toolbar, see Chapter 6.

Chapter Summary

The better you understand desktop publishing basics, the easier it is for you to use Excel to begin designing forms, newsletters, charts, and other desktop publishing documents.

This chapter covered the basic editing and formatting functions of Excel. You probably have determined by now that you can accomplish the same task in many ways. To include text in your document, you enter the text into a cell or a text box. The choice you make depends on what you want to do with the text. To enhance specific parts of the text with bold or italic formatting, you use a text box. If you want all text fully justified and bold, you enter the text into a cell.

Understanding how to align or realign data gives you the versatility to make your documents look exactly the way you perceive them. Changing columns and rows to adjust to your specific needs enables you to be precise on how data looks in a slide show or on the printed page. Some of the best features of Excel 4 include the eight optional toolbars and the

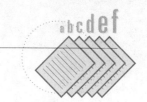

Shortcut menu. You also learned how to use the spell check feature to make sure that your documents do not contain misspelled words. After you have experimented with some of the features explained in this chapter, you can determine the best way to accomplish the editing and formatting tasks needed to produce professional documents.

In the next chapter, you will be able to take your basic worksheet and use printing techniques to enhance it even more.

Printing
with Excel

4

The final step for most desktop publishing applications is the
printed page. Excel includes very powerful but easy-to-use
print commands that enhance your worksheet and help
produce professional-looking documents.

Excel Print commands are extremely valuable and necessary in improving the appearance of your spreadsheets. Effectively using the Excel Print commands will result in professional-looking materials.

The major print commands are Print, Page Setup, Print Report, and Print Preview. You select these commands from the File menu, which you can access from the main menu (see fig. 4.1).

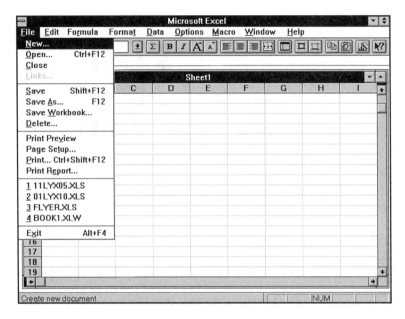

Fig. 4.1   The File print commands in Excel.

This chapter discusses the use of these three commands, along with installing and modifying print settings using the Windows Program Manager.

Using the Page Setup Commands

The easy-to-use File Page Setup command in Excel 4 is very important in helping create a professional-looking document. This command controls how your material looks on a printed page.

File Page Setup enables you to align and adjust text to fit correctly on pages and to determine the order in which pages are printed. In addition, this command enables you to select paper size, change orientation, set margins, and insert headers and footers. You also can control printer setup and print to the printer from this menu. Figure 4.2 shows the Page Setup dialog box.

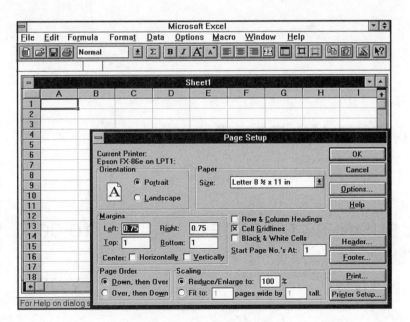

Fig. 4.2 The Page Setup dialog box.

Changing the Page Orientation

Excel enables you to print your documents in Portrait or Landscape mode. Figure 4.3 shows a worksheet printed in portrait mode, and figure 4.4 shows a worksheet printed in Landscape mode. You choose Portrait or Landscape mode by selecting the appropriate button in the Page Setup dialog box. Excel adjusts the document and uses the preset margins.

Selecting the Paper Size

The Paper Size option enables you to select one of several predefined paper sizes (see fig. 4.5). To see a list of the paper sizes available, click the arrow in the box and then select the paper size by clicking your choice. Excel adjusts your document for the new paper size and continues to use the current margins.

Spreadsheets that are wider than tall often will look better when printed in Landscape orientation.

BUSINESS MILEAGE

TOTAL BUSINESS MILEAGE   10,000
AIB MILEAGE
(INCL. IN TOTAL)   7,000

BEGINNING MILEAGE   9,200
CURRENT MILEAGE (3/15/92)   25,697
1992 MILES   1,700
TOTAL MILEAGE 1991   14,797

PCT. BUSINESS USE   67.58%

Fig. 4.3   A worksheet printed in Portrait orientation.

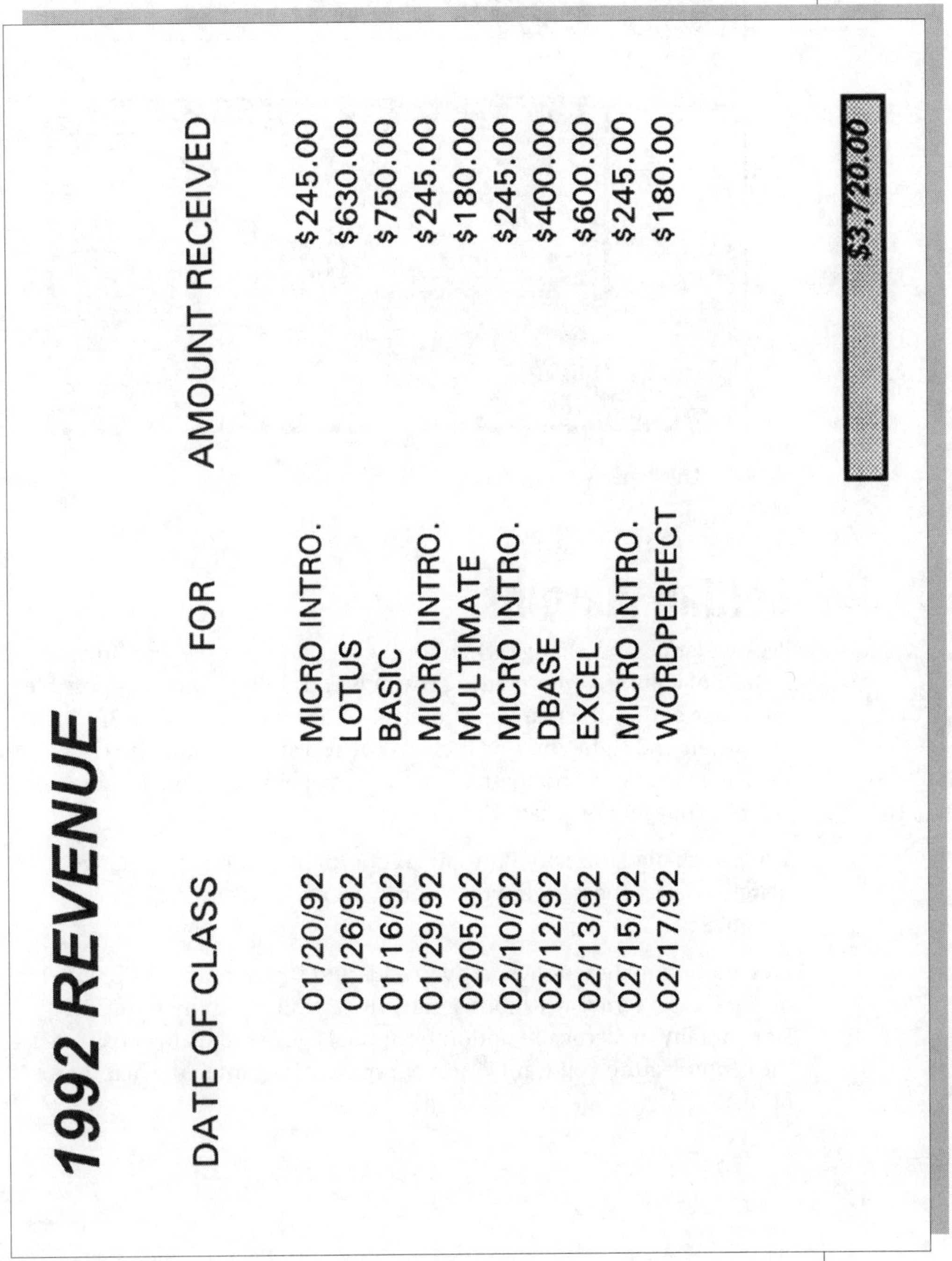

1992 REVENUE

DATE OF CLASS	FOR	AMOUNT RECEIVED
01/20/92	MICRO INTRO.	$245.00
01/26/92	LOTUS	$630.00
01/16/92	BASIC	$750.00
01/29/92	MICRO INTRO.	$245.00
02/05/92	MULTIMATE	$180.00
02/10/92	MICRO INTRO.	$245.00
02/12/92	DBASE	$400.00
02/13/92	EXCEL	$600.00
02/15/92	MICRO INTRO.	$245.00
02/17/92	WORDPERFECT	$180.00

$3,720.00

Fig. 4.4 A worksheet printed in Landscape orientation.

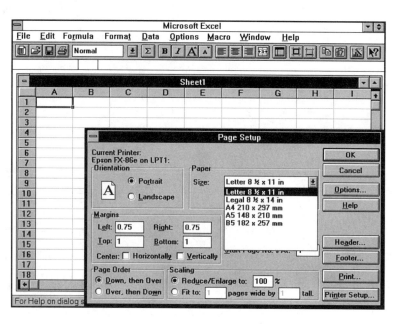

Fig. 4.5 The Paper Size options.

Setting Margins

Because letter sizes change when fonts are changed, Excel uses inches instead of columns when setting margins. Excel fits as much as possible on a page within the margins chosen. The default margins are 3/4 inch on the left and right and one inch on the top and bottom. These are relative margins—so no matter what font, paper size, or orientation you choose, your margins stay the same.

You can change the Top, Bottom, Left or Right Margins. To change margins, select the margin you want to change and enter the new margin size.

Presentation material, such as overheads and slides, normally is centered on a page. To center text horizontally or vertically, simply select the Horizontally or Vertically option from the Page Setup dialog box. Select the center feature you want, and your material is centered when it prints.

Scaling a Document

Presentation material, such as slides and overheads, is easier to read when it fills an entire page. Other documents you create in Excel also usually look better if they fit on one page or are scaled to an appropriate size.

To scale a document so that it meets your requirements, select the appropriate box in the scaling area of the Page Setup dialog box. You can choose the option that enables you to fit the document to one or more pages, or you can reduce or enlarge a document.

The easiest way to force a document to fit on one page is to select the Fit to box in the scaling area of the Page Setup dialog box. This box defaults to one page wide by one page tall and uses the current margins.

To adjust the size of the document manually, select the Reduce/Enlarge button. You may have to try several sizes to get the right fit when you use this option.

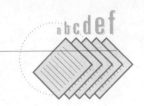

U se the Fit to Page command to make your spreadsheet fit on one page.

Sizing a Chart

If you are working with a chart, you are given options not seen in the normal Page Setup screen. You can, for example, select the Chart Size options (see fig. 4.6).

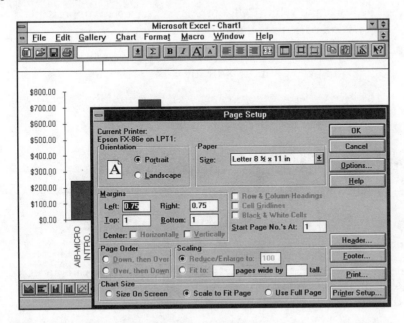

Fig. 4.6   The Page Setup dialog box for charts.

The Chart Size options follow:

- The Size On Screen option (at the bottom left corner of the dialog box) prints the chart the same size as it appears on your screen.

- The Scale to Fit Page option adjusts the size of the chart to fill as much of the page as possible while retaining the height-to-width ratio.

- The Use Full Page option adjusts the size of the chart to fill an entire page, changing height and widths appropriately.

Using Other Page Setup Features

The Page Setup box has several other useful features. Excel enables you to print gridlines, column headings, and row headings. You can suppress any colors or patterns that look good on-screen but would not look good when printed. Finally, the Page Setup features enable you to control page numbering and the order in which pages are printed. You may want to use the following options:

- The Page Setup dialog box enables you to display or suppress worksheet gridlines, row numbers, and column letters. Displaying cell gridlines and column headings is helpful in presentations if you will be referring to specific areas of the worksheet.

- The Black and White Cells option enables you to suppress any colors and patterns you may have in your worksheet.

- The Start Page No.'s At option enables you to control what page numbering you want to start with.

- The Page Order selections enable you to control the order in which pages print.

Inserting Headers and Footers

Excel enables you to set headers that print at the top of every page or footers that print at the bottom of every page. Headers or footers enable you to add titles, dates, times, file names, or page numbers to your worksheet.

Excel 4 divides headers and footers into three areas. You can put in information that will print on the left, center, or right part of your document. You can include in a header or footer any formatting or text you would include in a normal document. In addition, you can type as many lines as you want in each section. To insert a hard return to go to the next line, press Alt+Enter.

If you will be referring to specific cells when presenting information, print your spreadsheet with gridlines, column headings, and row headings.

The Header and Footer icons are quick and easy ways to insert the date and page number in printed spreadsheets.

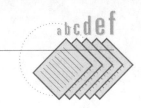

Figure 4.7 shows the Header dialog box. The screen contains six icons that are practical in a header or footer: font, page number, total pages, date, time, and file name.

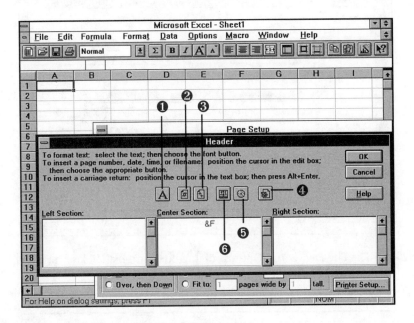

❶ Font
❷ Page number
❸ Page number of total pages
❹ File name
❺ Time
❻ Date

Fig. 4.7   The Page Setup Header dialog box.

Using the Page Setup Options Command

The File Page Setup Options command enables you to control print resolutions, darkness, and text quality. HP III models and later have a different Page Setup Options screen than other laser or dot-matrix printers (see figs. 4.8 and 4.9).

Page Setup for Dot-Matrix Printers and HP Models Other than HP IIIs

The Dithering options control the detail, or resolution, of your graphic images. Descriptions of these options follow:

- If you select None, graphics print in black and white only with no shading.

- If you use a resolution of 300 dpi or greater, select the Coarse option.

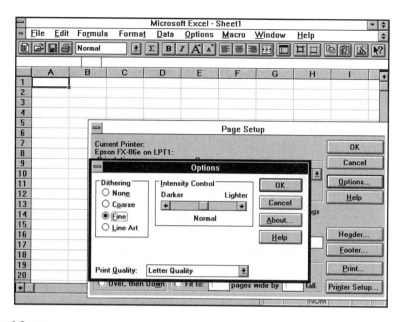

Fig. 4.8 The File Page Setup Options dialog box for most HP laser printers and all dot-matrix printers.

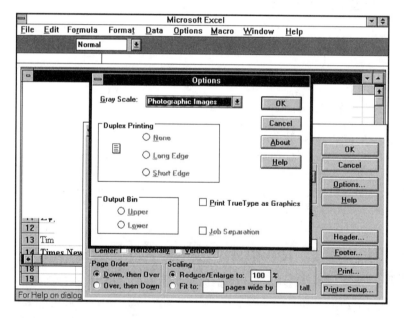

Fig. 4.9 The File Page Setup Options dialog box for HP III series printers.

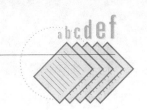

- If you have a resolution of 200 dpi or less, select the Fine option for smoother images.

- If you want well-defined borders between shades of gray, select the Line Art option.

If you want to lighten or darken your graphic images, select Intensity Control. Click the left arrow to make images darker and the right arrow to make them lighter.

If your printer supports it, you can use Print Quality to select the quality of print. If you have a laser printer, you will not have this option. You will, however, have a box to select that will print TrueType fonts or graphics. This will speed up the printing of TrueType fonts and save print memory.

Page Setup for HP III Series Laser Printers

The following options are available to you when using the HP III series laser printers:

- Gray Scale controls the type of pattern applied to printed images. You have three choices:

    Photographic Images controls soft contrasts between various shades of gray.

    Line Art Images controls sharp contrasts and solid lines between grays.

    HP ScanJet Images should be used with documents scanned through an HP ScanJet.

- The Duplex printing option is available only with HP LaserJet IIID printers or with HP LaserJet IIIsi printers. This feature enables you to select two-sided printing.

- The Output Bin option is available only with the HP LaserJet IIIsi printer. This feature enables you to output to the upper or lower output bin.

- The Job Separation option is available on HP LaserJet IIIsi printers. These printers have the capability to offset print jobs (shift the paper). This will occur if Job Separation is on.

- The Print TrueType Fonts as Graphics option enables you to print TrueType fonts as graphics rather than text. This may speed up printing and save printer memory if you are using a great deal of TrueType fonts.

The HP LaserJet III series printers have advanced features for controlling print quality. Certain models can print on both the front and back of a sheet of paper.

If you have a LaserJet IIID and use the Duplex Printing feature, you must use the upper output tray bin.

Using the Print Preview Command

U se the Print Preview screen to see how your document will look before sending it to the printer. This step will save you paper and money.

The File Print Preview command enables you to display your document in a format that is the same as you will see on paper (see figs. 4.10 and 4.11). From the Preview menu, you can move from page to page and select Zoom to zoom in or out on different areas. You can go to Page Setup and make any of the changes discussed in the previous sections. You even can change margins in the preview screen—an extremely valuable option for desktop publishing.

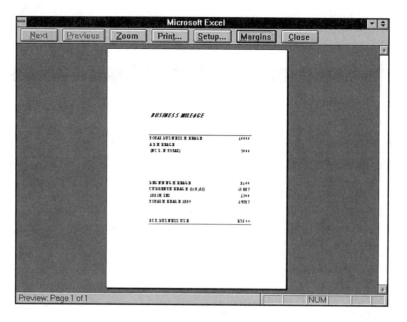

Fig. 4.10   The Print Preview screen.

Moving within a Page and between Pages

While previewing a document, you can move around the page by pressing the arrow keys or the other movement keys, such as PgUp and PgDn. These keys behave basically the same as they do in the Worksheet mode.

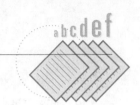

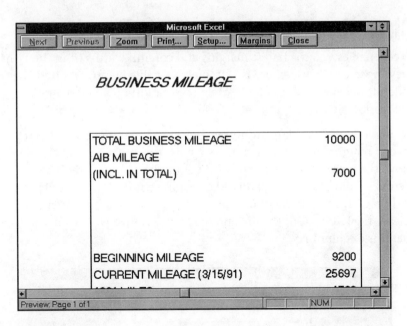

Fig. 4.11 The Zoom mode of the Print Preview screen.

To move to the next page in a multiple-page document, select the Next button at the top of the Print Preview screen. To move back a page, select the Previous button. The status bar at the bottom of the screen tells you what page you are on.

Using the Zoom Feature

The Print Preview screen has two modes. The Full Page mode is a screen that shows the entire page. This mode gives you a feel for how the document will look when it is printed. You can see how the text is balanced on the page and how the different formatting features work together. You probably will not be able to read the text in this screen, however.

The Zoom mode blows up the document so that you can see it better, but you can see only a portion of the document. To use Zoom mode, click the Zoom button at the top of the screen.

When you are in the Full Page mode, your mouse pointer looks like a magnifying glass. To zoom in on a particular area of text, position the mouse pointer on that area and click the left button, or click the document image.

When you are in Zoom mode, your mouse pointer is an arrow. Click the left button to go back to the Full Page mode.

Changing Margins in Print Preview

Excel enables you to change margins and column widths from the Print Preview screen. This feature is extremely valuable because it often is difficult to get the correct look for a presentation-quality document in the worksheet screen.

When you select margins from the choices at the top of your screen, several margin and column markers appear (see fig. 4.12). When you move the mouse pointer to one of these markers, the pointer changes to a cross symbol. You then can hold down the left button on your mouse and drag the margin or column marker to a new location. When you release the left button, the document is repositioned with your new margins or columns.

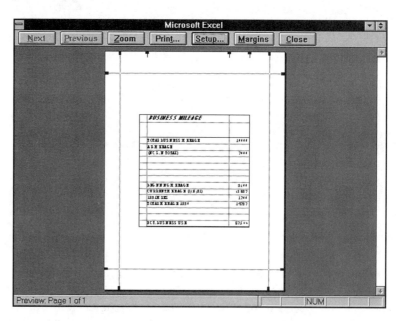

Fig. 4.12   The Print Preview screen with the column and margin markers displayed.

Printing to Paper

You can print by using the File Print command (or pressing Ctrl+Shift+F12), the File Print Preview command, or the File Page Setup command. Or you can simply click the Print tool in the Standard toolbar (see fig. 4.13).

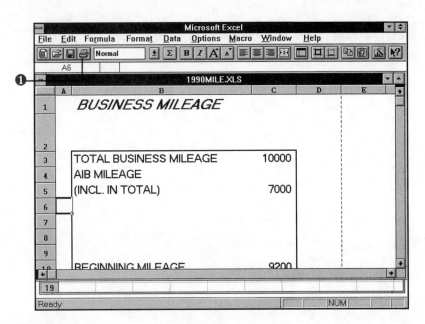

Fig. 4.13   The Print tool in the Standard toolbar.

When you print from anything but the Print tool, the Print box in figure 4.14 appears. This box enables you to select which parts of the worksheet you want to print, as well as the print quality. You also can use this box to suppress or print any notes or graphics you may have included in the worksheet.

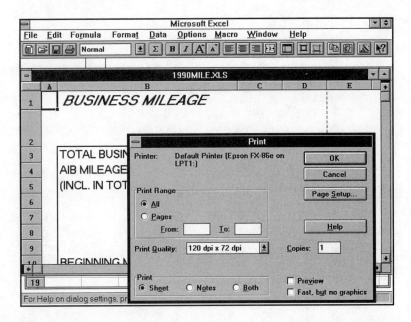

Fig. 4.14   The Print dialog box.

❶ Print tool

Selecting the Print Range

Excel assumes that you want to print your entire worksheet unless you tell it otherwise by setting a print range in the worksheet or with the **File Print** dialog box.

To select a print range in the worksheet, follow these steps:

1. Highlight the area of text you want to print.

To highlight, first move your mouse pointer to the beginning of the text that you want to block. While pressing the left mouse button, move the mouse until the area you want to print is highlighted. Then release the button.

2. Select Options from the main menu.

3. Select the Set Print Area option.

When you use this method to set a print range, you can select any amount of text. You also can set multiple ranges for printing. The process is the same as for a single print range, but you must select multiple ranges before choosing **Options Set Print Area**.

To set multiple ranges, highlight the first print range with the mouse, as described earlier in this section. Then, move the mouse to the next area to highlight, press the Ctrl key, and highlight this area. Both areas should be highlighted now. Repeat this procedure for as many areas as you want. Then select **Options Set Print Area**. Each block will be printed on a different sheet of paper.

To remove a print range, first select the entire worksheet by clicking the left mouse button on the blank square above the row numbers and to the left of the column headings. Then chose **Options Remove Print Area**. You also can press Ctrl+Shift+Space bar to select the entire spreadsheet.

You also can use the File Print dialog box to select a range to print. With this method, you can limit what you want to print—but by entire pages only.

- From the File Print dialog box (under Print Range), select **Pages** and specify the pages to print.

- If you want to print the entire worksheet, do not set a print range and leave the Print Range set to All in the File Print box.

After a print area has been defined, Excel inserts vertical and horizontal dashed page breaks.

Excel will print your entire worksheet unless you tell it otherwise by selecting a print range.

Choosing a Print Quality

To change the default print quality (for dot-matrix printers only), select File Print and click the arrow in the Print Quality box. Options available to you appear; click the option you want. You should select higher resolutions only when printing a final draft.

Printing Notes

Excel enables you to attach notes to cells as a reminder of what the cell contains, its purpose, and so on. Notes also are used for documentation. You create notes by using the Formula Note command.

To print any notes created in your worksheet, select File Print and then select Notes or Both. If you select Notes, only notes will print—not your worksheet data. To print notes and worksheet data, select Both.

Printing Titles on Multiple Pages

Worksheets often require more than one page to print. Frequently, you may need to carry row or column titles from the first page to subsequent pages.

To use the Options Set Titles command to print titles on multiple pages, follow these steps:

1. Select the Rows and Columns options to designate how many rows and columns you want to include on every page. Move your mouse pointer to the row or column designator at the beginning of the column or row you want to select and click your left mouse button. Or press Ctrl+Space bar to select columns and press Shift+Space bar for rows.

2. Select Options Set Print Titles.

If you are selecting specific areas to print using the Options Set Print Area commands, be careful—if you include in the print area any area designated as a title, Excel prints the title twice.

*S*etting print titles will make multiple-page spreadsheets easier to read. Print titles carry row and column headings from the first page to subsequent pages.

Using the Print Report Commands

The Print Report feature is an Excel add-in. It is installed when Excel is installed. Print Report enables you to put together a collection of views (ranges) that will print in sequence as one large report.

A *view* is basically a worksheet range that you have named. It will save the display and any print settings. You can create a view by using the **Window View** command.

To create a view, follow these steps:

1. Select the range you want to include as a view.

2. Choose **Window View**.

3. Choose Add.

4. Type the view name.

5. Select OK.

To create a report, follow these steps:

1. Select the File Print Report command.

2. Choose Add.

3. Type a report name.

4. Select a view from the pull-down menu list. Select the views in the order you want them printed.

5. Choose Add to add the view to the current list.

6. Repeat steps 4 and 5 to add more views to the report.

7. Press Enter or choose OK.

To print a report, follow these steps:

1. Select File Print Report.

2. Choose Print.

3. Enter the number of copies to print.

Using the Print Tool on the Standard Toolbar

To print in Excel, you can select any of the print-related options from the File menu or the Print tool from the Standard toolbar at the top of the screen.

The Print tool will print the entire worksheet or any print ranges that have been defined. It will not give you any other control over what will be printed. The Print tool sends information directly to the printer without any additional prompts.

Installing Printers

When you installed Microsoft Windows, you were asked to select the printers you use. You install or remove a printer through the Main window in the Program Manager.

To add or remove a printer, follow these steps:

1. Access the Program Manager in Windows.

2. Select the **W**indow command from the main menu.

3. Select the Main option from the **W**indow pull-down menu (see fig. 4.15).

I nstall all the printers you think you may use during the Windows installation. This will save you work later.

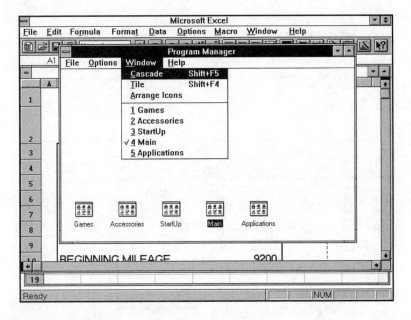

Fig. 4.15 The Window pull-down menu in the Program Manager.

4. Select the Control Panel icon (see fig. 4.16).

5. Select the Printers icon (see fig. 4.17).

6. To add or remove a printer, select the appropriate button from the Printers dialog box (see fig. 4.18).

The Add button lists the printers Windows supports. Select the printer you want to add by highlighting it. At this point, you probably will be asked to insert your Windows printer disk into drive A. To remove a printer, highlight the printer name and select the **R**emove button.

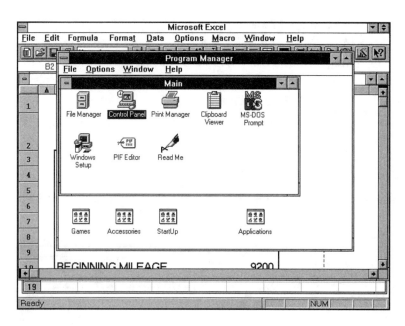

Fig. 4.16 The Control Panel icon in Windows.

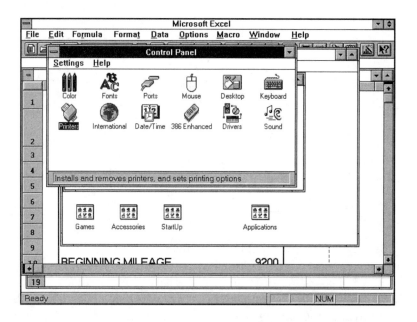

Fig. 4.17 The Printers icon in Windows.

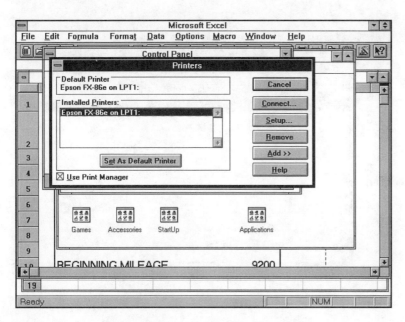

Fig. 4.18   The Printers dialog box in Windows.

The Connect button enables you to select the port your printer uses. The Setup button enables you to change the default settings of the printer you selected. The Help button gives you a brief explanation of each of the commands.

Using the Windows Print Manager

You can use the Windows Print Manager to check the status of Excel's print jobs. Like the Control Panel, it is accessed through the Main window of the Program Manager. Figure 4.19 shows the Print Manager box. This box tells you the status of all print jobs and makes you aware of any printing problems. The Help menu from the Print Manager main menu gives you additional information about the View and Options menus.

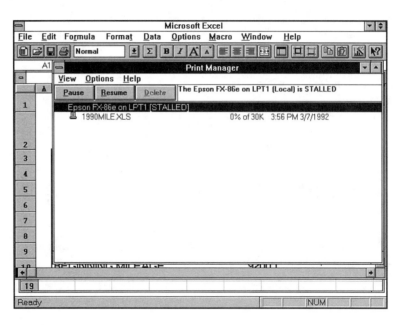

Fig. 4.19   The Print Manager dialog box.

Selecting a Printer

You can select an installed printer from Excel by using the File Page Setup command. To install a printer from within Excel, follow these steps:

1. Select File Page Setup.

2. Select Printer Setup.

3. Highlight the printer you want to use and select it. You can move up or down the list by clicking the arrows in the printer box (see fig. 4.20).

Select Setup from the Printer Setup dialog box to change printer defaults. Use Setup to adjust the resolution or to choose the paper size. You can tell your system how the paper will be fed by using the Paper Source option.

The Setup box also has an Options choice for additional default changes. These Excel default options were discussed in the Page Setup sections of this chapter. The commands in the Printer Setup dialog box are the same, except that changes made in the Page Setup dialog box are for the current document only. Changes made in the Printer Setup dialog box are default changes, and will be saved automatically.

Any changes made in the Printer Setup dialog box are default changes that will affect all documents created in the future.

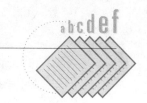

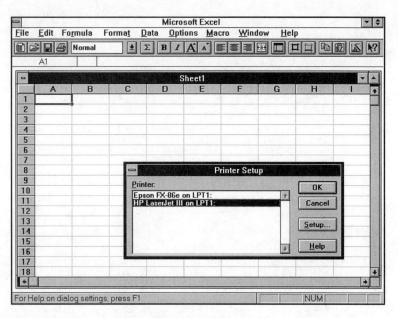

Fig. 4.20 The Printer Setup dialog box.

Chapter Summary

This chapter discussed the many features found in the File Print, File Page Setup, and File Print Preview commands. To successfully produce desktop publications in Excel, you need to understand the effective use of these commands.

The File Page Setup command is of particular importance in creating quality documents. It enables you to control page sizing and orientation, set margins, add headers and footers, control print quality, and much more.

The File Print Preview command not only enables you to see how the document will look when printed, but it also enables you to change margins and column widths before printing.

The chapter also discussed how to use Windows to add or remove printers and how to select a printer from within Excel.

The next chapter discusses charts. Excel has a very powerful, easy-to-use chart generator. This function enables you to present data in graphical form, which is often easier to understand than standard worksheets.

Using Excel To Create Charts

5

An Excel chart is a graphic representation of worksheet data. You can use charts for many purposes, including representing trends in data over time or showing the relationships among data. Charts visually tell the story that your numbers reflect—sometimes more persuasively than the numbers themselves. Charts therefore can be a very effective way of communicating a message.

Excel charts present data from worksheets in an attractive, easy-to-understand format. Charts show trends in data and the relationships among data. Charts present striking and persuasive visual images of data. With thoughtful use, charts and graphs can enable you to present large and complex data sets succinctly and coherently.

Creating a meaningful and expressive chart requires consideration and thought.

Attention to data, message, and audience must be considered when you are creating a chart. A well-conceived chart can provide a very dramatic effect that visually brings the point across to your audience. You must carefully consider several factors when creating a chart.

This chapter covers how to plan for and create effective and persuasive charts with Excel 4 for Windows' powerful charting features. In Chapter 6, you learn how to change the style and look of your chart. Chapter 6 also covers techniques and tips for enhancing your chart to make your message very clear.

Planning an Effective Chart

An effective chart presents a clear, concise message. It accurately represents your data. The message that you want to portray must be easily understood by your audience. You should plan carefully before you begin the charting process.

To create an effective chart, follow these steps:

1. Determine the data you want to chart and check for accuracy.
2. Interpret your data to determine the message you want to express.
3. Identify your audience.
4. Consider the form of presentation.
5. Choose an appropriate chart type.
6. Build the chart for accuracy.

Microsoft Excel offers several choices of charts and styles. You can select from a number of built-in formats for each chart type or you can add your own custom formatting to create exactly the type of chart you want. Even with all the features that Excel offers, an effective chart must be planned and constructed carefully. The following sections explain the preliminary stages to take when charting.

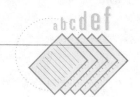

Determining the Data to Chart and Checking for Accuracy

The first step in creating an effective chart is to determine the data to be plotted. You must decide what information best represents the message you want to convey. Then determine what information you can leave out. The less data you select, the clearer the chart will be. Far too often, people build charts with unclear messages because they try to chart too much data. The audience becomes confused, and the message is lost. The less complex the chart, the clearer the message.

Examine the worksheet data carefully. Check the numbers for accuracy. We all know that with today's electronic mediums, inaccurate or skewed data can lead to false graphical representation. A visual examination of the data may uncover mistakes. Examine the calculations used to generate the data; check the data ranges for accuracy; look for dropped zeroes, missing decimal points, improbable numbers, and any other anomalies. Missing data can make a mess of even the most mathematically accurate results.

The first step when planning a chart is to determine your data and to check it for accuracy.

Determining the Message of the Chart

Now that you have identified the data to be charted, you need to interpret the data results to determine the chart's message. If you are assembling your own data, you already may be aware of the underlying message of the numbers. If you are interpreting someone else's data, however, you will need to carefully evaluate the data. Taking extra time at this point to understand what the data is representing will help you choose the correct chart type.

Interpret your data results to determine your message.

You now should have a good idea of what the numbers are "saying." At this point you need to determine the message that you want to represent in the chart. Stating your message clearly will guide you as you generate the chart. It is a good idea to write down the message. This clarity of purpose will help make your chart more direct, expressive, and consistent in its design and message.

The central message that you wrote down will help you create the title of the chart. A chart title should summarize the main point of the data. Your audience will grasp the message at first glance.

Identifying Your Audience

Knowing who your audience is will guide your chart's development.

It is important to identify your audience when planning a chart. Who will see your chart? Will you be presenting it to a large or small group of people? Are they literate on the subject? What is their level of sophistication with data and charts? Will they be receptive or hostile to the message? Are the viewers interested in finding a solution to an existing problem, or do you need to first attract them to your data? Answering questions like these will help you develop a much more effective chart.

Considering the Form of Presentation

The last of the preliminary steps in creating your chart is to consider how you will present it to your audience. If desktop publishing is your final output, you can create a chart with more detail and complexity. Your readers will have the time to examine the chart and identify its meaning. If your output is limited to black and white print, you need to use patterns instead of colors.

Slide presentations and desktop animation presentations require simpler charts. Your audience will have little time to decipher the message, so it must be direct and clear. If your data is complex, you may want to break a single chart into several separate charts, each illustrating a portion of the overall message. You also can use colors with this form of presentation to draw your audience's attention to specific data.

Once you have identified the form of presentation, you have completed the preliminary stages of planning the chart. Now you are ready to begin the physical process of producing the chart. Next you will choose the chart type most appropriate for the message you want to express.

Choosing an Appropriate Chart Type

Excel 4 offers 14 chart types—eight two-dimensional chart types, and six three-dimensional chart types.

Excel 3 offers 11 chart types to choose from—seven two-dimensional chart types, and four three-dimensional chart types. Excel 4 offers 14 chart types—eight two-dimensional chart types, and six three-dimensional chart types. By now, you should have a good idea of how you want your data to be represented and what message you want to present. Table 5.1 describes the type of charts you can use to express your data (see fig. 5.4 to see what each chart type looks like).

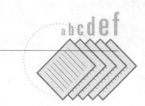

Table 5.1   Excel Charts

Chart Type	Illustrates
Area	Relative importance of data over a period of time. Area charts show the data in terms of its volume, or the area it consumes. The stacked format shows relationships to the whole area.
Bar	Individual figures at a certain period of time or draws comparisons between the data. The stacked and 100% stacked formats show relationships to a whole. The categories are organized vertically and the values are organized horizontally. There is more emphasis on comparisons and less emphasis on time passage.
Column	Variation over a designated amount of time or draws comparisons between items. The stacked and 100% stacked formats show relationships to a whole. The categories are organized horizontally and values are organized vertically.
Line	Trends or changes in data over a specific period of time. A line chart emphasizes time passage and rate of change, not the amount of change.
Pie	Relationship or proportion of parts to a whole; always contains only one data series.
Radar	Changes or frequencies of data relative to a center point and to each other. Each category has its own value axis extending from the center point. Lines connect all the data markers in the same series.
XY (scatter)	Relationship or degree of relationship between the numeric values in several data series, or plots two groups of numbers as one series of xy coordinates.
Combination	Related data that is measured in different units. You can use up to four axes in a combination chart. A combination chart is comprised of two charts: a main chart and an overlay chart. This chart enables you to superimpose one data series over another in order to show just how close the data series correspond.

continues

Table 5.1   Continued

Chart Type	Illustrates
3-D Area	3-D view of an area chart, which emphasizes the sum of data, and separates chart data series into distinct rows to show differences among the data series.
3-D Bar	3-D view of a bar chart, which emphasizes the values of individual items at specific times or draws comparisons among items. The stacked and 100% formats show relationships to a whole.
3-D Column	3-D view of a column chart. This chart compares data points along two axes: the category axis and the chart data series axis. This enables you to compare data within a data series more easily and still view data by category.
3-D Line	Data series as 3-D ribbons. This makes individual lines easier to view, even when they cross, while still showing all data series in one chart for comparison.
3-D Pie	3-D view of a pie chart. 3-D pie charts emphasize the data values in the front wedges.
3-D Surface	Data as a sheet of cellophane stretched over a 3-D column chart. This chart can show interrelationships between large amounts of data that otherwise may be difficult to see. The use of color indicates areas that are the same height, but it does not mark the data series.

Understanding Excel Charting Capabilities

The first row or column of your selection determines the series or category names.

Excel has a set procedure for interpreting selected worksheet data. The worksheet data must be a data series including any row or column labels you want to use in the chart. You define your selection by highlighting the data series on the worksheet. The shape of the selection determines whether the row or column is used for series names or category names. Excel will always create fewer data series than categories. If the user-defined selection has more columns than rows, Excel will plot each row as a chart data series.

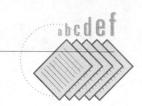

The basic function of Excel charting is to place charts directly into the worksheet. This capability provides an easy way to include charts with worksheet data and text. You can place charts at any location and in any combination on a page. Charts will be displayed and printed with the worksheet data. A chart created on a worksheet is a graphic object and is saved as part of the worksheet on which it was created. Excel 4 offers two new methods for creating embedded charts: ChartWizard and the Chart toolbar.

Excel also will create a chart as a separate document in its own window. Any embedded chart can be opened in a separate document within a window. You double-click the embedded chart, and it opens a window displaying the chart. You can add many enhancements to the chart through the new window. See Chapter 6 for more information.

Creating Embedded Charts with ChartWizard

Excel 4 expands on Excel 3's charting facilities with ChartWizard. (If you have Excel 3 for Windows and do not know how to create a chart, refer to Que's *Using Excel 4 for Windows*, Special Edition, which covers Versions 3 and 4.) ChartWizard displays a series of windows, enabling the user to select the chart type and add titles and legends. ChartWizard even enables you to select the data range to be plotted.

To use ChartWizard, follow these steps:

1. Highlight the range of data to use in a graph, including any row and column labels. To select nonadjacent cells, press Ctrl while highlighting these cells.

   If you select empty cells within your highlighted range, Excel uses them to define a series or category name. Sometimes, you may want this effect in order to help spread out the categories represented in a chart. Including empty cells in your range also can create a gap in your categories or series names, however, that is visually distracting and can cause your audience to misinterpret your data.

   Remember, the first row or column of your selection determines the series or category names. The shape of the selection determines whether the row or column is used for series names or category names. Excel always creates fewer data series than categories.

E mbedded charts provide an easy way to include worksheet data and text.

C hartWizard methodically guides the user through the commands needed to create or edit a chart.

Now that you have defined your data series, you can begin to create your chart. The Standard toolbar must be visible; it is the default toolbar that is displayed when you first load into Excel.

2. To display the Standard toolbar, pull down the Options menu and select Toolbars Standard. The Standard toolbar appears in the location where it was last displayed (see fig. 5.1).

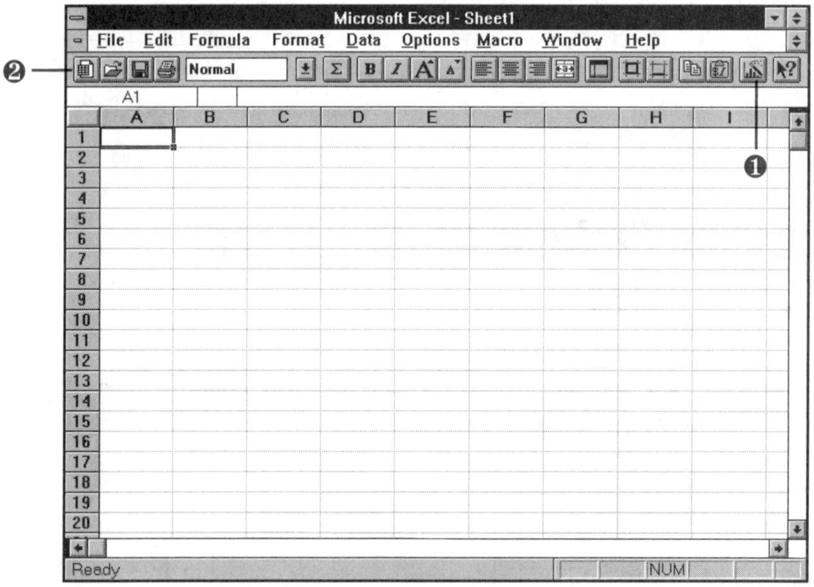

① ChartWizard tool

② Standard tool

Fig. 5.1 The Standard toolbar with the ChartWizard tool.

T he ChartWizard tool is the tool with the wand above the chart.

3. Select the ChartWizard tool, which is the second tool from the right end of the Standard toolbar. Your mouse pointer becomes a cross-hair pointer typical of the graphics drawing tool.

4. Using your mouse, point to where you want one corner of the chart to be located. Drag your mouse to draw a rectangle the size and shape you want the chart to be (see fig. 5.2). To plot the chart in a perfect square, press Shift while you drag the mouse. To align the chart to the cell grid, press Alt while you drag the mouse.

S tep 1 of the Chart-Wizard enables you to change your definition range of cells to be charted. Type in the new range.

5. After you designate the chart area, the ChartWizard Step 1 dialog box appears (see fig. 5.3). ChartWizard displays the cell reference numbers for the range of cells that you highlighted on your worksheet. If this is not the correct range to be charted, type the cell reference numbers for the range you want. You can choose the

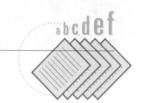

Cancel, Next>, or >> button. In the following dialog boxes—Step 2, 3, 4, and 5 of ChartWizard—you will have access to all six buttons displayed in figure 5.4. Select the Next > button to move to Step 2.

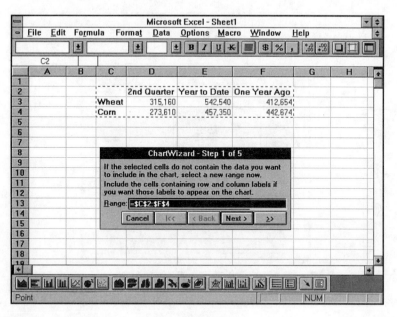

Fig. 5.2 Selecting the designated chart area.

Fig. 5.3 The ChartWizard - Step 1 of 5 dialog box.

Table 5.2 describes the action of each ChartWizard button.

Table 5.2   The ChartWizard Buttons

To do this	Choose this button
Move to next ChartWizard step	Next >
Return to previous ChartWizard step	< Back
Create a chart using options you have selected at that point and exit ChartWizard	>>
Return to beginning of ChartWizard	<<
Cancel ChartWizard and return to your worksheet	Cancel
Display Help information about options and tools	Help

ChartWizard enables you to select the chart format and style.

6. The ChartWizard Step 2 dialog box appears, asking you to select a chart type for displaying your data (see fig. 5.4). Keep in mind that certain chart types are more accurate at representing particular types of data than others. Refer to Table 5.1 for chart descriptions. Select the chart type you want by clicking that chart tool.

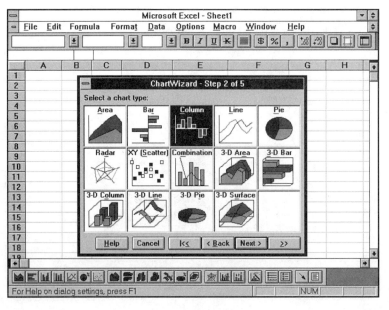

Fig. 5.4   The ChartWizard - Step 2 of 5 dialog box.

The ChartWizard Step 2 dialog box has six buttons at the bottom of the box. In addition to the previous five buttons displayed in Step 1 of the ChartWizard, now you have a **H**elp button and a < **B**ack button.

7. The ChartWizard Step 3 dialog box appears, asking you to choose a format for that chart type (see fig. 5.5). Remember, at any time you can go back to the preceding dialog box to change the chart type.

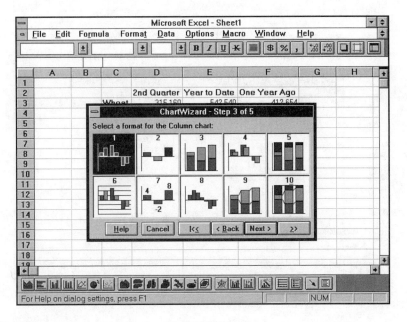

Fig. 5.5 The ChartWizard - Step 3 of 5 dialog box.

8. The ChartWizard Step 4 dialog box appears, displaying an example of your chart (see fig. 5.6). If you are not satisfied with the chart, click the **B**ack button to choose a new chart format or go two steps backward to change the chart type.

The Step 4 dialog box shows three options. The first set of radio buttons enables you to switch the range of cells that you selected for the data series. The second set of radio buttons turns on or off the category (x) axis. The third set offers you two choices—replacing the first column of the data series with legend text, or using the first column as a data point.

As you select your choices, notice that the sample chart changes to reflect those options. When you are satisfied, click the Next > button.

9. The ChartWizard Step 5 dialog box appears (see fig. 5.7). By selecting the options displayed, you can add a legend to your chart by clicking the Yes radio button, and you can create a chart title by typing a title in the Chart Title field. Step 5 also enables you to create category and value titles for the axis in the Axis Titles section. If your chart is a combination type chart and you have selected a chart format of 2 or 3 (Step 3 of 5), you can attach a name to your overlay by typing the title in the Overlay field. When you are satisfied with your chart's appearance, select the OK button.

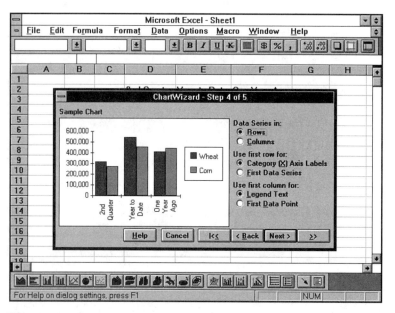

Fig. 5.6 The ChartWizard - Step 4 of 5 dialog box.

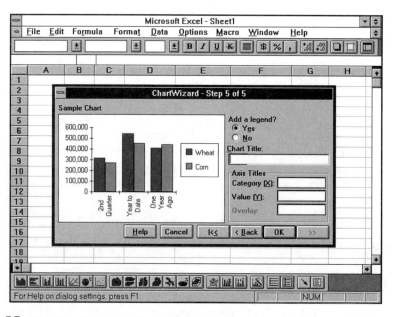

Fig. 5.7 The ChartWizard - Step 5 of 5 dialog box.

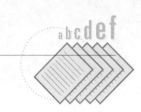

10. Click the OK button.

ChartWizard creates an embedded chart within the area you specified on your worksheet (see fig. 5.8).

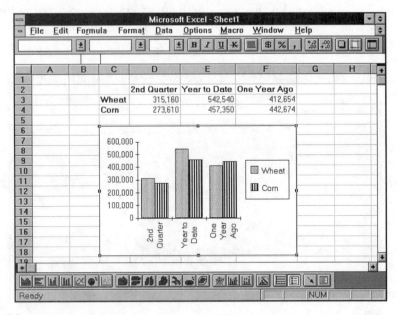

Fig. 5.8 A completed chart.

Creating an Embedded Chart with the Chart Tools

By selecting one of the 17 charting tools on the Chart toolbar, you can tell Microsoft Excel 4 to quickly create an embedded chart on the active worksheet. The charting tools correspond to the most commonly used formats for each chart type. If the tool you select does not reflect the chart type you want, you can create a different chart by clicking another charting tool.

To create an embedded chart on the active worksheet, follow these steps:

1. Select the range of worksheet cells that contain the data you want to plot, including any worksheet column or row labels that you want to use in the chart. Do not select empty cells outside the rows and columns you want to chart.

You can create an embedded chart just by clicking a tool on the Chart toolbar.

2. Click one of the charting tools on the Chart toolbar (see fig. 5.9). The mouse pointer changes to a cross-hair pointer. (If you are unfamiliar with the chart types, you can display the chart tool names in the status bar at the bottom far left corner of the worksheet window by pointing to any chart tool and pressing the left mouse button.) The chart name appears in the status bar for as long as you hold down the left mouse button.

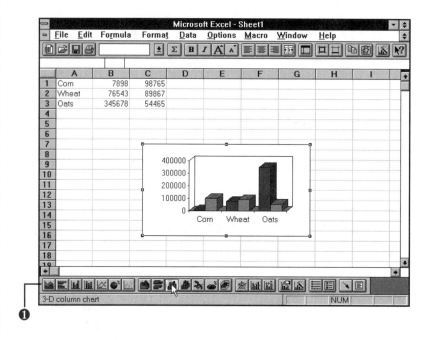

① Chart toolbar

Fig. 5.9 The Chart toolbar displaying the name of the Chart tool in the status bar.

3. Point to where you want one corner of the chart located and drag the mouse to draw a rectangle of the size and shape you want the chart to be.

When you release the mouse button, the chart appears in the designated area on your worksheet (see fig. 5.10).

Building the Chart for Accuracy

Computerized charting has made accurate portrayal of data a more complex issue than in the past. Charting programs enable you to quickly edit every aspect of a chart; therefore, you may inadvertently distort the message and portray the data invalidly. The chart in figure 5.11 portrays

Remember, to plot the chart in a perfect square, press Shift while you drag the mouse. To align the chart to the cell grid, press Alt while you drag the mouse.

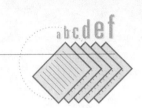

an example of *true scaling*. True scaling accurately reflects the message of the numbers. Figure 5.12 portrays distorted scaling. With the Category axis moved to cross the Value axis at the 2600 point, the chart inaccurately reflects a drastic increase from the first quarter to the fourth quarter.

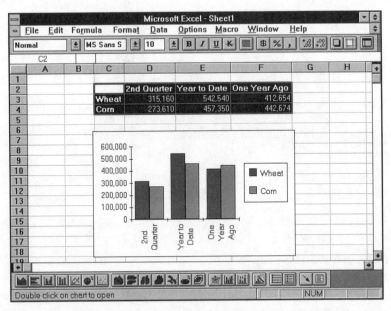

Fig. 5.10 Selecting the designated chart area.

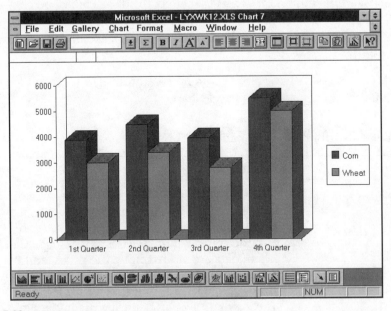

Fig. 5.11 True scaling.

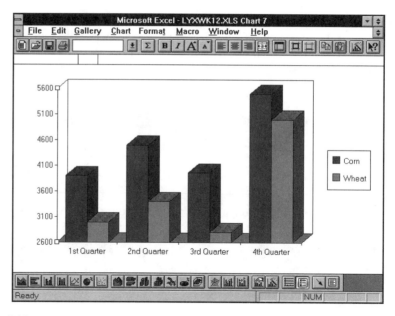

Fig. 5.12 Distorted scaling.

To effectively express your data graphically, you need to understand all parts of a chart. Your understanding of the parts of a chart will enable you to enhance and focus its message. To enhance a chart, you need to open the chart in a separate window. You can annotate the chart with text and objects such as arrows or lines; this enables you to highlight key trends or note important events that affect the data. Embedded charts and chart documents are linked to the worksheet data from which they were created. Therefore, if you change the worksheet data, the chart will reflect those changes.

All types of charts have certain common features. Figure 5.13 and table 5.3 illustrate the parts of an Excel Chart.

Table 5.3   The Parts of an Excel Chart

Part	Description
Axis	Line that serves as a major reference for charting data in a chart. Two-dimensional charts have two axes: the horizontal axis or category axis (x-axis) and the vertical axis or values axis (y-axis). Categories of data are plotted along the x-axis, and data values are plotted along the y-axis. Three-dimensional charts have the vertical axis as the z-axis. The x-axis and y-axis delineate the horizontal surface of the chart on the chart floor.

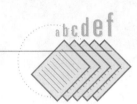

Part	Description
Chart data series	A group of related values, such as every data value in a single row or column of the worksheet selection. A chart can have one or more data series. Figure 5.13 shows two data series: Sales and Service.
Chart menu bar	When a chart is active, the menu bar displays the names of chart menus. When a chart is inactive, the menu bar at the top of the window displays the chart menu choices. You have access to the following new menu choices: Gallery and Chart. The other menu choices—File, Edit, Format, Macro, Window, and Help—have slight differences in their pull-down features.
Chart text	Text that describes the data or objects in a chart. *Attached text* is any label linked to a chart object such as an axis or a data marker. Attached text stays with the object if the object is moved. Attached text cannot be moved independently of the chart object. *Unattached text* is text you add with the Text Box tool on the Chart toolbar or just by typing whenever the chart is active and then pressing Enter. You can move unattached text anywhere on the chart.
Chart toolbar	Displays 17 charting tools and the ChartWizard tool. The charting tools correspond to the most commonly used formats for each chart type.
Data marker	A dot, area, bar, or symbol that marks one data point or value. A data series is signified by related data markers in a chart.
Gridlines	Lines that extend from the tick marks on an axis across the plot area. The grid is optional, but it can make it easier for you to view the data values.
Legend	Key that identifies the colors, patterns, or symbols associated with the markers of a chart data series and illustrates the data series name that corresponds to each data marker.
Plot area	Area in which your data is plotted. Includes all axes and markers that represent data points.

continues

Table 5.3   Continued

Part	Description
Series formula	Formula describing a chart data series. This formula shows a reference to the cell that contains the data series name, references to worksheet cells that contain the categories and values plotted in the chart, and the plot order of the series. A series formula also can contain the actual data used to create the chart.
Tick mark	Small line that crosses an axis and marks off a category, scale, or chart data series. A *tick-mark label* is attached text next to the tick mark.

1. Plot area
2. Gridlines
3. Chart menu bar
4. Chart text
5. Series formula
6. Legend
7. Axis
8. Chart toolbar
9. Axis
10. Tick mark
11. Chart data series
12. Data marker

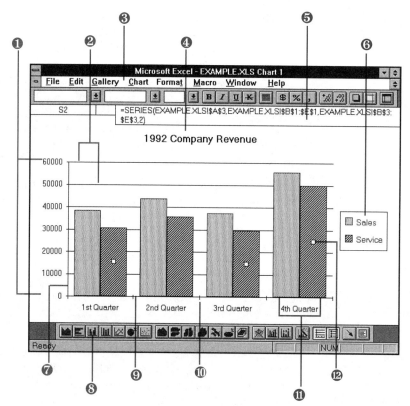

Fig. 5.13   The parts of a chart.

By understanding the function of all parts of a chart, you can effectively and accurately represent your worksheet data.

Chapter Summary

Through careful examination and interpretation of your data, you will be able to choose the best chart type to accurately represent your message. With your audience identified, you can further focus the chart to represent your point clearly and precisely.

The following chapter covers in detail how to add enhancements to your chart through text, arrows, and extra detail. These enhancements will enable you to bring the message to your audience in dramatic fashion.

Accurately representing your data is crucial to an effective chart and presentation.

6

Editing and Enhancing Charts

In Chapter 5, you learned how to create an effective and persuasive chart. This chapter focuses on adding enhancements and basic editing techniques that can help you further emphasize the chart message and bring the message home to your audience.

A void portraying too much information and detail in your chart. Keep the chart simple so that your message is more easily conveyed.

You should keep in mind some design considerations and techniques that guide the enhancement process. Changing the chart's content can be disastrous if not carefully planned. Through computer charting, you can change any part of a chart and add many additional features. Computer charting can help you create an ideal chart or a poorly designed chart. A poorly designed chart tries to portray too much detail and too much information (see fig. 6.1). This chapter discusses proper design techniques and design elements to use when enhancing and editing your chart.

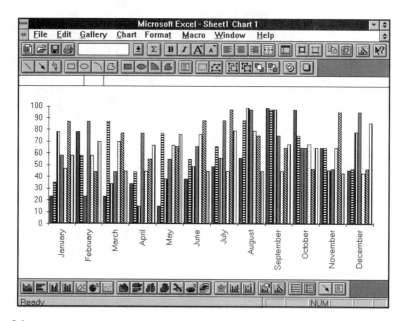

Fig. 6.1   A poorly designed chart.

Considering Design Elements

You should consider the following five design elements when creating a chart:

- *Clarity:* This is probably the most important design consideration when creating an effective chart. Your audience will perceive the message immediately from a well-planned chart. When you add enhancements and change default styles, clarity should be your main consideration.

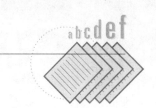

- *Emphasis:* Through Excel's editing features, you can change any part of a chart. You can place emphasis on certain features of the chart to reinforce your message. Be careful not to inadvertently change the chart's message by emphasizing the wrong data, however.

- *White Space:* This is a very important aspect of design. You can create a well-planned chart by effective use of white space. Far too often, people tend to cram too much information or too many messages into a chart. The audience cannot find the message because there is too much information being portrayed. Special attention to white space will help you create a much more persuasive chart.

- *Proportion:* Proportion in a chart is very important. If you have limited space to express an idea, one aspect of the chart can get lost or dominate the chart.

- *Consistency:* Consistency must be present in a chart's design. Consistency in font usage, patterns, and borders is a must. A poorly designed chart will be created through lack of consistency. Excel offers templates to help keep consistency throughout your charts.

This chapter addresses design considerations and techniques for editing a chart to effectively enhance your message.

Editing a Chart

Chapter 5 discusses how to create a chart by using the ChartWizard tool or by using the Chart toolbar. These two techniques embed the chart in the Excel worksheet. To edit and enhance an embedded chart, you need to open it into a chart window. By double-clicking the embedded chart, you can open a separate document that provides a graphic editing environment. The chart window resembles a dedicated graphics program and temporarily replaces the worksheet with just the chart document window and a new menu. Notice that you now have a new menu bar. Some commands on the menu bar will be familiar to users of desktop publishing and graphics programs.

The chart window resembles a dedicated graphics program and temporarily replaces the worksheet with just the chart document window and a new menu.

To open an embedded chart, follow these steps:

1. Double-click the embedded chart. The chart appears in a chart window (see fig. 6.2).

2. Resize or maximize the window by positioning the mouse on the window's edges or corners and dragging the frame out to the

dimensions that you need, or by clicking the Maximize button in the upper right corner of the chart window. The Maximize button is the button with the triangle that points up.

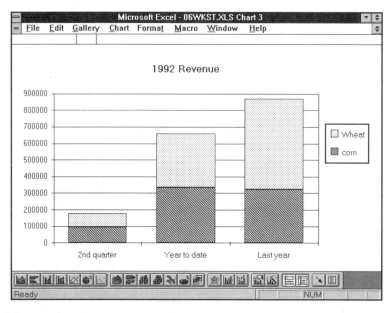

Fig. 6.2 The chart window.

If you move or resize the new chart window, you see the original embedded chart behind the chart window. Any changes you make in the chart window, except for the moving and sizing of the chart window, affect the embedded chart. All changes are reflected immediately in the embedded chart. All changes are saved when you save the worksheet. You also can save the chart as a separate document by using the chart window's File and Save command. If you delete the embedded chart, Excel closes the chart window.

A common problem with embedded charts is that the designated area in the worksheet is usually too small to properly display the chart. You will need to adjust many features of the chart. You also will face this problem when you enhance and edit a chart in the chart window. The space in the worksheet is usually smaller than the chart window. If you add arrows and text to the chart, when you exit from the chart window, you will see the changes reflected in the worksheet. If your worksheet chart area is too small, however, the changes may overlap and appear to be out of proportion.

Figure 6.3 shows a chart with a title in a large font size and arrows pointing to the column chart. When you exit the chart window, the font retains the applied font size in the smaller worksheet area, and the arrows are out of proportion with the rest of the plot area (see fig. 6.4).

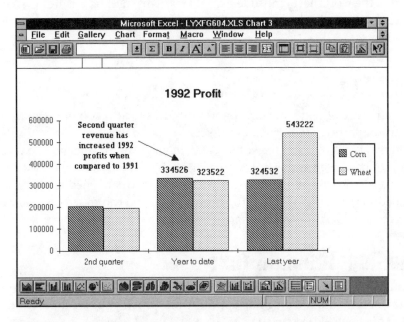

Fig. 6.3 The chart window displaying a chart with text and arrows.

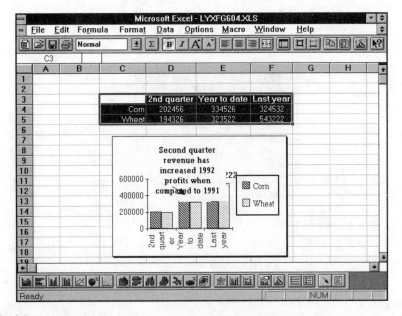

Fig. 6.4 An embedded chart displaying overlapped text and arrows.

As the example illustrates, you need to plan all enhancements and edits that you make to a chart. Always keep in mind that the smaller embedded chart will dictate what is incorporated into the chart within the chart windows. One solution is to resize the chart window to the same size as the worksheet embedded chart area. This method ensures that all edits and enhancements will be in proportion with the chart area in the worksheet.

Adding Chart Titles and Text

Effective use of text will allow important ideas to attract more attention than supporting arguments, examples, and facts. Excel enables you to add two types of text: *attached text* and *unattached text*. Attached text cannot be moved and is linked to a chart object such as an axis or data markers. The title of your chart is attached text. Unattached text can be added to your chart through the formula bar. You can move unattached text to any location on the chart.

Adding Attached Text

You can add attached text by selecting the Attach Text command from the Chart menu. A dialog box appears from which you can choose the type of attached text (see fig. 6.5).

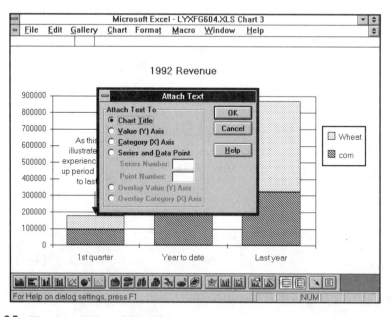

Fig. 6.5 The Attach Text dialog box.

Clarity and proportion are important design considerations when adding text. Adding a title to a chart will help your audience focus on the main idea of the chart.

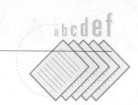

You can add a chart title by selecting Chart Title. Then, after you click OK, you see the word Title at the top of the chart with white handles surrounding it (see fig. 6.6). The white handles signify that the word is attached text and cannot be moved or manipulated. Notice that the word Title also appears in the formula bar. To add your title to the chart, highlight Title in the formula bar and type the message that you want to appear.

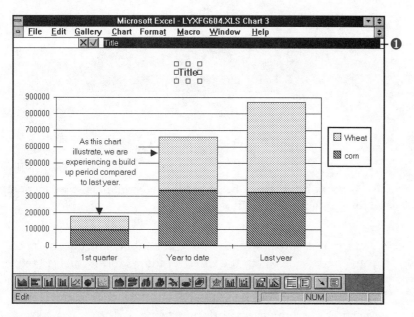

❶ Formula bar

Fig. 6.6 The formula bar and attached text.

You can add other attached text to the value, series and data Points, and category axes. You also can label the series numbers and the data points. Figure 6.7 shows a chart with these features. These labels can help emphasize your chart's message.

Adding Unattached Text

You can add unattached text to a chart by one of three methods:

- Select the Text Box tool from the Chart toolbar. The Text Box tool causes the word Text to appear in the middle of your chart. The formula bar also displays the word Text. To input the words, highlight Text in the formula bar and type the message you want.

- Just type the message you want. The formula bar displays the message. Then, after you press Enter, the message appears in the center of your screen.

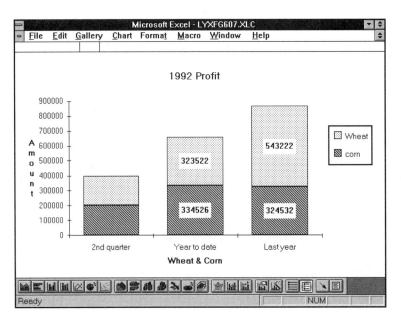

Fig. 6.7   A chart with all axes labeled and the series number and data points labeled for 1991 and 1992 profit series.

- You can link spreadsheet text from the supporting document to your chart. Type "=" in the Chart window's formula bar to tell Excel that you are going to link a cell to the chart. Then go to the supporting document by pulling down the **Window** menu and selecting the supporting worksheet name. Within this worksheet, select the cell that contains the text you want to appear on your chart. The absolute cell reference number appears in the Chart window's formula bar. Enter the formula bar data by pressing Enter. The worksheet cell text appears on your chart.

You easily can add unattached text to your chart by any one of these three methods. Once you have the text in your chart, you can begin to enhance it for a more aesthetically pleasing look.

Applying Rules of Typography

To effectively bring the message home, you need to be aware of typography rules and know how to apply them. The entire appearance of your chart can be affected by the selection of typefaces. Many characteristics such as masculinity, femininity, delicacy, and formality can be suggested through the typeface used. The first rule to follow is *type was*

Typeface and typography are powerful design tools.

designed to be read easily. You must consider the selection of the typeface and the size to be used to ensure the clarity of the message. Refer to Chapter 2 for more information about fonts and typography.

Paying attention to the following type considerations will help you express your message more effectively. You can achieve consistency and clarity through proper font usage and enhancement. Consider these guidelines for your charts:

- *Type size should reflect the importance of the various parts of your chart.* The title of the chart should be larger than the unattached text. The use of large type emphasizes the main message of the chart. Figure 6.8 shows a chart with inappropriate type sizes; figure 6.9 shows how much more effective your message is with the proper type sizes.

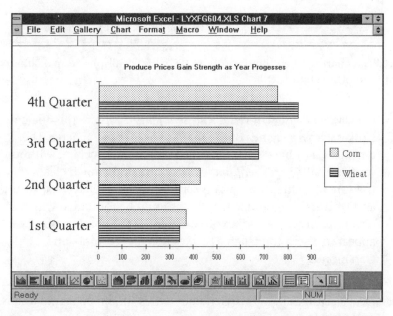

Fig. 6.8 A chart with large text emphasizing the quarters; the title of the chart is too small.

- *Vary type styles to emphasize important ideas or details of your chart.* Boldface type is authoritative. Italic type adds emphasis in a less authoritative way. Italic type provides a refined or elegant mood or irony and humor. Use italics with care—its primary purpose is for emphasis, not to be read in large blocks. Bold italic type conveys a sense of action.

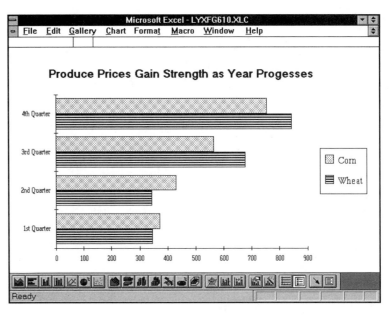

Fig. 6.9 A chart with emphasis on the title, which is displayed in a larger font than other chart text.

- *Know when to use serif verses sans serif fonts: Serifs* are the fine cross strokes across the ends of the main strokes of a character. The typefaces that have serifs are called *serif fonts.* Typefaces without serifs are called *sans serif fonts.* Chart titles look much cleaner if they are formatted with a sans serif face such as Helvetica, Futura, and Univers. Axes and legend text should be formatted with a sans serif face. Any attached text that describes the chart in detail can appear in a serif font such as Times Roman, Palatino, and Garamond.

- *Although the size of your fonts may change, limit the number of typefaces on each chart to two.* Generally, titles should appear in a sans serif font and the text should appear in a serif font.

- *Be consistent in labeling.* Keep text in the chart as uniform as possible. Label text that is set in a larger size or bolder typeface can cause the audience to think that a column or pie slice is more important than others. If this is not your intent, you have caused a misconception and the message is misunderstood. The column or slices have no greater significance than any others, but the viewer's eyes are drawn to them. Figure 6.10 shows a pie chart with misleading labeling.

Be consistent in your labeling. Label text set in a larger size or bolder typeface can cause the audience to perceive a column or pie slice to be more important than others.

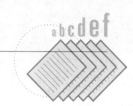

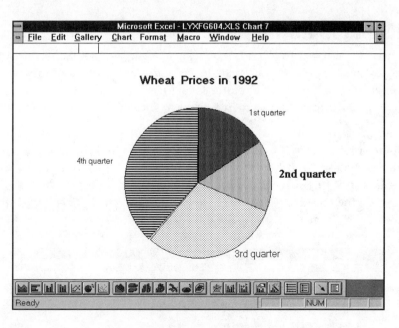

Fig. 6.10 The 2nd quarter pie slice stands out due to unequal label size.

- *Colors will attract or detract from the message.* When using colors, you must keep the whole design in mind. Your output must be supportive of color use. Red will attract your audience's eye and cause the message to stand out. Yellow is not suggested for text. You should use dark, vibrant colors for your text.

Your message will be conveyed easily through proper use of fonts and typography. Key points will stand out and underlying messages will be understood with correct typography enhancements.

Changing the Text Fonts

All text added to a chart will appear in the Excel default font MS Sans Serif. You can change any font by selecting the chart text block; to do this, click once on the text. You see the handles or dots appear around the text block, signifying that the text is active. From the Format menu, select Text. (Double-clicking the text box also brings up the Patterns dialog box, from which you can select the Text button.) A dialog box appears, listing your system fonts, type sizes, and text enhancement features. The lower right corner of the dialog box displays an example of the text features that you select. You can use font size or formatting enhancements to create more variation in the chart's fonts.

Y ou should never use more than two types of font styles in a chart—use one for the title and one for all other unattached and attached text in the chart.

Adding Multiline Text Blocks

When you add text to a chart, it appears in a single-line text block with the text flowing across your chart in a one-line segment. You can change a single-line text block to a multiline text block in which the text is broken into shorter line segments displayed underneath each other.

You can use multiline text blocks to present a message more clearly. It is much easier to lay out multiline text blocks on a chart than long, single-line text blocks. Multiline text blocks allow a cleaner distribution of text on a chart. White space is used effectively, enabling the audience to focus on the message. Figure 6.11 shows the ineffective use of single-line blocks, and figure 6.12 shows the effective use of multiline blocks.

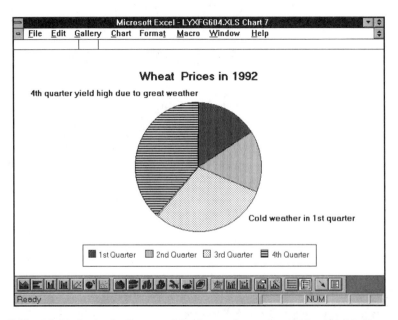

Fig. 6.11   Multiple single-line text blocks tend to create a cluttered look on a chart.

Text added to your chart appears in a single line. You easily can have multiline text blocks, however. You must make the text block active by clicking it once. To resize the text block, click a corner handle and drag the block. An outline of the text block appears, and the text is forced to flow within this area. Drag the block until you have the size rectangle that will display the text in the multiline format you want.

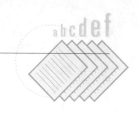

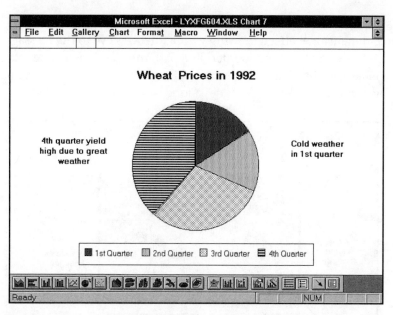

Fig. 6.12 Multiline text blocks help create a cleaner distribution.

Changing the Text Box Orientation

As Chapter 3 discussed, Excel displays text blocks in four orientation formats. You also can center text within the text block horizontally or vertically. To change the orientation, select the text block. Pull down the Format menu and select Text, or double-click the text box to display the Pattern dialog box and select the Text tool. You see the Text dialog box (see fig. 6.13).

Select the features that you want to display. If you border the text block, the message will look better centered vertically and horizontally within the box. Sometimes, to effectively use your white space, a short message can be oriented to flow vertically next to the chart. The value axis label looks better if it flows vertically along that axis. Text orientation can add variety and interest to a message, enhancing the white space of the chart.

Setting Off Text from the Background

Text can be difficult to read when it is positioned over other chart objects unless it is set off from the background in some manner. Borders draw your audience's eye to the message. Patterns add emphasis to text,

B orders, patterns, and shadows can help set text apart from the background.

making it stand out from the background. Shadows tend to create a three-dimensional effect, drawing your audience's eye to the message. Be aware of adding too many borders and patterns. Too much enhancing can make the chart look cluttered (see fig. 6.14). Clarity and white space are lost. A little enhancement goes a long way.

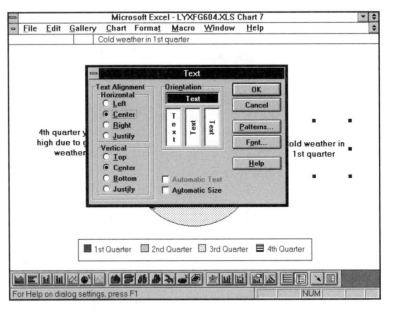

Fig. 6.13 The Text dialog box.

Patterns and borders help distinguish text from the background. When text is added to the chart, it occupies a single-line text block or a multiline text block. To make the text stand out from the chart, you can add a border that surrounds the text block. Select the text block to make it active. Then pull down the Format menu and select Patterns to display the Patterns dialog box (see fig. 6.15). Or, simply double-click the active text block. Both methods activate the Patterns dialog box.

The Patterns dialog box enables you to choose borders and area attributes. Therefore, you can apply the style of border you want to surround your text block, as well as a fill pattern within your text block.

To create a border, you have four options: Automatic, None, Custom, or Shadow. Descriptions of these options follow:

- The Automatic option creates a border with a style setting of a solid line, a color of black, and weight of 1-point line width. Notice that when you click the radio button next to Automatic, these default

settings are displayed next to the titles Style, Color, and Weight. Also, a sample of the border appears in the Sample box in the lower-right corner of the Patterns dialog box.

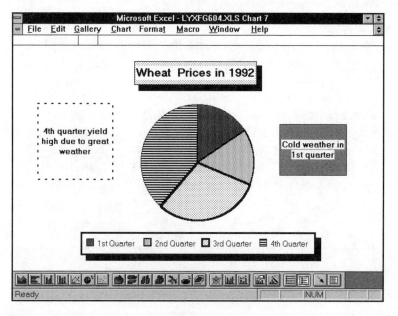

Fig. 6.14 A chart with too many enhancements.

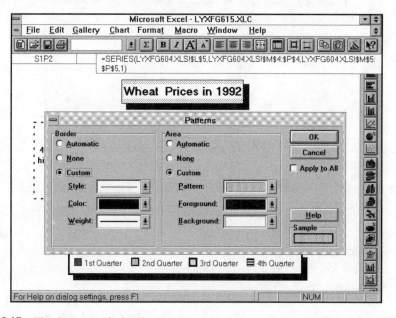

Fig 6.15 The Patterns dialog box.

- The None option creates no border around the text box. You can use this choice to delete an existing border around a text block. Click the radio button next to None to turn on this feature. Notice that the Sample box displays nothing.

- The Custom option enables you to completely customize the border you want to display. Click the radio button next to Custom. Now you can select the various options listed next to the Style, Color, and Weight options (see fig. 6.16). To change the Style option, click your mouse on the down arrow button next to the solid line attribute that is displayed. A list of other styles appears. Select the new line style by clicking it. That style replaces the solid line, and a sample border displaying this new line style appears in the Sample box in the lower-right corner of the Patterns dialog box. You can change the Color and Weight options in the same way. Click the down arrow button next to the option you want and then select the new color or line weight.

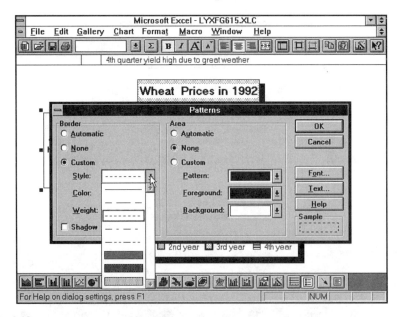

Fig. 6.16   The border Style choices displayed in the Patterns dialog box.

- The Shadow options enables you to apply a shadow to the text block. Click the button next to Shadow. The Sample box displays a shadow around the sample border.

You also can add a fill pattern to your text box by changing Area options. To create a fill pattern, you have the following options: Automatic, None, and Custom. Descriptions of these options follow:

- The Automatic option creates the default fill for the Area option. Click the radio button next to Automatic to turn on this feature. The default fill is a solid white color. Notice that the Sample box displays a solid white fill.

- The None option creates no fill pattern. Click the radio button next to None to turn on this feature. The Sample box displays no fill pattern, with the gray background of the Sample box showing through. This is a nice attribute to apply if you want to have the background of your chart show through a text block area.

- The Custom option enables you to create your own fill pattern. You can change the Pattern, Foreground, and Background options. Click the Custom radio button to turn on this option. To change the Pattern option, click the down arrow next to this selection. A menu appears, listing all the pattern attributes (see fig. 6.17). Click your mouse on the pattern with which you want to fill your text block. The Sample box displays this new fill pattern. You can change the Foreground and Background options in the same way. Click the down arrow button next to the attribute and then select the new foreground and background color. Notice that the Sample box shows you the combination of these colors reflected in the fill pattern you have chosen.

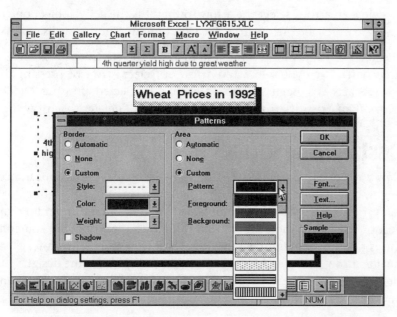

Fig. 6.17 The Patterns options displayed in the Patterns dialog box.

Through the Patterns dialog box, you have many options for adding a border and a fill pattern to your text blocks. You have many options and attributes that you can choose to create the exact effect that you need to enhance your chart and its message.

Adding Arrows and Lines

You easily can add arrows and lines to an Excel chart. Arrows and lines will further draw your audience's eyes to the message. You can use arrows and lines to point out important but subtle information, or to emphasize a trend in the data.

Creating Arrows on a Chart

Excel 4's Chart toolbar enables you to quickly add arrows. Simply click the Arrow tool and an arrow appears in your chart. You can add a second arrow by selecting the chart area and selecting the Arrow tool again. Or, you can select Add Arrow from the Chart menu. A second arrow appears on-screen.

Deleting an Existing Arrow or Line

To delete an arrow, select the arrow so that it is the active object on your chart. Select Delete Arrow from the Chart menu. The arrow disappears.

The keyboard equivalent command to add or delete an arrow is Alt-C (for Chart). Then you select Add Arrow or Delete Arrow by pressing the R key; R acts as a toggle switch. If the chart is selected, pressing R adds an arrow. If an existing arrow is selected, pressing R deletes the arrow.

Customizing Arrows or Lines

How you portray your arrow or line will affect your chart's appearance. A bright, colored line will attract attention, whereas a dull or light color can get lost. A thicker line weight will stand out, but a thinner line can be more elegant. A large arrow head will attract attention, but sometimes this is not the main message that you want to portray. Therefore, a smaller arrow head would be better. You must consider the design elements of clarity, emphasis, and white space when adding arrows and lines.

You can change an arrow to a line or customize the existing arrow through the Patterns dialog box. Select the arrow so that it is the active object on your chart. Double-click the arrow or select **Pattern** from the Format menu. The Patterns dialog box appears (see fig. 6.18).

Arrows and lines can add emphasis to your chart's message. Your audience's eye will be drawn to the data.

Lines and arrows with colors and various line weights can further draw your audience's eyes to the message.

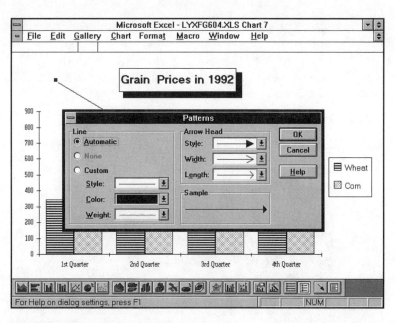

Fig. 6.18 The Patterns dialog box.

You can change the arrow to a line by altering the style in the Arrow Head section of the Patterns dialog box. The Arrow Head section also customizes any arrow that you have created on the chart. By using the Style, Width, and Length options, you can create arrows with many different features or a straight line.

Creating a Straight Line

You can use the Style option to change the style of the arrow to a straight line. You can make the arrow have a solid arrow head or a line arrow head. Or, you can select the straight line attribute to change the arrow to a straight line (see fig. 6.19). Notice that the Sample space displays the attributes you select.

If you change the arrow to a straight line, the other options of Width and Length do not apply to the straight line. These attributes alter the arrow head shape.

Altering Arrow Heads

The Arrow Head section of the Patterns dialog box enables you to change arrows to straight lines or to customize the arrow head. To customize the arrow head, you can use the Style, Width, and Length options. You can use the Style command to change the arrow head shape from a solid or line arrow head. You can use the Width option to change the width of the arrow head from a very thin head to a very wide head. The Sample space reflects any new attributes that you select. The Length option changes the length of the arrow head from the tip of the arrow to the base of the arrow head. The Sample space reflects any new attributes you select.

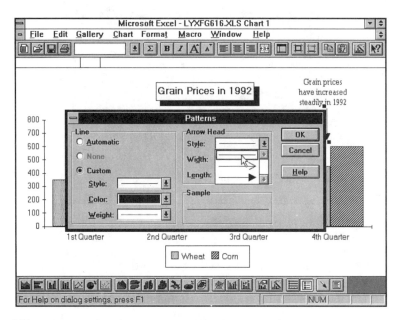

Fig. 6.19 Changing an arrow to a straight line.

Customizing the Line of an Arrow or a Straight Line

You can customize the line of any arrow or any straight line by using the attributes in the Line section of the Patterns dialog box. You have three choices: Automatic, None, and Custom. Descriptions of these choices follow:

- The Automatic option creates a line with a Style setting of a solid line, a Color setting of Black, and a Weight setting of 1-point line width. Notice that when you click the radio button next to Automatic, these default settings are displayed next to the titles Style, Color, and Weight. Also, a sample of the border appears in the Sample space in the lower right corner of the Patterns dialog box.

- The None button is grayed to show you that you cannot select this option. If you want to delete an arrow or line, you must select the arrow or line to make it active, and then choose Delete Arrow from the Chart menu. You cannot delete an arrow or line simply by selecting the None button.

- The Custom button enables you to completely customize the arrow or line that you want to display. Click the radio button next to Custom. Now you can select the various options listed next to the Style, Color, and Weight options. To change the Style option, click the down arrow next to the solid line attribute that is displayed. A list of other line styles appears (see fig. 6.20). Select the new line style by clicking it. That style replaces the solid line and the Sample space in the lower right corner of the Patterns dialog box displays your new line style. You can change the Color and Weight options in the same manner. Click the down arrow next to the option and then select the new color or line weight.

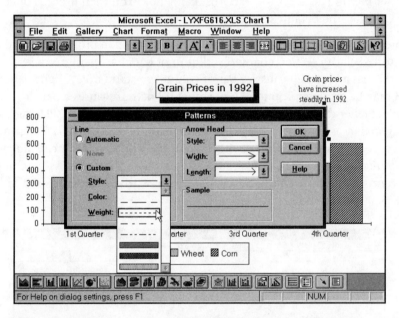

Fig. 6.20 The line Style choices displayed in the Patterns dialog box.

Through the Patterns dialog box, you have many options for customizing arrows and lines. The Custom option and its attributes of Style, Color and Weight enable you to create a line with many different looks. You have many options from which to choose to create the exact effect that you need to enhance your chart and its message.

Creating Borders and Patterns

As stated earlier, borders and patterns help accent a chart's message by drawing your audience's eyes to that area. You can add a border to the chart plot area to create a frame for that area. A pattern provides further contrast to the chart plot area, making it more distinctive. Excel enables you to add or change borders or patterns of almost any part of a chart.

You're probably finding that to edit any part of a chart, you have one of two choices:

- Double-click the part of the chart you want to change to bring up the dialog box.

- Make the part of the chart you want to change active and select **P**atterns from the Format menu.

Either method accesses the Patterns dialog box. You then use this dialog box to alter the default style of any part of the chart.

Borders and patterns sometimes may cause inaccurate proportions and distorted clarity. When changing column or bar chart patterns, keep in mind that a black fill causes a bar or column to stand out. A light pattern fill may be more appropriate. A diagonal fill pattern causes a bar to appear taller than it actually is, or a pie slice to appear larger. Placing two diagonal, cross-hatching patterns together can be perceived as flickering, because the patterns conflict with each other. This conflict is called *moire distortion* (see fig. 6.21). You should use only two or three cross-hatching patterns within any chart and separate them with a pattern of solid white, gray, or colors.

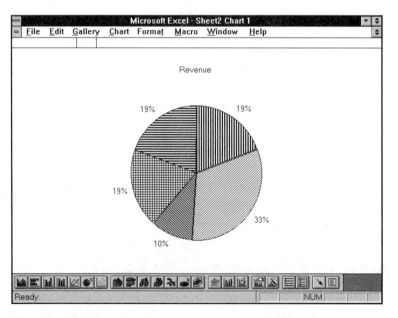

Fig. 6.21 A chart with moire distortion.

Creating and Deleting Gridlines

Excel can add gridlines to any chart but the pie chart. *Gridlines* are lines that extend from the axis across the plot area to help guide the reader's eye from the data marker to the corresponding value or category on the axis. Gridlines help add proportion and distinction to the chart plot area. Adding gridlines can make a chart much more readable, especially if the chart is very large. Compare figure 6.22, which shows a chart without gridlines, to figure 6.23, which shows a chart with gridlines.

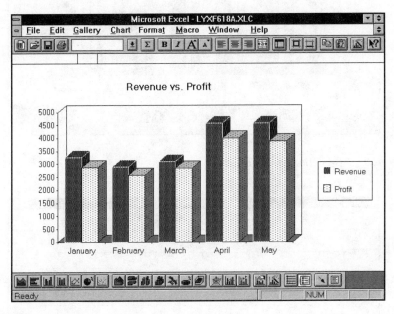

Fig. 6.22 A 3-D chart without gridlines.

The 3-D chart with the gridlines is more readable. The gridlines create an illusion of depth within the 3-D effect of the column chart.

You easily can create gridlines. Your chart must be in an active window so that the Chart toolbar is visible. Click the Gridline tool from the Chart toolbar (see fig. 6.24). Gridlines appear on-screen. To delete the gridlines, click the Gridline tool again. The existing gridlines disappear.

Gridlines can be guidelines for interpreting chart data, but in many cases they are not needed. If your audience can interpret the chart without the use of gridlines, leave them out. In many cases, the grid clutters the chart and removes any white space. Be careful when using gridlines with a line chart; the lines of the grid and the lines of the charted data can interfere, especially if the lines intersect (see fig. 6.24).

Gridlines can add proportion and more distinction to the chart plot area. Be careful, however, because gridlines may interfere with the data, especially if the chart lines and the gridlines intersect.

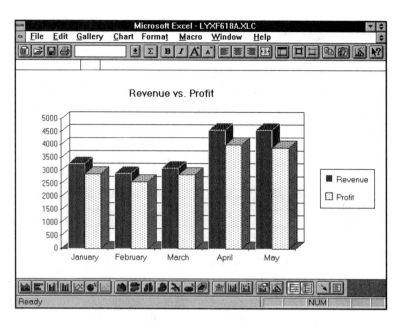

Fig. 6.23 A 3-D chart with gridlines.

❶ Gridline tool

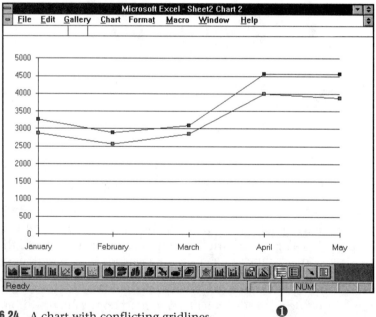

Fig. 6.24 A chart with conflicting gridlines.   ❶

You easily can create gridlines in Excel 4 for Windows. Some charts are enhanced with the addition of gridlines, because the data is more readable. Other charts can become cluttered when you apply gridlines—

they can cause the white space and clarity to be lost. If you want to apply gridlines, do so carefully. Always preview your chart after applying gridlines; check to see if they enhance your chart or make the data more readable. If they do not, delete them.

Adding Legends

Legends are used for identification of the chart's data series. Excel 4 offers two new legend features. You can add a legend to a chart by clicking the Legend tool on the Chart toolbar. The legend appears to the right of the chart. With Excel 4, you now can move the legend with your mouse. Click the legend to make it active and then drag it to the new location. Notice that when the legend is positioned at the very top, bottom, left, or right, a highlighted line appears next to the plot area. This line signifies that the legend will be inserted at this location, causing the chart to resize and allow room for the legend.

You should remember a few points when positioning a legend. Most designers agree that people will look from the top left of a page and work their way to the bottom right corner. Depending on the complexity of your data, you may want the audience to identify the data series first. Positioning the legend at the top of the chart or to the left therefore allows the audience to view it first.

Your legend always displays the Excel default font of MS Sans Serif. As discussed earlier in "Adding Chart Titles and Text," the legend text is attached text and can appear in a serif font. If you limit your chart to two types of fonts, you will achieve clarity.

Manipulating a 3-D Chart

A new feature of Excel 4 is the direct manipulation of any 3-D chart with your mouse. By changing the orientation of the chart, you can emphasize the message or downplay a numeric trend. You must have an idea of what you want to accomplish when you are manipulating the orientation of a 3-D chart.

The chart in figure 6.25 displays a 3-D column chart. There is a slight difference between revenue and profit in the months of January through May. If the chart is rotated so that the locations of Profit and Revenue are reversed, however, the month categories appear to have no difference in value (see fig. 6.26). The numerical data appears to be the same for each month in the Revenue and Profit data series. This is very misleading and another example of distorted scaling. (See Chapter 5 for more information.)

By changing the orientation of the chart, you can emphasize the message or downplay a numeric trend.

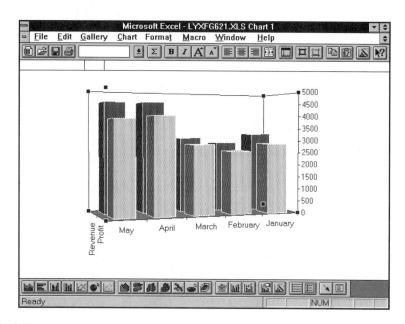

Fig. 6.25 A chart portrayed in a normal, default 3-D orientation.

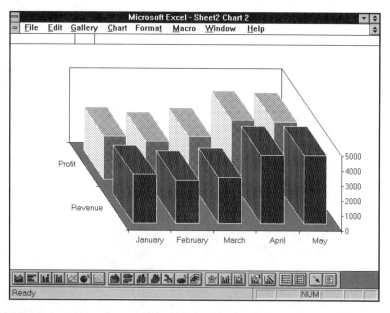

Fig. 6.26 A chart that appears to have no difference in numbers, due to manipulation of the chart view.

To manipulate a 3-D chart, follow these steps:

1. With your mouse, click the intersection point of the x, y, or z axes. Black dots or handles appear in the corners of the chart area.

2. With your mouse, click and drag a handle to change the orientation of the chart. An outline of the chart will be displayed in schematic form, representing the chart's new position.

Manipulating a 3-D chart can radically affect the message of the data by creating distorted scaling. Sometimes the distorted scaling further emphasizes the message the chart is representing by increasing the scale between the categories. Other times, the scaling can appear to be equal due to the chart's orientation. Always examine the chart carefully to check for accuracy after you rotate it.

Creating a Chart Template

Once you have a chart designed with the correct fonts and the desired patterns and borders, you can create a template of the chart and its characteristics. You can apply these saved template formats to new data being charted. This template will save time, because you will not need to re-create all the previously used formats. The template also will help you establish consistency throughout a presentation composed of many charts.

To create a template, follow these steps:

1. After you have the chart formatted with the enhancements you want, select Save As from the Chart menu. The Save As dialog box appears (see fig. 6.27).

2. Select the path by choosing the drive and directory in which you want to save the file. Use your mouse to select the path by clicking the drive letter under the Drives option and the correct directory location under the Directories option.

3. In the lower left corner of the Save As dialog box, you can choose a file type under the Save file as Type option. Click the down arrow to display the different file types and select the Template option.

4. Name your template file by typing a name in the File Name field.

5. Save the file by clicking the OK button. The file is saved as a template file in the directory you selected.

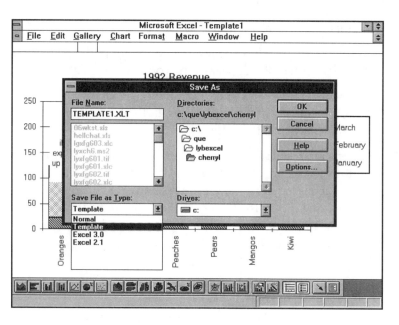

Fig. 6.27 The Save or Save As dialog box with the Template file format chosen.

After you have created the template, you can apply it to any worksheet data for charting. The new chart appears with the previously created enhancements. If you had any text blocks saved on the chart that you used to create the template, these exact text blocks will appear on the new chart.

To create a new chart using a template, follow these steps:

1. Select the worksheet data to be charted by highlighting the cells to be charted. (See Chapter 5 for more information.)

2. Select Open from the File menu. A dialog box appears (see fig. 6.28). Select the drive where the template file is located by clicking the Drives option and choosing the drive letter. Under the Directories option, select the directory in which the template was saved by clicking the folder name that contains the template file. Locate the template file under the File Name option. Click the template file name to select it.

3. Click OK. The worksheet data is charted, using the previously defined enhancements.

Template files can save you time and energy. When you apply template files to data being charted, the new chart will have all the formats of the template chart. You can achieve consistency throughout multiple slides. Templates are ideal for presentations consisting of many slides.

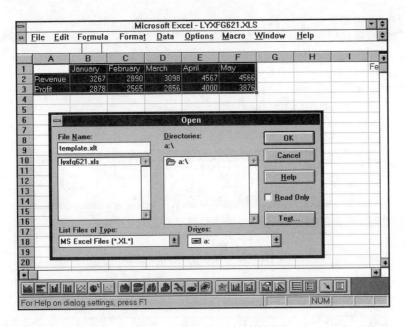

Fig. 6.28 A dialog box to apply a template to a chart.

Adding a Chart to the Worksheet

As shown in Chapter 5, charts usually are created in the worksheet and then edited and enhanced in the chart window. Once you have completed this editing and enhancing, you easily can return to the worksheet by closing the chart window. Your chart appears in the worksheet in the area that you previously designated. All enhancements and edits you have added to the chart are present in the worksheet version. At this point, you can further emphasize your chart's message and integrate the chart with the worksheet data by using Excel's drawing tools.

By simply clicking tools on the Drawing toolbar, you can add shapes to a worksheet or chart, group and ungroup shapes, rearrange layers, reshape a polygon, and even add a drop shadow. These graphics capabilities help to integrate and enhance a chart's message within the whole worksheet page. The chart must be embedded in the worksheet if you want to add any of the shapes on the Drawing toolbar.

Excel 4 offers you simple but powerful graphics capabilities. The new Drawing toolbar enables you to directly access these capabilities.

Using the Excel Drawing Tools

The Drawing toolbar contains seven major drawing tools and nine tools that enable you to directly access graphic manipulation. Figure 6.29 shows the Drawing toolbar, and table 6.1 describes these tools, in the order they appear on the toolbar.

① Line
② Arrow
③ Freehand
④ Rectangle
⑤ Oval
⑥ Arc
⑦ Freehand Polygon
⑧ Filled Rectangle
⑨ Filled Oval
⑩ Filled Arc
⑪ Filled Freehand Polygon
⑫ Text Box
⑬ Selection
⑭ Reshape
⑮ Group
⑯ UnGroup
⑰ Bring to Front
⑱ Send to Back
⑲ Color
⑳ Drop Shadow

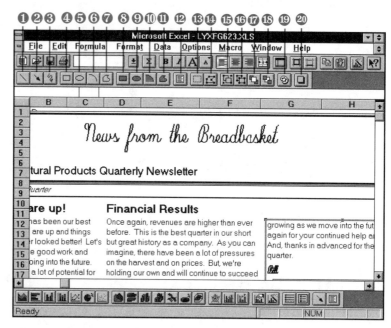

Fig. 6.29   The Drawing toolbar.

Table 6.1   The Drawing Toolbar

Name	Description
Line	Creates a line.
Arrow	Creates an arrow.
Freehand	Enables you to draw freehand shapes.
Rectangle	Creates squares and rectangles.
Oval	Creates circles and ovals.
Arc	Creates arcs and quarter circles.
Freehand Polygon	Enables you to create any shape of polygon—closed or unclosed.
Filled Rectangle	Creates squares and rectangles with a fill pattern.

Name	Description
Filled Oval	Creates circles and ovals with a fill pattern.
Filled Arc	Creates arcs and quarter circles with a fill pattern.
Filled Freehand Polygon	Creates a polygon of any shape—closed or unclosed—with a fill pattern.
Text Box	Creates a text box.
Selection	Enables you to select multiple graphic shapes.
Reshape	Enables you to reshape any polygon or freehand shape.
Group	Groups many shapes as one object.
UnGroup	Ungroups grouped objects.
Bring to Front	Moves one shape in front of another shape.
Send to Back	Moves one shape behind another shape.
Color	Causes the active shape to display another color. When pressed in succession, you circulate through the Excel color palette.
Drop Shadow	Adds a drop shadow behind the active shape.

Creating and Selecting Techniques

You can use some tricks and techniques when creating graphic shapes that will make your work easier. The shape needs to be active in order for you to be able to perform the following techniques.

Creating Perfect Squares, Circles, Arcs, and Straight Lines

You can create perfect geometric shapes by pressing Shift while you create the shape. If you want the shape to align with the grid, press Alt while creating the shape. This is a trick for creating straight vertical and horizontal lines.

When selecting a shape in the worksheet, you must position your mouse directly on the line of the shape. Click to make the shape active. A common problem is to miss selecting the shape and to select the worksheet cell behind the shape.

To select more than one shape, press Shift while selecting the second shape.

Selecting Multiple Shapes

Aside from using the Selection tool to select multiple shapes, you can use the Shift key. Select a shape to make it active. Before you select the next shape, hold down Shift and then click on the next shape. Shift enables you to choose more than one shape. If you use Shift to select an active shape a second time, you will deselect that shape. After you have a group of shapes selected, you can group or resize them proportionately.

Editing Shapes

Excel enables you to change the pattern, color, and line weight of any shape. To access the Pattern dialog box, double-click the shape or choose **P**atterns from the Forma**t** menu. Or, click the shape with the right mouse button and select **P**atterns. The Pattern dialog box appears. Select the border options and the fill options you want the shape to have. Then click OK. The shape will display these new attributes. (See "Creating Borders and Patterns," earlier in this chapter, for more information.)

A nice effect is to add a drop shadow behind the embedded chart. This causes the chart to stand out from the worksheet. Your audience's eye will be drawn to the chart. Select the chart to make it active and then select the Drop Shadow tool on the Drawing toolbar. Figure 6.30 shows an example of a drop shadow used with a chart.

 Drop Shadow tool

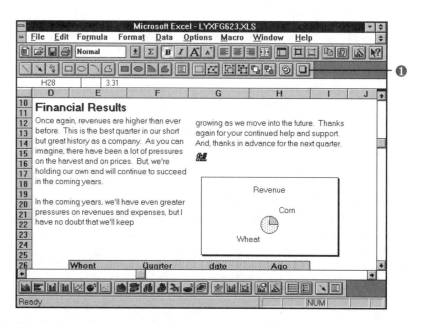

Fig. 6.30   A drop shadow appears behind the embedded chart.

Adding shapes to a worksheet enhances the worksheet and embedded chart. The shapes can further draw your reader's eye to the data you want to emphasize. Your message will stand out from the rest of the worksheet and be portrayed loud and clear to your audience.

Importing Clip Art and Graphics

As you develop and enhance your chart, you may want to include a company logo or diagram within the chart or on the worksheet page. Unfortunately, you cannot import a graphic directly into a chart. You must have the chart embedded in the worksheet. Then you can place the graphic on top of the embedded chart. Using the layering tools from the Drawing toolbar, you can create any appearance with the graphic and other worksheet objects that you want.

Excel 4 can import a graphic into the worksheet so that you can place it on a chart. You can add graphics and clip art to any worksheet. Clip art libraries are available from a variety of sources in a variety of file formats. See Chapter 12 for detailed instructions on importing graphics from other software packages.

You also can use the Clipboard to import a graphic. Copying the graphic from another program places the graphic on the Clipboard. Then you can paste the graphic into the Excel worksheet. By using the Clipboard, you can import almost any graphic or chart regardless of the file format in which it is created.

Creating a Picture Chart

A *picture chart* is a chart that has graphics representing its data markers. As discussed in this chapter, you can format the border, fill pattern, and color of your data markers. You can control the line or border style, color, and weight used for data markers. You also can control the markers' pattern and foreground and background colors. The options available in the Format menu and Patterns dialog box vary depending on the type of marker you select. You also can import a picture to use as the data series markers for the column, bar, and line charts.

You can use clip art, graphics, and simple shapes as data markers. You can import your graphic into Excel by using the Insert Object command from almost any program. (See Chapter 12 for more information on importing graphics.) Using pictures as your data markers can further enhance your chart and dramatically convey a message.

Y ou can add graphics and clip art to a chart if the chart is embedded on the worksheet. You can use graphics to replace a data series marker.

A *picture chart* is a chart with graphics representing its data series markers.

Replacing a Data Marker with a Graphic

A picture chart is created from an existing chart. You can use certain chart types, including Bar, Column, 3-D Bar and Column, and Line charts. You must create your graphic and import it into the Excel worksheet. The graphic should be about the size of the data markers you will be creating. If the graphic is too large or small, its appearance can be affected by Excel trying to shrink or stretch it to fit the data mark area. It is a good idea to select or create a graphic that is approximately the size the data markers.

To create a picture chart, follow these steps:

1. Activate the application or the document containing the picture you want to use as a data series marker.

2. Copy the graphic by selecting it and choose Copy from the Edit menu. The graphic is placed on the Clipboard.

3. Activate the Excel chart in which you want to use the picture.

4. To select a single data marker—not the entire series—press Ctrl while clicking a data marker.

   Handles appear on the edges of the single data marker, indicating that it is active.

5. Select Paste from the Edit menu.

   The graphic replaces the single data marker (see fig. 6.31). Excel stretches or shrinks the picture to show the numeric value.

You can replace the markers of a data series by selecting the entire series and selecting Paste from the Edit menu. The graphic replaces all data markers for that series (see fig. 6.32).

Specifying Whether a Picture Marker is Stacked or Stretched

You can specify whether Excel stretches a single picture, stacks multiple copies of a picture, or stacks scaled copies of a picture to represent larger or smaller values in a bar or column chart. (In a line chart, each marker represents a value and therefore, the graphic represents one value.)

Excel formats the picture to stretch if it is the first marker picture you copy into a bar or column chart. You also can paste other pictures to replace the data markers for other series in the same chart. Excel formats any additional pasted pictures as stacked or stretched, the same way you formatted the most recently formatted picture. You cannot overlap stacked pictures.

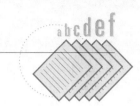

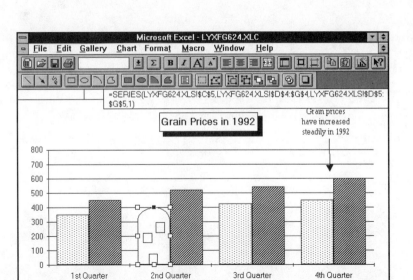

Fig. 6.31 A picture replacing one data marker.

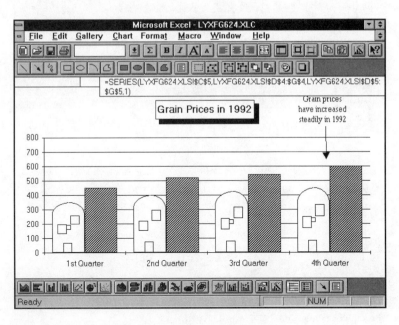

Fig. 6.32 Pictures replacing all markers of a data series.

To format the picture marker, follow these steps:

1. Select the picture marker or data series you want to format and choose **P**atterns from the Forma**t** menu. Or, double-click the marker or series or click a marker with the right mouse button to display the menu and select **P**atterns. The Patterns dialog box appears, asking you which formatting option you want: St**r**etch, St**a**ck, or Stack and S**c**ale (see fig. 6.33).

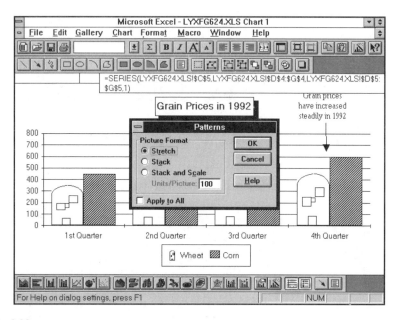

Fig. 6.33   The Picture markers' Patterns dialog box.

2. Select the option you want by clicking the radio box next to the option. If you have only one data marker selected, you still can apply the new attribute by selecting the Apply to All button.

3. Select OK.

Your data marker or data series marker is formatted.

The Stretched, Stacked, or Stack and Scale format can very effectively present your message. Experiment with the three formats so that you can select the most clear representation.

Clearing a Data Marker Picture

Excel will remove a picture from the data marker or data series and will format the marker or series to the original format. Select the marker or

data series and choose Clear from the Edit menu. Excel formats the marker or data series with the original format, prior to the picture being pasted into the chart.

A picture chart is a very effective way to represent data. Pictures add further interest to a chart and make the message more understandable.

Chapter Summary

Excel 4 and Windows 3.1 combine to provide very powerful graphics capabilities. This chapter introduced the concepts of enhancing and annotating charts in Excel, and provided a number of tips for using the chart capabilities. Excel is nearly as capable as a presentation graphics program. You can work with existing graphics or create your own drawings. The result is Excel worksheets and documents that are interesting to look at and make your point clearly and concisely.

Excel Office Applications

LaserPro Corporation
Balance Sheet
December 31, 1992

Assets

	This Year	Last Year	Change
Current Assets			
Cash	$247,886	$126,473	96%
Accounts receivable	863,652	524,570	65%
Inventory	88,328	65,508	35%
Investments	108,577	31,934	240%
Total current assets	$1,308,443	$748,485	75%
Fixed Assets			
Machinery and equipment	$209,906	$158,730	32%
Vehicles	429,505	243,793	76%
Office furniture	50,240	36,406	38%
(Accumulated depreciation)	(101,098)	(64,394)	57%
Total fixed assets	$588,553	$374,535	57%
Total Assets	**$1,896,996**	**$1,123,020**	**69%**

Liabilities and Shareholders' Equity

	This Year	Last Year	Change
Current Liabilities			
Accounts payable	$426,041	$332,845	28%
Notes payable	45,327	23,486	93%
Accrued liabilities	34,614	26,026	33%
Income taxes payable	88,645	51,840	71%
Total current liabilities	$594,627	$434,197	37%
Noncurrent Liabilities			
Long-term debt	$488,822	$349,253	40%
Deferred federal tax	147,844	92,101	61%
Total noncurrent liabilities	$636,666	$441,354	44%
Shareholders' Equity			
Common stock	$1,000	$1,000	0%
Retained earnings	664,703	246,469	170%
Total shareholders' equity	$665,703	$247,469	169%
Total Liabilities and Equity	**$1,896,996**	**$1,123,020**	**69%**

Includes

7. Enhancing Excel Worksheets

8. Creating Business Memos, Letters, and Reports

9. Creating Business Forms

7

Enhancing Excel Worksheets

A worksheet, like any other document, must communicate
information. The content, of course, is the most important
part of the document. If your worksheet is among many
competing documents that someone may look at, however,
how do you get that person to review the worksheet in the
first place? Also, because of the large amount of information
in many worksheets, the reader can easily become lost in the
detail. How do you show what is important in the mass of
data?

Here is where you can take advantage of the desktop-publishing features of Excel. You can produce professional quality worksheets that are inviting to read. With the enhanced features of Excel you also can highlight important parts of the worksheet so that anyone reviewing your work can quickly get to the point and save time. Figure 7.1 shows a worksheet printed with the standard capabilities of Excel, and figure 7.2 shows a worksheet printed with the desktop-publishing features of Excel.

This chapter shows you how to apply the desktop-publishing capabilities of Excel to your worksheets in order to improve the print quality, which will make your worksheets easier to read and understand. Specifically, this chapter teaches you how to do the following: prepare the worksheet to produce the printed output you want, format your worksheet for a professional look and make the worksheet easy to read and understand, add graphs to your worksheet, create user-named formats, create templates, and use AutoFormat to automate the process of producing desktop-published quality worksheets.

This chapter presents techniques and directions for applying the basic concepts explained in Chapters 1 through 3 for producing desktop-published quality worksheets. If you have not used the desktop-publishing capabilities of Excel much, read Chapters 1 through 3 before reading this chapter. Using these elements—fonts, boldface, italic, underlining, boxes, shading, and graphics—are all presented in Chapters 2 and 3. This chapter explains exactly how to use these elements to produce worksheets that look as if they have been professionally designed, laid out, and typeset by a desktop-publishing expert.

Understanding Format and Layout

The terms *format* and *layout* are used throughout this chapter, and throughout the book. To help you understand the references to format and layout, remember these definitions:

Format refers to the form of the numeric and text information on the page—the type and size of font, including the use of boldface or italic. Format also refers to the use of capitalization, the use of underlining, or the use of special graphical characters within the text.

Layout refers to the position of numeric and text information on the page. Layout includes, for example, how information is presented in blocked, columnar fashion or how information is indented. Layout also refers to how information is positioned in relation to white space, including left, right, top, and bottom margins.

```
LaserPro Corporation
Balance Sheet
December 31, 1992
```

Assets	This Year	Last Year	Change
Current Assets			
Cash	$247,886	$126,473	96%
Accounts receivable	863,652	524,570	65%
Inventory	88,328	65,508	35%
Investments	108,577	31,934	240%
	---------	---------	
Total current assets	$1,308,443	$748,485	75%
Fixed Assets			
Machinery and equipment	$209,906	$158,730	32%
Vehicles	429,505	243,793	76%
Office furniture	50,240	36,406	38%
(Accumulated depreciation)	(101,098)	(64,394)	57%
	---------	---------	
Total fixed assets	$588,553	$374,535	57%
Total Assets	$1,896,996	$1,123,020	69%

Liabilities and Shareholders Equity	This Year	Last Year	Change
Current Liabilities			
Accounts payable	$426,041	$332,845	28%
Notes payable	45,327	23,486	93%
Accrued liabilities	34,614	26,026	33%
Income taxes payable	88,645	51,840	71%
	---------	---------	
Total current liabilities	$594,627	$434,197	37%
Noncurrent Liabilities			
Long-term debt	488,822	349,253	40%
Deferred federal tax	147,844	92,101	61%
	---------	---------	
Total noncurrent liabilities	$636,666	$441,354	44%
Shareholders' Equity			
Common stock	1,000	1,000	0%
Retained earnings	664,703	246,469	170%
	---------	---------	
Total shareholders' equity	$665,703	$247,469	169%
	---------	---------	
Total Liabilities and Equity	$1,896,996	$1,123,020	69%
	=========	=========	

Fig. 7.1 A worksheet printed with the standard capabilities of Excel.

LaserPro Corporation

Balance Sheet
December 31, 1992

Assets			

	This Year	Last Year	Change
Current Assets			
Cash	$247,886	$126,473	96%
Accounts receivable	863,652	524,570	65%
Inventory	88,328	65,508	35%
Investments	108,577	31,934	240%
Total current assets	$1,308,443	$748,485	75%
Fixed Assets			
Machinery and equipment	$209,906	$158,730	32%
Vehicles	429,505	243,793	76%
Office furniture	50,240	36,406	38%
(Accumulated depreciation)	(101,098)	(64,394)	57%
Total fixed assets	$588,553	$374,535	57%
Total Assets	**$1,896,996**	**$1,123,020**	**69%**

Liabilities and Shareholders' Equity			

	This Year	Last Year	Change
Current Liabilities			
Accounts payable	$426,041	$332,845	28%
Notes payable	45,327	23,486	93%
Accrued liabilities	34,614	26,026	33%
Income taxes payable	88,645	51,840	71%
Total current liabilities	$594,627	$434,197	37%
Noncurrent Liabilities			
Long-term debt	$488,822	$349,253	40%
Deferred federal tax	147,844	92,101	61%
Total noncurrent liabilities	$636,666	$441,354	44%
Shareholders' Equity			
Common stock	$1,000	$1,000	0%
Retained earnings	664,703	246,469	170%
Total shareholders' equity	$665,703	$247,469	169%
Total Liabilities and Equity	**$1,896,996**	**$1,123,020**	**69%**

Fig. 7.2 A worksheet that uses the desktop-publishing features of Excel.

Preparing the Worksheet for Presentation-Quality Output

One of the great advantages of Excel is that you can see and evaluate the desktop-publishing changes you make to your worksheet as you enter the worksheet data and add formatting and layout features. Another advantage of Excel is its capability to set up the worksheet so that you can tell immediately whether the formatting and layout elements will produce a printed worksheet exactly as you want (for example, to make sure that your worksheet prints on one page). Setting up your worksheet before entering text and numbers will help you determine what your worksheet will look like. The following sections present techniques and tricks for preparing your worksheet for the kind of printed output you want with Excel.

Giving Your Worksheet a Professional Look

You will have the most success using Excel if you remember to use its capabilities to communicate information presented in your worksheet. Although using the desktop-publishing features of Excel to impress your readers may be helpful, you will get the most impact from Excel by using its features to draw the readers' attention to certain information, to show how information is organized and subordinated to other information, and to make finding and reading information easy. This chapter presents a few key concepts that will help you produce impressive-looking worksheets that communicate the information in an easy-to-follow form. The key ingredients to producing a professional-looking worksheet include the following guidelines of good desktop-publishing design and layout:

- Determine how you want the worksheet information communicated (what should be emphasized or de-emphasized, and what relationships between information you should show).

- Opt for simplicity; for example, avoid using too many fonts or formatting elements.

- Establish consistency in the format and layout of your worksheets so that regular readers of your work can easily and quickly find and understand information. Special elements also will have the desired effect.

Use Excel's features to draw the reader's attention to certain information, to show how information is organized and sub-ordinated to other information, and to make finding and reading information easy.

- Use page format and layout to show contrast when you want certain elements in a worksheet to stand out in relation to all other information, or when you want one worksheet to stand out in relation to other worksheets.

Following these basic guidelines will help you make the right choices when you are trying to decide which desktop-publishing elements to include in your worksheets. The example worksheet shown in figure 7.2 illustrates these basic concepts.

The layout and format of figure 7.2 illustrate the developer's intention to show clearly two main parts of the balance sheet—the `Assets` section and the `Liabilities and Shareholders' Equity` section. First, the use of boldface, shading, solid black rule, and large font for `Assets` and `Liabilities and Shareholders' Equity` segment the two main parts of the balance sheet. Second, the use of boldface shows each of the main sections under the `Assets` and `Liabilities and Shareholders' Equity` parts of the balance sheet. Third, the use of boldface and underlining calls attention to the rows of the balance sheet containing totals for the overall `Assets` and `Liabilities and Shareholders' Equity` sections.

To achieve simplicity, the balance sheet in figure 7.2 uses one type of font for everything but the company name, `LaserPro Corporation`, at the top of the worksheet. Also, except for the company name, the worksheet uses only two sizes of fonts—11 point for the main information and 13 point for the subheadings—`Balance Sheet; December 31, 1991; Assets;` and `Liabilities and Shareholders' Equity`.

Maintaining consistency in the format and layout of the balance sheet in figure 7.2 is important for the following reasons. Setting consistency in format and layout conventions will help readers more easily read and understand other reports you produce. Being consistent in the way you present the main headings of your worksheets, such as the `Current Assets` heading in figure 7.2, will help readers quickly see the structure of your worksheet. Consistency in a worksheet like the balance sheet in figure 7.2 also is important if you plan to develop a series of balance sheets over time, or if you need to develop many balance sheets for different divisions of your company.

Contrast is used within the elements of a single worksheet and distinguishes one worksheet from another. The balance sheet in figure 7.2 shows contrast through the use of boldface, point size, position of headings, and underlining in the balance sheet. If you need to distinguish one balance sheet from among a series of others, you may, for example, box the contrasting balance sheet with a drop shadow to call

Setting consistency in format and layout conventions will help readers more easily read and understand other reports you produce.

attention to the balance sheet. Figure 7.3 shows how one balance sheet can stand out from the others by using the Excel features for creating boxes and drop shadows.

By following the simple desktop-publishing guidelines for professional worksheets presented in this chapter, you can apply the Excel capabilities to your best advantage.

Designing the Layout of Your Worksheet

The initial steps for developing a desktop-published quality worksheet with Excel include spending time planning the layout and format for your worksheet before entering data. First, make a mental or written note of what you want to communicate through the information presented in the worksheet. What do you want to emphasize? What do you want readers to grasp easily? What do you want to persuade readers of? How do you want to communicate the organization of the worksheet? Second, how can you keep the format and layout of your worksheet simple, but also show contrast and consistency?

After you have made decisions about what information the worksheet should convey and how to format and lay out your worksheet, you can use Excel's Format Border command to create a grid on-screen so that you easily can lay out the worksheet on the page. This grid can be as simple as showing only the boundaries of your page so that you can tell whether your worksheet will fit on one page, or where the best place is to break information if you must print on two or more pages.

Remember, if you want to keep the length of the worksheet to one page, you can use a small font size for all or parts of the worksheet. You can do this automatically through the File Page Setup Fit to command. Avoid using too many point sizes and make certain that the worksheet will be readable, even if a poor photocopy blurs or lightens the characters on the page. A more complex grid can show the center points of your page to help you balance different parts of the worksheet on the page (see fig. 7.4).

Using a grid to lay out the worksheet shown in figure 7.2, for example, helps to determine how much space to give to the information at the top of the page and how to position the two major sections of the balance sheet. If you create a page border (see "Displaying the Page Border," later in this chapter) before beginning to enter data, you can avoid having to move data on the page because it does not fit or because information is not balanced. Creating a page border before entering your worksheet data also helps you determine how much white space you can include.

You can use Excel's Format Border command to create a grid on-screen so that you easily can lay out the worksheet on the page.

LaserPro Corporation
Balance Sheet
December 31, 1992

Assets			
	This Year	Last Year	Change
Current Assets			
Cash	$247,886	$126,473	96%
Accounts receivable	863,652	524,570	65%
Inventory	88,328	65,508	35%
Investments	108,577	31,934	240%
Total current assets	$1,308,443	$748,485	75%
Fixed Assets			
Machinery and equipment	$209,906	$158,730	32%
Vehicles	429,505	243,793	76%
Office furniture	50,240	36,406	38%
(Accumulated depreciation)	(101,098)	(64,394)	57%
Total fixed assets	$588,553	$374,535	57%
Total Assets	**$1,896,996**	**$1,123,020**	**69%**

Liabilities and Shareholders' Equity			
	This Year	Last Year	Change
Current Liabilities			
Accounts payable	$426,041	$332,845	28%
Notes payable	45,327	23,486	93%
Accrued liabilities	34,614	26,026	33%
Income taxes payable	88,645	51,840	71%
Total current liabilities	$594,627	$434,197	37%
Noncurrent Liabilities			
Long-term debt	$488,822	$349,253	40%
Deferred federal tax	147,844	92,101	61%
Total noncurrent liabilities	$636,666	$441,354	44%
Shareholders' Equity			
Common stock	$1,000	$1,000	0%
Retained earnings	664,703	246,469	170%
Total shareholders' equity	$665,703	$247,469	169%
Total Liabilities and Equity	**$1,896,996**	**$1,123,020**	**69%**

Fig. 7.3 Contrasting one balance sheet from others by placing a box and drop shadow around it.

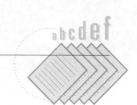

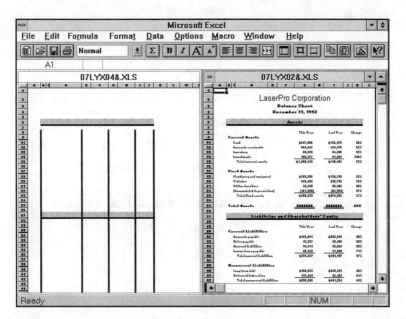

Fig. 7.4 The outline grid for the LaserPro balance sheet displayed in a window next to a reduced version of the balance sheet.

Using White Space

If you have enough room on the page, reserve columns of white space between columns of data, and reserve rows of white space to divide sections of the worksheet. White space between columns of data also can help create balance when columns of data vary in column width.

Figure 7.5 shows the layout of the balance sheet in figure 7.2, which contains 10 columns. Two columns are used for the labels on the left side of the balance sheet; three columns for numerical data; and five columns for white space (two of these are used for additional margin space on the left and right sides of the worksheet).

Displaying the Page Border

Excel provides two ways of knowing whether your worksheet data will fit on one page. First, when you select the Options Display Automatic Page Breaks command, Excel displays dashed lines around the borders of page breaks (see fig. 7.6). Second, the File Print Preview command displays a *picture* of the printed page on-screen so that you can preview the page before it is printed.

Use white space to make your worksheet information easier to read and to show contrast between elements.

Keep in mind that when you shrink text or decrease column widths, you may be sacrificing readability, balance, or enough white space in your document.

	A	B	C	D	E	F	G	H	I	J	K
1											
2				**LaserPro Corporation**							
3				Balance Sheet							
4				December 31, 1992							
5											
6						Assets					
7											
8						This Year		Last Year		Change	
9/10				**Current Assets**							
11				Cash		$247,886		$126,473		96%	
12				Accounts receivable		863,652		524,570		65%	
13				Inventory		88,328		65,508		35%	
14				Investments		108,577		31,934		240%	
15				Total current assets		$1,308,443		$748,485		75%	
16											
17/18				**Fixed Assets**							
19				Machinery and equipment		$209,906		$158,730		32%	
20				Vehicles		429,505		243,793		76%	
21				Office furniture		50,240		36,406		38%	
22				(Accumulated depreciation)		(101,098)		(64,394)		57%	
23				Total fixed assets		$588,553		$374,535		57%	
24											
25				**Total Assets**		**$1,896,996**		**$1,123,020**		**69%**	
26											
27						Liabilities and Shareholders' Equity					
28											
29						This Year		Last Year		Change	
30/31				**Current Liabilities**							
32				Accounts payable		$426,041		$332,845		28%	
33				Notes payable		45,327		23,486		93%	
34				Accrued liabilities		34,614		26,026		33%	
35				Income taxes payable		88,645		51,840		71%	
36				Total current liabilities		$594,627		$434,197		37%	
37											
38/39				**Noncurrent Liabilities**							
40				Long-term debt		$488,822		$349,253		40%	
41				Deferred federal tax		147,844		92,101		61%	
42				Total noncurrent liabilities		$636,666		$441,354		44%	
43											
44/45				**Shareholders' Equity**							
46				Common stock		$1,000		$1,000		0%	
47				Retained earnings		664,703		246,469		170%	
48				Total shareholders' equity		$665,703		$247,469		169%	
49											
50				**Total Liabilities and Equity**		**$1,896,996**		**$1,123,020**		**69%**	
51											

Fig. 7.5 The white space for figure 7.2.

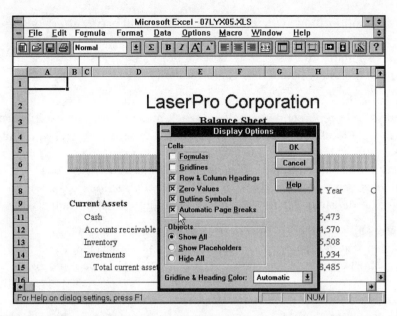

Fig. 7.6 Select Automatic Page Breaks to display dashed lines where page breaks will occur.

If you find that your data range extends beyond the boundaries of the page break lines, you have a few choices. First, you can delete columns or rows or change the column widths. Second, you can split the document so that it fits on more than one page. Third, you can choose to have the worksheet automatically fit on one page with the File Page Setup Fit to command. In some cases, it may be appropriate to consolidate data. Finally, when you print, Excel will bring up a dialog box that says how many pages will be printed with a Page 1 of x message where x is the number of pages. If you are quick, you may be able to stop printing by selecting Cancel from the dialog box.

Creating a Single- versus Multiple-Page Report

Selecting Options Display Automatic Page Breaks before you enter data into a worksheet will help you determine what point sizes to use if you want to fit all information on one page. Options Display Automatic Page Breaks is also an advantage when you are creating multiple-page reports. This command helps you divide your worksheet into *page grids*. If you are creating one large worksheet with many columns and need to see at which column a new page will begin, selecting the Automatic Page

Breaks option shows where these page breaks will occur. After you know how many columns of data will fit onto a page, you can lay out columns as appropriate. You also can use the Options Set Page Break command to control manually where new pages should begin.

Suppose that you need to create a worksheet containing 18 columns of data. A sales report showing sales for each month, totals for each quarter, the yearly total, and labels for the product lines, for example, would use 18 columns. If you enter the data in a single worksheet, you can use Options Display Automatic Page Breaks to determine where page breaks will occur and organize your data into quarterly sections according to the page divisions. Figure 7.7 shows a diagram of such a worksheet.

Using Options Display Automatic Page Breaks to show page borders enables you to organize your worksheet so that data is laid out in the worksheet exactly as you want it to flow from page to page. If, for example, you want each page to begin with data for a new quarter—first quarter on the first page, second quarter on the second, and so forth— you can enter columns where appropriate according to the page borders.

Laying Out and Formatting Your Worksheet

So far, this chapter has covered the beginning steps of spreadsheet publishing. These steps include planning your worksheet by considering how you can best communicate its information and using the features available with Excel. The chapter also has covered the mechanics of getting started to create a professional-looking, quality worksheet with Excel. You can show page breaks and even create divider lines separating sections of your worksheet to make laying out worksheet data easier. Through examples, the following sections present step-by-step instructions for creating professional, desktop-published worksheets using the WYSIWYG feature.

Two examples are used throughout the remaining sections of the chapter to show you how to lay out and format professional-looking worksheets. To help you follow the discussion and provide a single reference of page layout and design specifications, the following tables list all features used in the examples. Table 7.1 presents the specifications for the balance sheet example shown in figures 7.2 and 7.8. Table 7.2 presents the specifications for the one-page sales report shown in figures 7.9 and 7.10.

Using Options Display Automatic Page Breaks to show page borders enables you to organize your worksheet so that data is laid out in the worksheet exactly as you want it to flow from page to page.

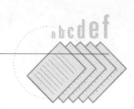

	Page 1				Page 2				Page 3				Page 4				
	Jan-92	Feb-92	Mar-92	1st Q	Apr-92	May-92	Jun-92	2nd Q	Jul-92	Aug-92	Sep-92	3rd Q	Oct-92	Nov-92	Dec-92	4th Q	Total
SERIES 1000																	
Model 1010	6,000	6,000	7,500	19,500	6,000	6,000	7,500	19,500	6,000	6,000	7,500	19,500	6,000	6,000	7,500	19,500	78,000
Model 1011	3,500	1,500	455	5,455	364	364	455	1,183	364	364	455	1,183	364	364	455	1,183	9,004
Model 1012	4,000	2,000	455	6,455	364	364	455	1,183	364	364	455	1,183	364	364	455	1,183	10,004
Model 1013	615	615	769	1,999	615	615	769	1,999	615	615	769	1,999	615	615	769	1,999	7,996
Model 1014	530	530	662	1,722	530	530	662	1,722	530	530	662	1,722	530	530	662	1,722	6,888
Model 1015	192	192	240	624	192	192	240	624	192	192	240	624	192	192	240	624	2,496
Model 1016	769	769	962	2,500	769	769	962	2,500	769	769	962	2,500	769	769	962	2,500	10,000
Model 1017	0	0	4,200	4,200	3,800	457	571	4,828	457	457	571	1,485	457	457	571	1,485	11,998
Model 1018	0	0	3,500	3,500	2,500	229	286	3,015	229	229	286	744	229	229	286	744	8,003
Model 1019	0	0	2,500	2,500	1,500	400	500	2,400	400	400	500	1,300	400	400	500	1,300	7,500
Model 1020	0	0	0	0	0	538	673	1,211	538	538	673	1,749	538	538	673	1,749	4,709
Model 1021	0	0	0	0	0	0	0	0	4,500	3,000	694	8,194	556	556	694	1,806	10,000
Total Series 1000	15,606	11,606	21,243	48,455	16,634	10,458	13,073	40,165	14,958	13,458	13,767	42,183	11,014	11,014	13,767	35,795	166,598
SERIES 2000																	
Model 2010	5,000	2,000	0	7,000	821	821	1,026	2,668	821	821	1,026	2,668	821	821	1,026	2,668	15,004
Model 2011	0	0	0	0	0	0	0	0	2,500	2,000	833	5,333	667	667	833	2,167	7,500
Model 2012	0	0	6,250	6,250	3,250	971	1,214	5,435	971	971	1,214	3,156	971	971	1,214	3,156	17,997
Model 2013	0	0	0	0	0	5,500	3,000	8,500	815	815	1,019	2,649	815	815	1,019	2,649	13,798
Model 2014	0	0	0	0	0	3,500	3,500	7,000	615	615	769	1,999	615	615	769	1,999	10,998
Total Series 2000	5,000	2,000	6,250	13,250	4,071	10,792	8,740	23,603	5,722	5,222	4,861	15,805	3,889	3,889	4,861	12,639	65,297
SERIES 3000																	
Model 3010	0	0	0	0	0	0	1,875	1,875	1,875	682	852	3,409	682	682	852	2,216	7,500
Model 3011	0	0	0	0	0	0	5,000	5,000	1,000	273	341	1,614	273	273	341	887	7,501
Model 3012	0	0	0	0	0	0	0	0	3,500	2,500	556	6,556	444	444	556	1,444	8,000
Model 3013	0	0	0	0	0	0	0	0	2,500	2,000	556	5,056	444	444	556	1,444	6,500
Model 3014	0	0	0	0	0	0	0	0	0	2,000	1,500	3,500	215	215	269	699	4,199
Model 3015	0	0	0	0	0	0	0	0	0	625	625	1,250	43	43	54	140	1,390
Total Series 3000	0	0	0	0	0	0	6,875	6,875	8,875	8,080	4,430	21,385	2,101	2,101	2,628	6,830	35,090
TOTAL	20,606	13,606	27,493	61,705	20,705	21,250	28,688	70,643	29,555	26,760	23,058	79,373	17,004	17,004	21,256	55,264	266,985

Fig. 7.7   A single worksheet showing a multiple-page layout.

	A	B	C	D	E	F	G	H	I	J	K
1											
2				**LaserPro Corporation**							
3				Balance Sheet							
4				December 31, 1992							
5											
6						Assets					
7											
8						This Year		Last Year		Change	
10				Current Assets							
11				Cash		$247,886		$126,473		96%	
12				Accounts receivable		863,652		524,570		65%	
13				Inventory		88,328		65,508		35%	
14				Investments		108,577		31,934		240%	
15				Total current assets		$1,308,443		$748,485		75%	
16											
18				Fixed Assets							
19				Machinery and equipment		$209,906		$158,730		32%	
20				Vehicles		429,505		243,793		76%	
21				Office furniture		50,240		36,406		38%	
22				(Accumulated depreciation)		(101,098)		(64,394)		57%	
23				Total fixed assets		$588,553		$374,535		57%	
24											
25				Total Assets		$1,896,996		$1,123,020		69%	
26											
27						Liabilities and Shareholders' Equity					
28											
29						This Year		Last Year		Change	
30				Current Liabilities							
32				Accounts payable		$426,041		$332,845		28%	
33				Notes payable		45,327		23,486		93%	
34				Accrued liabilities		34,614		26,026		33%	
35				Income taxes payable		88,645		51,840		71%	
36				Total current liabilities		$594,627		$434,197		37%	
37											
38				Noncurrent Liabilities							
40				Long-term debt		$488,822		$349,253		40%	
41				Deferred federal tax		147,844		92,101		61%	
42				Total noncurrent liabilities		$636,666		$441,354		44%	
43											
44				Shareholders' Equity							
46				Common stock		$1,000		$1,000		0%	
47				Retained earnings		664,703		246,469		170%	
48				Total shareholders' equity		$665,703		$247,469		169%	
49											
50				Total Liabilities and Equity		$1,896,996		$1,123,020		69%	
51											

Fig. 7.8 A balance sheet with the column and row references displayed.

LaserPro Corporation
1992 Sales Report
(Units)

	Jan-92	Feb-92	Mar-92	1st Q	Apr-92	May-92	Jun-92	2nd Q	Jul-92	Aug-92	Sep-92	3rd Q	Oct-92	Nov-92	Dec-92	4th Q	Total
SERIES 1000																	
Model 1010	6,000	6,000	7,500	19,500	6,000	6,000	7,500	19,500	6,000	6,000	7,500	19,500	6,000	6,000	7,500	19,500	78,000
Model 1011	3,500	1,500	455	5,455	364	364	455	1,183	364	364	455	1,183	364	364	455	1,183	9,004
Model 1012	4,000	2,000	455	6,455	364	364	455	1,183	364	364	455	1,183	364	364	455	1,183	10,004
Model 1013	615	615	769	1,999	615	615	769	1,999	615	615	769	1,999	615	615	769	1,999	7,996
Model 1014	530	530	662	1,722	530	530	662	1,722	530	530	662	1,722	530	530	662	1,722	6,888
Model 1015	192	192	240	624	192	192	240	624	192	192	240	624	192	192	240	624	2,496
Model 1016	769	769	962	2,500	769	769	962	2,500	769	769	962	2,500	769	769	962	2,500	10,000
Model 1017	0	0	4,200	4,200	3,800	457	571	4,828	457	457	571	1,485	457	457	571	1,485	11,998
Model 1018	0	0	3,500	3,500	2,500	229	286	3,015	229	229	286	744	229	229	286	744	8,003
Model 1019	0	0	2,500	2,500	1,500	400	500	2,400	400	400	500	1,300	400	400	500	1,300	7,500
Model 1020	0	0	0	0	0	538	673	1,211	538	538	673	1,749	538	538	673	1,749	4,709
Model 1021	0	0	0	0	0	0	0	0	4,500	3,000	694	8,194	556	556	694	1,806	10,000
Total Series 1000	15,606	11,606	21,243	48,455	16,634	10,458	13,073	40,165	14,958	13,458	13,767	42,183	11,014	11,014	13,767	35,795	166,598
SERIES 2000																	
Model 2010	5,000	2,000	0	7,000	821	821	1,026	2,668	821	821	1,026	2,668	821	821	1,026	2,668	15,004
Model 2011	0	0	0	0	0	0	5,000	5,000	2,500	2,000	833	5,333	667	667	833	2,167	7,500
Model 2012	0	0	6,250	6,250	3,250	971	1,214	5,435	971	971	1,214	3,156	971	971	1,214	3,156	17,997
Model 2013	0	0	0	0	0	5,500	3,000	8,500	815	815	1,019	2,649	815	815	1,019	2,649	13,798
Model 2014	0	0	0	0	0	3,500	3,500	7,000	615	615	769	1,999	615	615	769	1,999	10,998
Total Series 2000	5,000	2,000	6,250	13,250	4,071	10,792	8,740	23,603	5,722	5,222	4,861	15,805	3,889	3,889	4,861	12,639	65,297
SERIES 3000																	
Model 3010	0	0	0	0	0	0	1,875	1,875	1,875	682	852	3,409	682	682	852	2,216	7,500
Model 3011	0	0	0	0	0	0	5,000	5,000	1,000	273	341	1,614	273	273	341	887	7,501
Model 3012	0	0	0	0	0	0	0	0	3,500	2,500	556	6,556	444	444	556	1,444	8,000
Model 3013	0	0	0	0	0	0	0	0	2,500	2,000	556	5,056	444	444	556	1,444	6,500
Model 3014	0	0	0	0	0	0	0	0	0	2,000	1,500	3,500	215	215	269	699	4,199
Model 3015	0	0	0	0	0	0	0	0	0	625	625	1,250	43	43	54	140	1,390
Total Series 3000	0	0	0	0	0	0	6,875	6,875	8,875	8,080	4,430	21,385	2,101	2,101	2,628	6,830	35,090
TOTAL	20,606	13,606	27,493	61,705	20,705	21,250	28,688	70,643	29,555	26,760	23,058	79,373	17,004	17,004	21,256	55,264	266,985

Fig. 7.9 A sales report formatted on one page.

LaserPro Corporation
1992 Sales Report
(Units)

	Jan-92	Feb-92	Mar-92	1st Q	Apr-92	May-92	Jun-92	2nd Q	Jul-92	Aug-92	Sep-92	3rd Q	Oct-92	Nov-92	Dec-92	4th Q	Total
SERIES 1000																	
Model 1010	6,000	6,000	7,500	19,500	6,000	6,000	7,500	19,500	6,000	6,000	7,500	19,500	6,000	6,000	7,500	19,500	78,000
Model 1011	3,500	1,500	455	5,455	364	364	455	1,183	364	364	455	1,183	364	364	455	1,183	9,004
Model 1012	4,000	2,000	455	6,455	364	364	455	1,183	364	364	455	1,183	364	364	455	1,183	10,004
Model 1013	615	615	769	1,999	615	615	769	1,999	615	615	769	1,999	615	615	769	1,999	7,996
Model 1014	530	530	662	1,722	530	530	662	1,722	530	530	662	1,722	530	530	662	1,722	6,888
Model 1015	192	192	240	624	192	192	240	624	192	192	240	624	192	192	240	624	2,496
Model 1016	769	769	962	2,500	769	769	962	2,500	769	769	962	2,500	769	769	962	2,500	10,000
Model 1017	0	0	4,200	4,200	3,800	457	571	4,828	457	457	571	1,485	457	457	571	1,485	11,998
Model 1018	0	0	3,500	3,500	2,500	229	286	3,015	229	229	286	744	229	229	286	744	8,003
Model 1019	0	0	2,500	2,500	1,500	400	500	2,400	400	400	500	1,300	400	400	500	1,300	7,500
Model 1020	0	0	0	0	0	538	673	1,211	538	538	673	1,749	538	538	673	1,749	4,709
Model 1021	0	0	0	0	0	0	0	0	4,500	3,000	694	8,194	556	556	694	1,806	10,000
Total Series 1000	15,606	11,606	21,243	48,465	16,634	10,458	13,073	40,165	14,956	13,468	13,767	42,183	11,014	11,014	13,767	36,795	166,598
SERIES 2000																	
Model 2010	5,000	2,000	0	7,000	821	821	1,026	2,668	821	821	1,026	2,668	821	821	1,026	2,668	15,004
Model 2011	0	0	0	0	0	0	0	0	2,500	2,000	833	5,333	667	667	833	2,167	7,500
Model 2012	0	0	6,250	6,250	3,250	971	1,214	5,435	971	971	1,214	3,156	971	971	1,214	3,156	17,997
Model 2013	0	0	0	0	0	5,500	3,000	8,500	815	815	1,019	2,649	815	815	1,019	2,649	13,798
Model 2014	0	0	0	0	0	3,500	3,500	7,000	615	615	769	1,999	615	615	769	1,999	10,998
Total Series 2000	5,000	2,000	6,250	13,250	4,071	10,792	8,740	23,603	6,722	6,222	4,861	15,805	3,889	3,889	4,861	12,639	65,297
SERIES 3000																	
Model 3010	0	0	0	0	0	0	1,875	1,875	1,875	682	852	3,409	682	682	852	2,216	7,500
Model 3011	0	0	0	0	0	0	5,000	5,000	1,000	273	341	1,614	273	273	341	887	7,501
Model 3012	0	0	0	0	0	0	0	0	3,500	2,500	556	6,556	444	444	556	1,444	8,000
Model 3013	0	0	0	0	0	0	0	0	2,500	2,000	556	5,056	444	444	556	1,444	6,500
Model 3014	0	0	0	0	0	0	0	0	0	2,000	1,500	3,500	215	215	269	699	4,199
Model 3015	0	0	0	0	0	0	0	0	0	0	925	1,250	43	43	54	140	1,390
Total Series 3000	0	0	0	0	0	0	6,876	6,876	8,876	8,080	4,430	21,386	2,101	2,101	2,628	6,830	35,090
TOTAL	20,606	13,606	27,493	61,705	20,706	21,250	28,688	70,643	29,666	26,760	23,058	79,373	17,004	17,004	21,266	55,264	266,985

Fig. 7.10 A sales report with the column and row references displayed.

Using an Existing Worksheet versus Creating a New Worksheet

Although you can achieve exactly the same output whether you are applying Excel to an existing worksheet or creating a new one, working with an existing worksheet may require some precautions. You need to be careful of the effect that adding new columns and rows and moving data may have in an existing worksheet. You need to make sure, for example, that formulas will not be affected if you decide to insert columns for additional white space on the page. Using an existing worksheet can be a big timesaver, however, because it saves you the time you would spend creating a new worksheet.

When enhancing a worksheet, be careful not to ruin existing formulas. Be sure to keep a backup copy.

When working with an existing worksheet, you also need to consider whether the changes you make by applying desktop publishing techniques will affect the way a worksheet is used by others. If the worksheet you are changing, for example, is used by someone else for combining data from many worksheets, make sure that your changes will not cause errors when the worksheet is combined. Be careful with worksheets containing formulas that refer to worksheets in other files. Similarly, be careful when changing one Excel worksheet that is linked to worksheets or documents.

Finally, remember that the more you use the desktop-publishing features of Excel, the more likely you will be to move or erase data, sometimes erasing data accidentally. If you are using an existing worksheet, keep a backup copy and take precautions to avoid losing data or causing errors in a complex application—particularly an application consisting of linked files.

Table 7.1 Balance Sheet Layout and Format Specifications for Figures 7.2 and 7.8

Fonts

Main Headings	
LaserPro Corporation	Arial, 24 point, bold
Balance Sheet	Times New Roman, 14 point, bold
December 31, 1992	Times New Roman, 14 point, bold
Assets	Times New Roman, 14 point, bold
Liabilities...	Times New Roman, 14 point, bold
Column Headings	Times New Roman, 12 point, normal
Labels	Times New Roman, 12 point, normal
Numeric Data	Times New Roman, 12 point, normal

White Space

Rows	1, 5, 7, 10, 16, 18, 24, 26, 28, 31, 37, 39, 43, 45, 49, 51
Columns	A, E, G, I, K

Format Borders

Thin Bottom	F14, H14, F22, H22, F35, H35, F41, H41, F47, H47
Double Bottom	F25, H25, F50, H50
Thick Bottom	B6:J6, B27:J27
Format Patterns (4th)	B6:J6, B27:J27
Row Height of 2	10, 18, 31, 39, 45

Table 7.2 Sales Report Layout and Format Specifications for Figures 7.9 and 7.10

Fonts

Main Headings	
LaserPro Corporation	Arial, 14 point, bold
1992 Sales Report	Arial, 14 point, bold

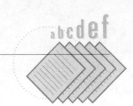

Fonts

(Units)	Arial, 8 point, normal
SERIES 1000	Arial, 10 point, bold
SERIES 2000	Arial, 10 point, bold
SERIES 3000	Arial, 10 point, bold
Column Headings	Arial, 8 point, normal
Labels (excluding totals)	Arial, 8 point, normal
Numeric Data (excluding totals)	Arial, 8 point, normal
Totals (labels and data)	Arial, 8 point, bold
Diamonds	Symbol (Char(0168))

Formulas for Diamonds

Rept(Char(0168)&" ",9)	A3
Rept(" "&Char(0168),9)	M3

White Space

Rows	1, 7, 9, 11, 24, 26, 28, 34, 36, 38, 45, 47

Underlining

Single	C23:S23, C33:S33, C44:S44

Format Borders

Bottom	C8:S8, C48:R48
Right	F8:F48, J8:J48, N8:N48, R8:R48
Format Pattern (2nd)	A2:G2, M2:S2, A4:G4, M4:S4
Row Height of 2	2, 4
Row Height of 6	11, 24, 28, 34, 38, 45
Format Alignment Vertical Center	A2, M2

Using Columns and Rows Effectively

Without the desktop-publishing features of Excel, the options for how to use columns and rows in the worksheet are limited. Determining the number of columns your worksheet application should contain is a matter of determining how many columns of data you have and how many columns you need for labels. Similarly, determining the number of rows needed for your worksheet is a matter of knowing the type and amount of data your worksheet will include. The desktop-publishing features of Excel, however, present many other ways for using rows and columns. You can use rows for creating solid black rules, space around boxes, graphics, or shaded elements. You can use columns for displaying graphs or graphics alongside worksheet data or for creating extra white space around and within the worksheet. This section describes the ways to use columns and rows when laying out your desktop-published worksheet.

Laying out a worksheet to achieve a high quality desktop-published look includes using columns for white space, using columns to position labels, reserving columns for special text notations, and using columns for graphs and graphics. The worksheet shown in figure 7.8, for example, uses columns for positioning labels and for white space, in addition to columns used for numeric data.

Columns used for white space in the worksheet in figure 7.8 include columns A, E, G, I, and K. See "Using Columns and Rows for White Space," later in this chapter, for tips on how to use white space effectively in your worksheet design.

Determining how wide to make worksheet columns involves not only considering the width needed for data, but also the layout of the worksheet page. The column widths of the worksheet in figure 7.8, for example, were determined by four factors: the positions of the labels to the left of the numeric data, the amount of white space needed to balance elements on the page, the width needed to ensure that numeric and text data would have enough room to display and print, and the width needed for numbers to display in their columns.

Using Different Levels of Label Headings

The columnar structure of Excel and the ability to change column widths make entering different levels of labels very easy in Excel. A worksheet containing main headings with subheadings, such as the

Determining how wide to make worksheet columns involves not only considering the width needed for data, but also the layout of the worksheet page.

Use a separate column to indent sections.

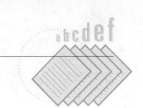

labels in the worksheet in figure 7.8, are very easy to enter. You can assign a new column for each new level of heading, for example, rather than reserving one very wide column and creating indentations by using the space bar to space labels to the right of the left margin. Notice in particular that columns B, C, and D help delineate different sections of information. Column C is used to indent the entries under each subsection of the `Assets` and `Liabilities and Shareholders' Equity` sections. Column D indents the total for each subsection.

An alternative to using columns to delineate sections is to add spaces before text. You could type four spaces for the first indent and 2 spaces for the second indent in figure 7.8, for example. However, this method is not recommended. First, if you use a nonproportional font such as Arial or Times New Roman, spaces are not equivalent to characters and you may have a problem lining up each section of data—especially if you change typefaces or type sizes. Second, it is difficult to tell how many spaces you typed. If you need to edit the worksheet later or if you make a mistake in the number of spaces, you may spend a significant amount of time correcting the worksheet. Third, if you need to change the spacing, it is much easier to change the column width than to change the number of spaces for each label.

As shown in later chapters, Excel is easier to use than a word processor when the document you are creating contains a lot of tabular information requiring that data be indented at certain points. Excel is also easier to use than a word processor when labels are numbered or preceded by bullets, icons, or other types of graphics. The examples in figure 7.11 contain columns reserved for the numbers, icons, and graphics that precede the text.

When you are laying out your worksheet, remember to account for columns that you will use to enter various levels of indented information or to enter numbers, icons, or graphics preceding information.

Using Columns and Rows for White Space

Considering how much and where to use white space is an important part of designing and laying out professional-looking worksheets. White space plays an important part in giving a balanced look to the page and in conveying the contrast among elements. White space used effectively can contribute to making a worksheet, or any other document, easier to read.

To create white space, add rows or columns or increase the width of columns or height of rows.

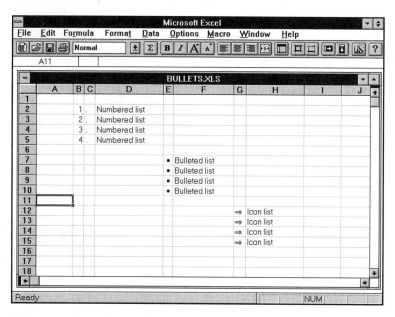

Fig. 7.11 Reserving columns for the numbers, icons, or graphics preceding tabular information.

The balance sheet in figure 7.8 is a good example of using columns and rows for white space. Specifically, this worksheet uses columns A, E, G, I, and K for vertical white space and rows 1, 5, 7, 10, 16, 18, 24, 26, 28, 31, 37, 39, 43, 45, 49, and 51 for horizontal white space. White space borders the worksheet with blank columns A and K and blank rows 1 and 51. This white space helps make the box around the balance sheet stand out and also helps make LaserPro Corporation and the headings in column B more distinct. The remaining blank columns, E, G, and I help to set off the labels on the left and make the columns of numeric data easier to read—particularly when a reader is focusing on one column of data. Blank rows used for white space help to distinguish the separate sections of the balance sheet and also set off headings and rows containing totals.

Excel users also can change the height of rows. You can change the height by using the Format Row Height command or by dragging the bottom boundary of the row in the worksheet frame. One of the valuable uses for this capability is for varying white space between rows of data or lines of text. This feature makes it possible to have different leading between blocks of text, headings and text, text and graphics,

or boxed and unboxed text and graphics. Format **R**ow Height is used in the balance sheet in figure 7.8 to shorten rows that were added for white space between main headings and the labels that follow. Blank rows were inserted at rows 10, 18, 31, 39, and 45 to help make the headings above these rows stand out. In figure 7.10, shortened rows were used to add white space but also to keep each series together. Short rows 11 and 24 keep the title SERIES 1000 and the Total for the series with the model numbers. The short rows still provide enough white space to enable the reader to focus on the title and the total, yet there is a difference in height between rows 26 and 36 which distinguishes each series of models.

Notice the difference between figure 7.12 and the original balance sheet shown in figure 7.2. Figure 7.12 excludes the use of additional columns and rows for white space. Although still readable, the second balance sheet fails to show the contrast and readability of the original sheet.

Creating Numbered Lists

If you are entering a column of labels or other information preceded by numbers, such as the numbered list in figure 7.11, you easily can enter the numbers using the **D**ata Series and **E**dit Fill Down commands. To enter numbers this way, follow these steps:

1. Reserve two columns for the numbers—one for the number itself, and the other for the period following the number. Set the column width for each column to two characters.

2. Type the beginning number in the first cell.

3. Select the range of rows for your list of numbered items.

4. Choose **D**ata Series. The Data Series dialog box appears.

5. Enter the step number and select OK. The numbers are entered down the column.

6. Enter a period (.) in the column to the right of the first number.

7. Copy the period down the column to the last number. You now can enter headings or other information in the column directly to the right of the column containing the periods.

To remove the space to the right of the number, use the Format **N**umber #,##0 selection. If you select #,##0_), Excel will insert an extra space between the number and the period.

To create a numbered list, use the Data Series command.

Centering Headings in the Worksheet

Normally, centering headings is as simple as highlighting the characters you want to center and the range over which you want them centered. You then select the Center Across Columns tool. Additionally, follow these tips when centering headings in your worksheet:

- Place the text in the leftmost column of the range.

- Use the **O**ptions **D**isplay Automatic Page **B**reaks command to determine the area within which you want to center your heading.

- Set the font size for your heading before centering it, so that you can more accurately tell if the heading is truly centered.

- If the centered heading will be placed within an area that is boxed, contains vertical lines on the left, or any other entries in cells to the left of the centered heading, add these elements to the worksheet before you center the heading.

- When you center a heading with the Center Across Columns tool, highlight the range inside the box or the range to the right of other entries left of the heading (see fig. 7.13).

Centering Symbols Vertically within a Row

Unlike other spreadsheet programs, Excel enables you to center characters vertically within a cell. The diamond border for the Sales Report in figure 7.9 was centered within a row by selecting Forma**t** Alignment and marking Center in the Vertical box. You also can align characters to the top or bottom of the cell (see fig. 7.14).

Determining Fonts and Font Sizes for Worksheets

Be consistent in your use of typeface and type style.

As explained in Chapter 2, Excel supplies different fonts, depending on your printer and version of Windows. Chapter 2 also explains the differences between serif fonts (Times New Roman) and sans serif fonts (Arial). Review Chapter 2 for an understanding of the basics of fonts. This section focuses on examples of how fonts are used in worksheets and a discussion of the reasons for choosing certain fonts.

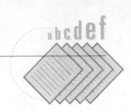

LaserPro Corporation
Balance Sheet
December 31, 1992

Assets

	This Year	Last Year	Change
Current Assets			
Cash	$247,886	$126,473	96%
Accounts receivable	863,652	524,570	65%
Inventory	88,328	65,508	35%
Investments	108,577	31,934	240%
Total current assets	$1,308,443	$748,485	75%
Fixed Assets			
Machinery and equipment	$209,906	$158,730	32%
Vehicles	429,505	243,793	76%
Office furniture	50,240	36,406	38%
(Accumulated depreciation)	(101,098)	(64,394)	57%
Total fixed assets	$588,553	$374,535	57%
Total Assets	**$1,896,996**	**$1,123,020**	**69%**

Liabilities and Shareholders' Equity

	This Year	Last Year	Change
Current Liabilities			
Accounts payable	$426,041	$332,845	28%
Notes payable	45,327	23,486	93%
Accrued liabilities	34,614	26,026	33%
Income taxes payable	88,645	51,840	71%
Total current liabilities	$594,627	$434,197	37%
Noncurrent Liabilities			
Long-term debt	$488,822	$349,253	40%
Deferred federal tax	147,844	92,101	61%
Total noncurrent liabilities	$636,666	$441,354	44%
Shareholders' Equity			
Common stock	$1,000	$1,000	0%
Retained earnings	664,703	246,469	170%
Total shareholders' equity	$665,703	$247,469	169%
Total Liabilities and Equity	**$1,896,996**	**$1,123,020**	**69%**

Fig. 7.12   A balance sheet without extra white space added.

As mentioned in Chapter 2, remembering a few guidelines about using fonts will help you avoid producing worksheets that are hard to read or that look unprofessional. The most important rule is to be consistent in typeface and type style. Being consistent means avoiding using too many different typefaces and type styles in the same worksheet. *Typeface* refers to the kind of font—Arial, Times New Roman, Courier, and so on. *Type style* refers to normal, bold, italic, bold italic, and so on. *Consistency* means following typeface and type style conventions within a single document or among many worksheets produced by the same department or the same company.

Notice the typefaces and type styles used in the two examples shown in figures 7.15 and 7.16. Figure 7.15 is the original balance sheet used throughout this chapter; the dominant typeface is Times New Roman and the only changes in type style occur in the main headings. Figure 7.16 shows the same balance sheet with the Arial typeface used throughout. Although both are equally readable, the serif Times New Roman typeface in figure 7.15 is slightly lighter because characters do not have the same thickness at all points as do the sans serif Arial characters.

Make certain that you have opted for the most readable typeface, given the amount of information and layout of your worksheet.

Whether you use a serif or sans serif typeface as the primary typeface for your worksheet depends on a few factors. First, select a dominant typeface for the worksheet depending on the environment in which the worksheet will be presented. Your typeface decision may be very different if the worksheet is going to be read as a single, isolated document rather than as part of a report, newsletter, letter, or memo. If your worksheet will be presented with text around it (sentences and paragraphs), you should use serif text—an easy-to-read typeface for body copy; you then can use a sans serif typeface for the dominant typeface for the worksheet data, making it distinct from the body copy around it.

A second factor to consider when choosing the typeface for your worksheet is readability. If you need to use a small type size to fit all the data onto one page, for example, you may want to use a sans serif typeface, because it is slightly more open between characters. This selection of typeface may increase readability, especially if you are going to photocopy the text (see fig. 7.17).

① Heading with symbols to the left

② Heading within a box

③ Heading with design element to the left

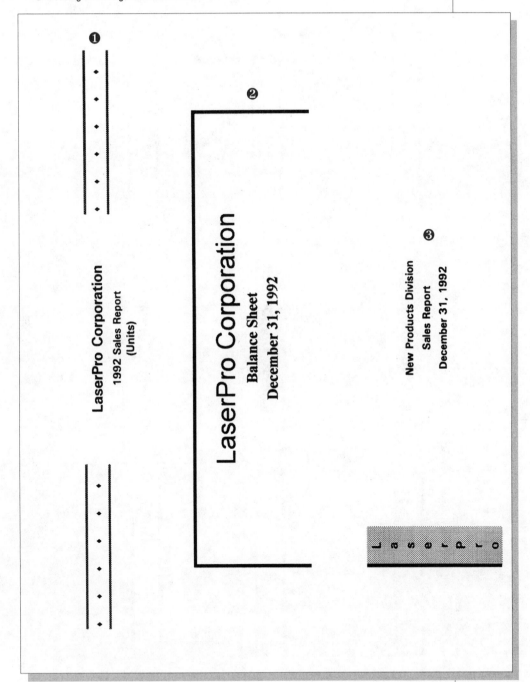

Fig. 7.13 Centering headings within boxes or to the right of other entries.

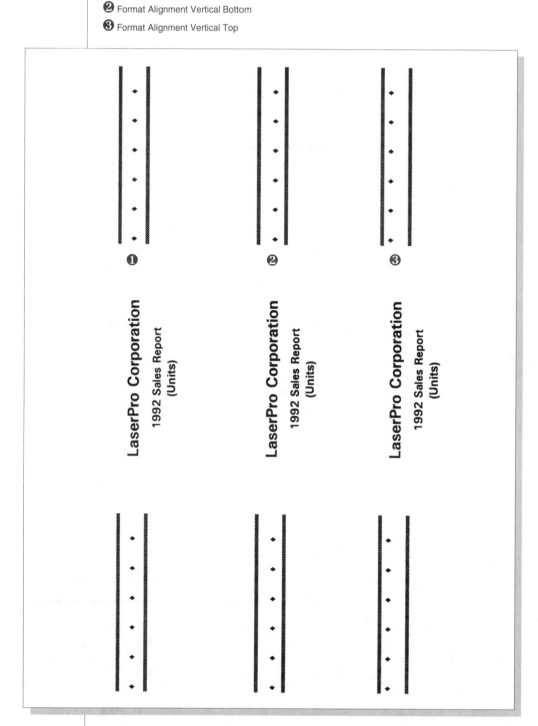

❶ Format Alignment Vertical Center

❷ Format Alignment Vertical Bottom

❸ Format Alignment Vertical Top

Fig. 7.14 Aligning diamonds in the center, at the top, and at the bottom of the row.

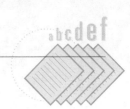

LaserPro Corporation
Balance Sheet
December 31, 1992

Assets			
	This Year	Last Year	Change
Current Assets			
Cash	$247,886	$126,473	96%
Accounts receivable	863,652	524,570	65%
Inventory	88,328	65,508	35%
Investments	108,577	31,934	240%
Total current assets	$1,308,443	$748,485	75%
Fixed Assets			
Machinery and equipment	$209,906	$158,730	32%
Vehicles	429,505	243,793	76%
Office furniture	50,240	36,406	38%
(Accumulated depreciation)	(101,098)	(64,394)	57%
Total fixed assets	$588,553	$374,535	57%
Total Assets	$1,896,996	$1,123,020	69%

Liabilities and Shareholders' Equity			
	This Year	Last Year	Change
Current Liabilities			
Accounts payable	$426,041	$332,845	28%
Notes payable	45,327	23,486	93%
Accrued liabilities	34,614	26,026	33%
Income taxes payable	88,645	51,840	71%
Total current liabilities	$594,627	$434,197	37%
Noncurrent Liabilities			
Long-term debt	$488,822	$349,253	40%
Deferred federal tax	147,844	92,101	61%
Total noncurrent liabilities	$636,666	$441,354	44%
Shareholders' Equity			
Common stock	$1,000	$1,000	0%
Retained earnings	664,703	246,469	170%
Total shareholders' equity	$665,703	$247,469	169%
Total Liabilities and Equity	$1,896,996	$1,123,020	69%

Fig. 7.15 A balance sheet using Times New Roman as the primary typeface.

LaserPro Corporation
Balance Sheet
December 31, 1992

Assets			
	This Year	Last Year	Change
Current Assets			
Cash	$247,886	$126,473	96%
Accounts receivable	863,652	524,570	65%
Inventory	88,328	65,508	35%
Investments	108,577	31,934	240%
Total current assets	$1,308,443	$748,485	75%
Fixed Assets			
Machinery and equipment	$209,906	$158,730	32%
Vehicles	429,505	243,793	76%
Office furniture	50,240	36,406	38%
(Accumulated depreciation)	(101,098)	(64,394)	57%
Total fixed assets	$588,553	$374,535	57%
Total Assets	**$1,896,996**	**$1,123,020**	**69%**

Liabilities and Shareholders' Equity			
	This Year	Last Year	Change
Current Liabilities			
Accounts payable	$426,041	$332,845	28%
Notes payable	45,327	23,486	93%
Accrued liabilities	34,614	26,026	33%
Income taxes payable	88,645	51,840	71%
Total current liabilities	$594,627	$434,197	37%
Noncurrent Liabilities			
Long-term debt	$488,822	$349,253	40%
Deferred federal tax	147,844	92,101	61%
Total noncurrent liabilities	$636,666	$441,354	44%
Shareholders' Equity			
Common stock	$1,000	$1,000	0%
Retained earnings	664,703	246,469	170%
Total shareholders' equity	$665,703	$247,469	169%
Total Liabilities and Equity	**$1,896,996**	**$1,123,020**	**69%**

Fig. 7.16 A balance sheet using Arial as the primary typeface.

LaserPro Corporation
1992 Sales Report
(Units)

	Jan-92	Feb-92	Mar-92	1st Q	Apr-92	May-92	Jun-92	2nd Q	Jul-92	Aug-92	Sep-92	3rd Q	Oct-92	Nov-92	Dec-92	4th Q	Total
SERIES 1000																	
Model 1010	6,000	6,000	7,500	19,500	6,000	6,000	7,500	19,500	6,000	6,000	7,500	19,500	6,000	6,000	7,500	19,500	78,000
Model 1011	3,500	1,500	455	5,455	364	364	455	1,183	364	364	455	1,183	364	364	455	1,183	9,004
Model 1012	4,000	2,000	455	6,455	364	364	455	1,183	364	364	455	1,183	364	364	455	1,183	10,004
Model 1013	615	615	769	1,999	615	615	769	1,999	615	615	769	1,999	615	615	769	1,999	7,996
Model 1014	530	530	662	1,722	530	530	662	1,722	530	530	662	1,722	530	530	662	1,722	6,888
Model 1015	192	192	240	624	192	192	240	624	192	192	240	624	192	192	240	624	2,496
Model 1016	769	769	962	2,500	769	769	962	2,500	769	769	962	2,500	769	769	962	2,500	10,000
Model 1017	0	0	4,200	4,200	3,800	457	571	4,828	457	457	571	1,485	457	457	571	1,485	11,998
Model 1018	0	0	3,500	3,500	2,500	229	286	3,015	229	229	286	744	229	229	286	744	8,003
Model 1019	0	0	2,500	2,500	1,500	400	500	2,400	400	400	500	1,300	400	400	500	1,300	7,500
Model 1020	0	0	0	0	538	538	673	1,211	538	538	673	1,749	538	538	673	1,749	4,709
Model 1021	0	0	0	0	0	0	0	0	4,500	3,000	694	8,194	556	556	694	1,806	10,000
Total Series 1000	15,606	11,606	21,243	48,455	16,634	10,458	13,073	40,165	14,958	13,458	13,767	42,183	11,014	11,014	13,767	35,795	166,598
SERIES 2000																	
Model 2010	5,000	2,000	0	7,000	821	821	1,026	2,668	821	821	1,026	2,668	821	821	1,026	2,668	15,004
Model 2011	0	0	0	0	0	0	0	0	2,500	2,000	833	5,333	667	667	833	2,167	7,500
Model 2012	6,250	0	6,250	6,250	3,250	971	1,214	5,435	971	971	1,214	3,156	971	971	1,214	3,156	17,997
Model 2013	0	0	0	0	0	5,500	3,000	8,500	815	815	1,019	2,649	815	815	1,019	2,649	13,798
Model 2014	0	0	0	0	0	3,500	3,500	7,000	615	615	769	1,999	615	615	769	1,999	10,998
Total Series 2000	5,000	2,000	6,250	13,250	4,071	10,792	8,740	23,603	5,722	5,222	4,861	15,805	3,889	3,889	4,861	12,639	65,297
SERIES 3000																	
Model 3010	0	0	0	0	0	0	1,875	1,875	1,875	682	852	3,409	682	682	852	2,216	7,500
Model 3011	0	0	0	0	0	0	5,000	5,000	1,000	273	341	1,614	273	273	341	887	7,501
Model 3012	0	0	0	0	0	0	0	0	3,500	2,500	556	6,556	444	444	556	1,444	8,000
Model 3013	0	0	0	0	0	0	0	0	2,500	2,000	556	5,056	444	444	556	1,444	6,500
Model 3014	0	0	0	0	0	0	0	0	0	2,000	1,500	3,500	215	215	269	699	4,199
Model 3015	0	0	0	0	0	0	0	0	0	625	625	1,250	43	43	54	140	1,390
Total Series 3000	0	0	0	0	0	0	6,875	6,875	8,875	8,080	4,430	21,385	2,101	2,101	2,628	6,830	35,090
TOTAL	20,606	13,606	27,493	61,705	20,705	21,250	28,688	70,643	29,555	26,760	23,058	79,373	17,004	17,004	21,256	55,264	266,985

Fig. 7.17 Using sans serif typeface with small type size.

Using Boldface, Italic, and Underlining for Emphasis

Applying elements such as boldface, italic, and underlining requires good planning to ensure that your worksheet highlights the information you want emphasized. To effectively call attention to parts of your worksheet, you need to follow the rules described in a previous section, "Giving Your Worksheet a Professional Look." Specifically, you should strive for simplicity, consistency, and contrast. Remember that these last two goals—consistency and contrast—are not contradictions. Italic type used sparingly can call attention to an important heading or important data, as long as a normal typeface is used consistently for most of the worksheet. This section explains how you can use underlining, boldface, italic, and contrast effectively to emphasize different pieces of information.

When determining what information to emphasize with boldface, italic, and underlining, keep in mind the message you want to convey to those who will review your worksheet. If you want to emphasize the sales totals for the quarter rather than individual months, for example, using italic and boldface together for the quarterly data would contrast and emphasize the information (see fig. 7.18).

Apart from the common use of underlining for Total lines, the only special use of underlining in the worksheet in figure 7.18 is the use of bold borders as underlines to highlight months.

Using Lines, Boxes, and Shading for Emphasis

To emphasize a large block of information, select Format Border to create different kinds of bordering lines and boxes.

Using boldface, italic, and underlining may be effective for emphasizing a small number of elements in a worksheet. To emphasize a larger block of information, however, select Format Border to create different kinds of bordering lines and boxes, and use Format Patterns to create shaded or solid colored areas.

If you want to emphasize the sales results of a new product line in contrast to the sales results of existing product lines, you can highlight the sales data for the new product line by boxing the data (see fig. 7.19).

Another way to emphasize sales data for the new product line in figure 7.19 is by using rules (see fig. 7.20).

Shading is used in figures 7.19 and 7.20 to highlight the Product Total line at the bottom of the worksheet.

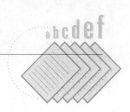

LaserPro Corporation
SALES REPORT
(Units)

	Jan-92	Feb-92	Mar-92	1st Quarter Total
SERIES 1000				
Model 1010	6,000	6,000	7,500	*19,500*
Model 1011	3,500	1,500	455	*5,455*
Model 1012	4,000	2,000	455	*6,455*
Model 1013	615	615	769	*1,999*
Model 1014	530	530	662	*1,722*
Model 1015	192	192	240	*624*
Model 1016	769	769	962	*2,500*
Model 1017	0	0	4,200	*4,200*
Model 1018	0	0	3,500	*3,500*
Model 1019	0	0	2,500	*2,500*
Model 1020	0	0	0	*0*
Model 1021	0	0	0	*0*
Total Series 1000	15,606	11,606	21,243	*48,455*
SERIES 2000				
Model 2010	5,000	2,000	0	*7,000*
Model 2011	0	0	0	*0*
Model 2012	0	0	6,250	*6,250*
Model 2013	0	0	0	*0*
Model 2014	0	0	0	*0*
Total Series 2000	5,000	2,000	6,250	*13,250*
SERIES 3000				
Model 3010	0	0	0	*0*
Model 3011	0	0	0	*0*
Model 3012	0	0	0	*0*
Model 3013	0	0	0	*0*
Model 3014	0	0	0	*0*
Model 3015	0	0	0	*0*
Total Series 3000	0	0	0	*0*
Product Total	20,606	13,606	27,493	*61,705*

Fig. 7.18 Using italic and boldface to emphasize quarterly sales data.

LaserPro Corporation
SALES REPORT
(Units)

	Jan-92	Feb-92	Mar-92	1st Quarter Total
SERIES 1000				
Model 1010	6,000	6,000	7,500	19,500
Model 1011	3,500	1,500	455	5,455
Model 1012	4,000	2,000	455	6,455
Model 1013	615	615	769	1,999
Model 1014	530	530	662	1,722
Model 1015	192	192	240	624
Model 1016	769	769	962	2,500
Model 1017	0	0	4,200	4,200
Model 1018	0	0	3,500	3,500
Model 1019	0	0	2,500	2,500
Model 1020	0	0	0	0
Model 1021	0	0	0	0
Total Series 1000	15,606	11,606	21,243	48,455
SERIES 2000				
Model 2010	5,000	2,000	0	7,000
Model 2011	0	0	0	0
Model 2012	0	0	6,250	6,250
Model 2013	0	0	0	0
Model 2014	0	0	0	0
Total Series 2000	5,000	2,000	6,250	13,250
SERIES 3000				
Model 3010	0	0	0	0
Model 3011	0	0	0	0
Model 3012	0	0	0	0
Model 3013	0	0	0	0
Model 3014	0	0	0	0
Model 3015	0	0	0	0
Total Series 3000	0	0	0	0
Product Total	20,606	13,606	27,493	61,705

Fig. 7.19 Boxing data to emphasize sales of a new product.

LaserPro Corporation
SALES REPORT
(Units)

	Jan-92	Feb-92	Mar-92	1st Quarter Total
SERIES 1000				
Model 1010	6,000	6,000	7,500	19,500
Model 1011	3,500	1,500	455	5,455
Model 1012	4,000	2,000	455	6,455
Model 1013	615	615	769	1,999
Model 1014	530	530	662	1,722
Model 1015	192	192	240	624
Model 1016	769	769	962	2,500
Model 1017	0	0	4,200	4,200
Model 1018	0	0	3,500	3,500
Model 1019	0	0	2,500	2,500
Model 1020	0	0	0	0
Model 1021	0	0	0	0
Total Series 1000	15,606	11,606	21,243	48,455
SERIES 2000				
Model 2010	5,000	2,000	0	7,000
Model 2011	0	0	0	0
Model 2012	0	0	6,250	6,250
Model 2013	0	0	0	0
Model 2014	0	0	0	0
Total Series 2000	5,000	2,000	6,250	13,250
SERIES 3000				
Model 3010	0	0	0	0
Model 3011	0	0	0	0
Model 3012	0	0	0	0
Model 3013	0	0	0	0
Model 3014	0	0	0	0
Model 3015	0	0	0	0
Total Series 3000	0	0	0	0
Product Total	20,606	13,606	27,493	61,705

Fig. 7.20 Using rules to emphasize sales of a new product.

Adding Charts to Your Worksheet

Make sure that you add charts to communicate information—not just to enhance the appearance of your documents.

As introduced in Chapter 1 and covered in detail in Chapter 5, the desktop-publishing capabilities of Excel enable you to display and print charts along with worksheets. You can position a chart anywhere in the worksheet and use charting commands to enhance the chart. If you have not used charting commands, read Chapter 5 to learn how to place, edit, and enhance charts. Chapter 5 also explains how you can use the commands to create special charts or import charts created by other programs or included with programs like Harvard Graphics as part of the program's clip art collection. This section discusses techniques for positioning and enhancing charts in Excel worksheets.

The guidelines to follow when adding graphs to your worksheets are similar to those covered throughout this chapter for good worksheet layout and design. Use the chart to help communicate the information you need to your readers. Use the layout of the page and format the chart as part of the overall consistent design of the page, or use the chart as a contrasting element to call attention to information not emphasized within the worksheet. Figures 7.21 and 7.22 show how you can use graphs to extend and emphasize worksheet data.

The graphs in figure 7.21 are incorporated into the printout as part of the overall design. Notice that the layout of the page emphasizes two sets of data—first quarter sales of Series 1000 products and first quarter sales of Series 2000 products. The graphs are placed within the boxes designed for the two categories of products; these graphs show how sales of different products compare to each other at the end of the first quarter—a comparison not easily conveyed by the sales totals listed in the last column of each worksheet. The graph in figure 7.22, on the other hand, dominates the page and emphasizes the comparative sales of different international markets. The graph also emphasizes the sales of Great Britain as part of the European market—information not shown by the worksheet.

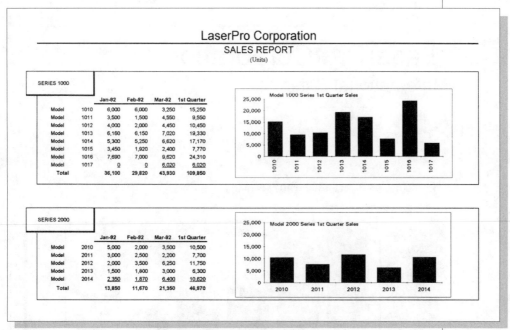

Fig. 7.21   Graphs used to complement worksheet data.

Using Named Styles and Automatic Formatting

Chapter 3, "Using Excel To Enter and Edit Text," describes the ways you can automate desktop publishing with Excel. As Chapter 3 explains, these methods include creating styles with the Format Style command, saving files as templates, and using the automatic formatting capabilities of Excel. This section describes examples of named styles and automatic formatting that you can use for spreadsheet publishing. Read Chapter 3 for specific explanations.

File templates are useful when you will be repeating the same format for a number of files.

LaserPro Corporation
International Sales

1st, 2nd, and 3rd Quarter 1992 Revenues

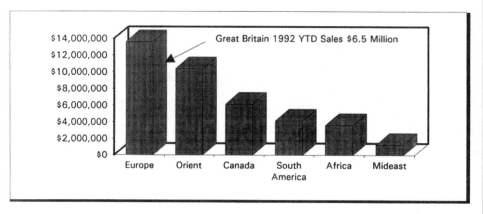

Region	$ Sales	Units	% Increase
Europe	$13,574,447	174,143	32%
Orient	$10,370,858	133,045	36%
Canada	$6,116,347	78,465	22%
South America	$4,121,762	52,877	28%
Africa	$3,595,989	46,132	24%
Mideast	$1,246,187	15987	-26%

Fig. 7.22 A graph positioned for emphasis.

File templates are helpful when you are preparing repetitive monthly reports or presentations. After you create the worksheet, you can use a template file when you are duplicating the layout and format of an original worksheet. To create a file template, follow these general guidelines:

1. Save the file as a normal Excel file.

2. Save the file you will use for a template as a template file by selecting the Template option on the Save File As Type text box.

3. If you need to create new sales worksheets that follow the exact form of the template, open the file and edit it.

4. When you save the file by clicking on the Save File tool or selecting File Save, Excel prompts you for a new file name.

Named styles can speed up and make creating new worksheets much easier. The balance sheet discussed throughout this chapter is a good example of how to use the Excel Format Style Define command to automate formatting different parts of the worksheet. Creating the following six styles for the balance sheet in figure 7.15 will speed up formatting the balance sheet and help when you format other worksheets (see fig. 7.23). Table 7.3 lists the styles shown in figure 7.23.

Table 7.3   Worksheet Styles

Name	Description	Style
Title	Style for company name title	Arial, 24 point
Sub	Subtitles below company name	Times New Roman, 14 point, bold
Mhead	Main headings separating two sections of balance sheet	Times New Roman, 14 point, bold, 4th format pattern, thick bottom border
Rtotal	Row total entries	Default font with single underline
Rhead	Outdented row headings	Default font (Times New Roman, 12 point), bold
Stotal	Totals at bottom of each main section	Default font, bold, double underline

❶ Title   ❹ Rhead

❷ Sub   ❺ Rtotal

❸ Mhead   ❻ Stotal

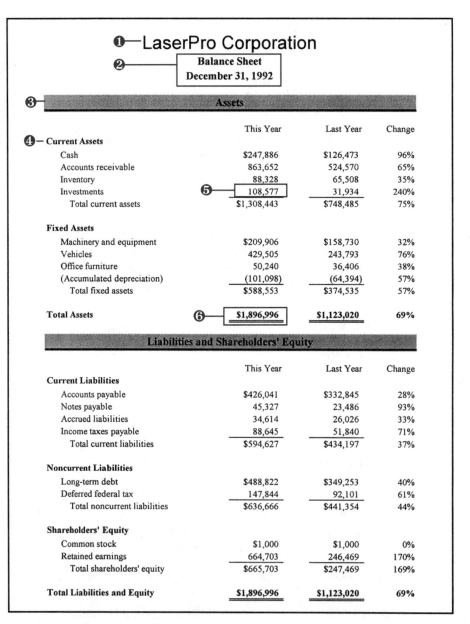

❶—LaserPro Corporation

❷——
Balance Sheet
December 31, 1992

❸—— **Assets**

	This Year	Last Year	Change
❹— **Current Assets**			
Cash	$247,886	$126,473	96%
Accounts receivable	863,652	524,570	65%
Inventory	88,328	65,508	35%
Investments ❺	108,577	31,934	240%
Total current assets	$1,308,443	$748,485	75%
Fixed Assets			
Machinery and equipment	$209,906	$158,730	32%
Vehicles	429,505	243,793	76%
Office furniture	50,240	36,406	38%
(Accumulated depreciation)	(101,098)	(64,394)	57%
Total fixed assets	$588,553	$374,535	57%
Total Assets ❻	$1,896,996	$1,123,020	69%

Liabilities and Shareholders' Equity

	This Year	Last Year	Change
Current Liabilities			
Accounts payable	$426,041	$332,845	28%
Notes payable	45,327	23,486	93%
Accrued liabilities	34,614	26,026	33%
Income taxes payable	88,645	51,840	71%
Total current liabilities	$594,627	$434,197	37%
Noncurrent Liabilities			
Long-term debt	$488,822	$349,253	40%
Deferred federal tax	147,844	92,101	61%
Total noncurrent liabilities	$636,666	$441,354	44%
Shareholders' Equity			
Common stock	$1,000	$1,000	0%
Retained earnings	664,703	246,469	170%
Total shareholders' equity	$665,703	$247,469	169%
Total Liabilities and Equity	$1,896,996	$1,123,020	69%

Fig. 7.23   Styles for the balance sheet in figure 7.15.

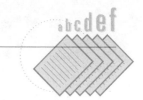

After you establish named styles for elements of your worksheet that have special formatting, use the Style Box tool to save keystrokes, particularly when you are formatting a cell containing two or more format changes (such as different fonts, bold, and underlining). Also, remember that you can format noncontiguous cells by pressing Ctrl as you highlight each range.

In addition to using named styles, you can use the automatic formatting capabilities available in Excel 4. Follow these steps:

1. Highlight the range of data (include column and row titles—see fig. 7.24).

2 Select Format AutoFormat.

   Excel provides you with a dialog box that lists the possible formats and an example of each one (see fig. 7.25).

3. Select one of the formats.

Notice in figure 7.26 that most of the formatting has been done for you (Classic 1 was chosen as the Table Format in this example). All you need to do is change the titles at the top of the page and possibly change the number format and column width.

By looking at the many AutoFormat choices, you can get an idea of what the designers of Excel think are good spreadsheet designs (see fig. 7.27). Compare these designs the basics of desktop publishing that you have learned so far.

Use the Style Box tool to save keystrokes.

Use AutoFormat to quickly format a worksheet.

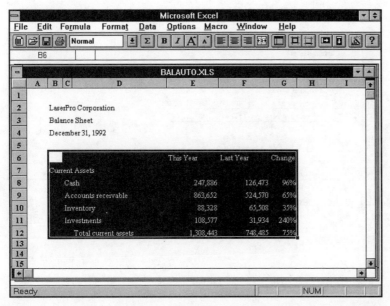

Fig. 7.24 A portion of the LaserPro balance sheet before using AutoFormat.

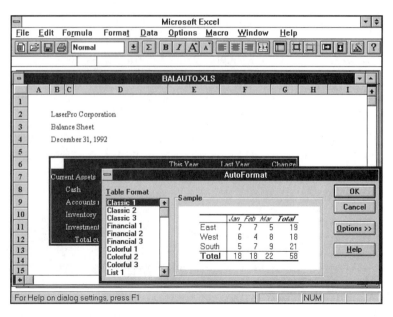

Fig. 7.25 The AutoFormat dialog box.

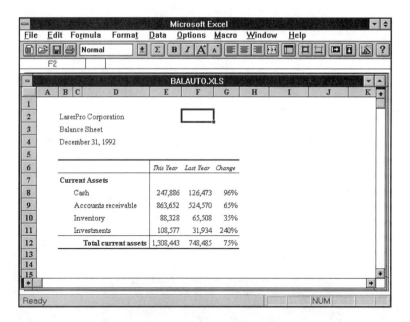

Fig. 7.26 The LaserPro balance sheet after using AutoFormat.

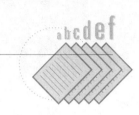

Classic 1 Format

Current Assets	This Year	Last Year	Change
Cash	247,886	126,473	96%
Accounts receivable	863,652	524,570	65%
Inventory	88,328	65,508	35%
Investments	108,577	31,934	240%
Total current assets	1,308,443	748,485	75%

Classic 2 Format

Current Assets	This Year	Last Year	Change
Cash	247,886	126,473	96%
Accounts receivable	863,652	524,570	65%
Inventory	88,328	65,508	35%
Investments	108,577	31,934	240%
Total current assets	1,308,443	748,485	75%

Classic 3 Format

Current Assets	This Year	Last Year	Change
Cash	247,886	126,473	96%
Accounts receivable	863,652	524,570	65%
Inventory	88,328	65,508	35%
Investments	108,577	31,934	240%
Total current assets	1,308,443	748,485	75%

Financial 1 Format

Current Assets	This Year	Last Year	Change
Cash	247,886	126,473	96%
Accounts receivable	863,652	524,570	65%
Inventory	88,328	65,508	35%
Investments	108,577	31,934	240%
Total current assets	1,308,443	748,485	75%

Financial 2 Format

Current Assets	This Year	Last Year	Change
Cash	247,886	126,473	96%
Accounts receivable	863,652	524,570	65%
Inventory	88,328	65,508	35%
Investments	108,577	31,934	240%
Total current assets	1,308,443	748,485	75%

Financial 3 Format

Current Assets	This Year	Last Year	Change
Cash	247,886	126,473	96%
Accounts receivable	863,652	524,570	65%
Inventory	88,328	65,508	35%
Investments	108,577	31,934	240%
Total current assets	1,308,443	748,485	75%

List 1 Format

Current Assets	This Year	Last Year	Change
Cash	247886	126473	0.95999146
Accounts receivable	863652	524570	0.64639991
Inventory	88328	65508	0.3483544
Investments	108577	31934	2.40004384
Total current assets	1308443	748485	0.74812187

List 2 Format

Current Assets	This Year	Last Year	Change
Inventory	88,328	65,508	35%
Investments	108,577	31,934	240%
Total current assets	1,308,443	748,485	75%

List 3 Format

Current Assets	This Year	Last Year	Change
Cash	247,886	126,473	96%
Accounts receivable	863,652	524,570	65%
Inventory	88,328	65,508	35%
Investments	108,577	31,934	240%
Total current assets	1,308,443	748,485	75%

3D Effects 1 Format

Current Assets	This Year	Last Year	Change
Cash	247,886	126,473	96%
Accounts receivable	863,652	524,570	65%
Inventory	88,328	65,508	35%
Investments	108,577	31,934	240%
Total current assets	1,308,443	748,485	75%

Fig. 7.27 Examples of different AutoFormat choices.

Chapter Summary

The desktop publishing capabilities of Excel provide you with the tools to produce high quality, desktop-published output. Using Excel commands along with learning how to visualize and use the worksheet area as a page will help you easily produce high quality reports.

As this chapter explains, the steps to producing reports include determining what you want to communicate through the worksheet data; deciding which Excel elements will best help you to communicate the information; and setting up the worksheet so that as you enter headings, labels, formulas, and data, the information will display and print as desired.

This chapter also presented the concepts and techniques that result in worksheets that look their best. With these concepts and techniques, you can produce an impression beyond what the worksheet data itself can convey.

In the next chapter you'll learn how to continue taking advantage of the capabilities available in Excel by producing your office correspondence with Excel.

Creating Business Memos, Letters, and Reports

Although Excel does not have all the word processing capabilities of a word processor such as Microsoft Word or WordPerfect, you can use Excel for most letters, memos, and reports—especially if you have added graphs and tables. Many spreadsheet users prefer not to quit Excel and start a word processing program to create a memo or letter. The awkwardness and inefficiencies of using earlier versions of Excel as a word processor gave them no choice, however.

With the new desktop capabilities of Excel 3 and 4, users have all the functionality they need to create most business memos, letters, and reports from Excel alone. This chapter shows examples of business memos, letters, and reports created with Excel, as well as how to create similar types of business documents for your needs.

Specifically, this chapter shows you how to prepare the worksheet for specific kinds of office correspondence, how to enter and edit body text, how to use tables and columnar information in correspondence, how to import a worksheet into your correspondence and reports, and how to use graphics in your correspondence.

If you have not used the desktop capabilities of Excel, read Chapter 3, "Using Excel To Enter and Edit Text" before beginning this chapter.

Understanding Word Processing with Excel

Use the text box feature when you have a lot of text on your worksheet.

When you use Excel to create office correspondence, you must learn to use the program's word processing capabilities. Although never promoted as a program with word processing features, earlier versions of Excel always included the capabilities for limited word processing. The latest version extends these capabilities and provides a text box feature that enables you to turn the worksheet into a word processing display. The text box alone, however, does not provide all the capabilities needed for most word processing tasks. When you use Excel as a word processor, you also must use other worksheet commands to achieve the results you want. This section discusses how you can combine frequently used commands and the text box feature to create word processing documents.

Your use of the text box feature will vary depending on your type of document and whether your document contains mostly conventional paragraph text (see fig. 8.1), a mixture of conventional paragraph text with information presented in columnar or tabular format (see fig. 8.2), or text presented with graphs and illustrations positioned beside text (see fig. 8.3).

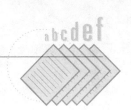

Capital City
Printing

December 12, 1992

Mr. John Richards
1003 Connecticut Avenue
Washington, D.C. 50527

Dear Mr. Richards:

My staff and I wish you a very happy holiday season. Thank you for your patronage during the past year. Capital City Printing is committed to giving you the highest quality printing. We guarantee that your printing will be quick and efficient.

With the beginning of the new year, Capital City Printing will expand its service to include new binding services and new color copying capabilities. Also, beginning in January, we will make available over one hundred new options for types and color of paper for your printing needs. With all of our expanded service and copying options, we guarantee you the same discounts on volume orders available to you in the past.

Please review the enclosed brochure describing the new services and products available from Capital City Printing beginning on January 2, 1993. If you would like to see actual samples of our new copying options, we would be very glad to schedule a meeting for you with one of our sales representatives.

The best of this holiday season to you and your family and, again, our warmest thanks for being a customer and friend of Capital City Printing.

Sincerely,

Doug Herbert
President

Enc.: Brochure

876 Connecticut Avenue ♦ Washington, DC 50034 ♦ (202) 745-3433

Fig. 8.1 A letter created with a text box in Excel.

MEMO TO: Rob Michaels

FROM: Frank O'Conner

DATE: 11-Feb-93

SUBJECT: **November Sales**

The November sales figures for your division just arrived. Because of a new Excel networked application, we are now able to process month end sales figures in record time! It looks like more of the sales people in your division had a good month. Even though Goldman's sales were down for October, he still met his quota for the month. After such spectacular results in October ($125,000), it would have been difficult for Goldman to achieve the same level in November. I am worried, however, about Smith. His sales have been steadily decreasing over the past year. Please call to schedule an appointment to discuss this issue.

Here is a summary of the November sales figures for the sales people in your division:.

Jones	$75,000
Smith	36,000
Black	68,000
Johnson	77,000
Goldman	85,000
	$341,000

Remind your sales people about the following items as soon as possible:

- The retail price of product line A will increase by 10%. All other prices will remain the same until further notice.

- Beginning in January, quotas will increase by 15% over this year's quotas.

- Because of cash flow problems, no bonuses will be given this year.

Keep up the good work, Rob. Please remember to call about the meeting to talk about Smith's performance.

Fig. 8.2 A memo containing paragraph text and columnar information.

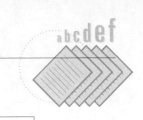

Agricultural Products International

Revenue and Production Summary

Financial Highlights

Revenue for the past year has continued up to expectations. We've seen expected seasonal variations in both availability of grains and price. Because we planned well, we were able to continue to fill our commitments at the highest available price.

For the first time, revenue from wheat exceeded corn. There are many reasons for this but it was not expected. Lower prices for corn has had an impact, but overall the increases come from higher demand.

Expenses, while not shown here, are in line with inflation and increases in commodity prices. If anything, we're in a better position than ever before. This could be our most profitable year yet.

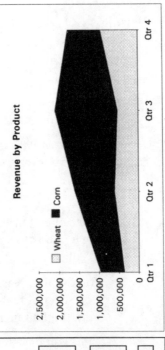

4th Quarter Revenue by Grain

Revenue by Product

	Fourth Quarter	This Year	Last Year
Wheat			
Bushels	315,160	1,236,150	1,200,150
$ per bu.	2.99	1.98	2.57
Revenue	$942.328	$2,447.577	$3,084.386
Corn			
Bushels	273.610	1,116,510	1,500,675
$ per bu.	2.98	3.54	3.05
Revenue	$815.358	$3,952.445	$4,577.059
Total	$1,757,686	$6,400,022	$7,661,444

Fig. 8.3 A report with a graph placed beside paragraph text.

Excel 4 now has a new feature that turns your spreadsheet even more into a word processor. You now can check spelling on your spreadsheet as well as on your charts. You can access this feature through the **Op-tions Spelling** command or by clicking the Check Spelling tool on the Utility toolbar. For more discussion on the spell checker, see Chapter 3.

Using Excel as a word processor also requires the creativity of knowing how to use standard worksheet commands to edit text in your document. Keep the following tips in mind as you create letters, memos, and reports with Excel:

- Mark the edges of a page with the **Options Display Automatic Page Breaks** command.

- Because of its text-wrapping capabilities, you should use the text box whenever entering text that extends beyond two or three lines on-screen. The Text Box tool is on the Chart, Utility, Drawing, and Microsoft Excel 3.0 toolbars.

- You can edit directly in the worksheet in the text box by clicking the text box to select it and then highlighting the text you want to edit.

- You can most easily move, copy, and erase large blocks in the worksheet or text box by selecting **Copy**, **Cut**, **Paste**, and **Clear** from the Edit menu.

- Once you have text in a text box, you easily can move the text box anywhere in the worksheet or resize the box by dragging the text box or stretching the handles that surround the text box when it is selected.

- You can reformat text outside the text box with the **Format Justify** command.

Once text is in a text box, it is easy to manipulate—you can move, copy, and delete the text box quickly.

Creating Office Correspondence and Reports with Excel

If you spend much of your computing time using Excel for spreadsheet applications and are familiar with using Excel for entering and editing data in an application, you easily can extend your use of Excel to letters, memos, and reports without sacrificing quality or efficiency. Using Excel for word processing and desktop publishing, as well as spreadsheet applications, also can help reduce the amount of training required when your staff must learn multiple packages to accomplish the same tasks.

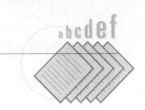

The following sections provide the techniques required for creating professional, high-quality letters, memos, and reports with Excel.

Creating Memos and Letters

When you use Excel to create letters and memos, you can develop template files to store on your computer or network to make the templates available to employees when needed. Designing a memo or letter template with Excel is fairly easy, particularly if you decide not to include any graphics in the letterhead or memo heading design. Even when you decide to create special graphics for your company's letterhead or for memo headings, you easily can create professional memo and letter templates whenever you work with graphics. The following sections explain how to design professional letter and memo templates with and without special graphics.

Creating Basic Memo Templates

By using the font, border, and pattern capabilities in Excel, you can create a memo template that you can print on your company's existing letterhead paper or on plain white paper. Figures 8.4 and 8.5 show two standard memo designs that you can use for your own templates.

To create the memo template shown in figure 8.4, follow these steps:

1. Set the column widths for the worksheet area you will use for the template.

   Because most of the columns used in the template in figure 8.4 are five characters in width, you can select Format Column Width Standard Width to set the column width to 5. Next, as shown in figure 8.6, change the column width of column D to 18 to provide space for a long date format. To balance the memo on the page, change the widths of columns A and M to 3 by choosing Format Column Width, typing 3 in the Column Width text box, and selecting OK.

2. Change the height of row 12 from its default height of 14 to 3 by selecting Format Row Height, typing 3 in the Row Height text box, and selecting OK. Changing the height enables you to create the thin black rule shown in figure 8.6.

3. To change the default font to a large readable font, such as Times New Roman 12 point, select Format Style and select the Normal style. Choose the Define button, select Font, and choose a serif font.

Use Excel to create letter and memo templates you can use over and over again.

MEMORANDUM

TO: CC:

FROM: Danny Winter

DATE: September 30, 1993

SUBJECT:
_____

Fig. 8.4 A basic memo template created with Excel.

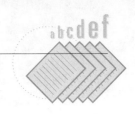

MEMORANDUM

TO: CC:

FROM: Danny Winter

DATE: September 30, 1993

SUBJECT:

Fig. 8.5 A basic memo template with a shaded pattern created with Format Patterns.

4. Select Options Display Automatic Page Breaks to create a border on your screen showing the page boundaries of your memo template.

The page boundaries for the template in figure 8.4 span the range A1:M45.

5. Keep the default margins on File Page Setup as the following:

Left margin	.75	Top margin	1
Right margin	.75	Bottom margin	1

Also, in addition to retaining the default margin settings of the File Page Setup command, use columns A and M in your template for additional margin space.

To center and bold the heading MEMORANDUM at the top of the memo, follow these steps:

1. Enter the heading in cell B2.

2. Highlight the range B2:L2, including the heading.

3. Select the Center Align and Center Across Columns tools.

4. Select the Bold tool.

5. Next, enter the headings in columns B and H (see fig. 8.6). If the same person will be using the memo, enter that person's name in D7 following the FROM: heading.

	A	B	C	D	E	F	G	H	I	J	K	L	M
1	3	5	5	18	5	5	5	5	5	5	5	5	3
2				MEMORANDUM									
3													
4													
5		TO:						CC:					
6													
7		FROM:		Danny Winter									
8													
9		DATE:		September 30, 1993									
10													
11		SUBJECT:											
13													
14													
15													
16													
17													

Fig. 8.6   A memo template showing column and row indicators.

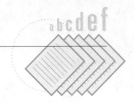

If you want the date to display each time you retrieve the memo template, follow these steps:

1. Enter the formula =**NOW**( ) into cell D9.

2. To format the cell, select Forma**t** Number.

   The Format Number dialog box appears.

3. In the **C**ategory box, select Date and select one of the dates.

4. If you want a new format, select the **C**ode text box and edit or type a new code. In this example, to spell out the month, day, and year type **mmmm d, yyyy**.

Next, to add the solid black rule in row 12, follow these steps:

1. Highlight the range B12:L12.

2. Select Forma**t** Patterns.

3. Select the Pattern pull-down menu and choose the solid black pattern. Select OK.

Finally, you can set off the top section of your memo by shading the section, as shown in figure 8.5. Highlight the range and select Forma**t** Patterns Pattern. Then select the fifth pattern from the pull-down menu.

Before saving the template, make sure that all of the standard settings you will need to use for creating and printing memos are set in the template file. Also, be sure to print a sample memorandum, to ensure that the margins, spacing of text, and use of fonts appear correct. The following types of settings stored in the template file will save you from having to enter settings every time you or someone else creates a memo:

- Automatic page breaks.

- Standard print settings you will use for every memo, including margin settings, headers and footers, copies to be printed, and so on.

- Display settings you want to use for every memo, including type of frame around the memo area and text and background colors.

- Any named styles you plan to use when creating memos.

Also, before you save your template file, position the cell pointer where you or others will first enter text. If the first text is entered, for example, into cell D5 to the right of the TO: heading, move the cell pointer to this cell before saving the template file. See "Entering Text into a Letter or Memo Template," later in this chapter, for specific tips on how to use the template for creating business correspondence. When you save the

U se the formula =**NOW**( ) to enter today's date in a letter or memo.

B e sure to print a sample memorandum to ensure that the margins, text spacing, and font use appears correct.

worksheet, be sure to select File Save As and select template Type. When you save the file as a template file, the next time you save the file, you will avoid overwriting the template file with the File Save command or tool.

Creating a Basic Letter Template

Creating a template for business letters is similar to the procedure described earlier for creating a memo template. This procedure includes the following steps:

- Change the column widths and row heights where needed

- Use the Options Display Automatic Page Breaks command to display the page borders of the letter

- Enter settings that you will use for every letter

- Create any named styles you plan to use

- Set the text range where you or others will enter new text into the letter

- Print a sample letter to determine if all settings are correct

- Save the file as a template type to avoid overwriting the template

With Excel, you can create a template that will print letters on your company's existing letterhead stationery, or you can use Excel to create a template with a letterhead design that displays on-screen and prints on blank stationery. The samples in figures 8.7 and 8.8 show company letterhead designs created with Excel. You can create a professional-looking letterhead, such as a very basic design shown in figure 8.7, and a more elaborate design shown in figure 8.8. For small businesses or for companies that need to have many versions of letterhead, letterhead designs created with Excel can save you expensive design and printing costs.

Creating a basic letterhead design like the one shown in figure 8.8 involves using Excel's Arial or a similar sans serif font, setting the default font, and creating a solid black rule at rows 8 and 54 (see fig. 8.9). The company name in the upper right corner of the page is positioned in cells J3, J4, and J5 and uses 12-point Arial in bold. As figure 8.8 shows, you can place the company address information at the bottom of the page (B55 and centered along B55:L55). A standard column width setting of 5 is used in the example in figure 8.9. Figure 8.7 is a slight variation of figure 8.8, which does not use reverse text and includes the address at the top of the page.

U se Excel to create your own stationery or to use existing letterheads.

U se Excel's reverse text and background feature for interesting letter effects with the Symbol font.

**STANDARD
INTERNATIONAL
CORPORATION**

1714 Market Street
Denver, CO 80221
(303) 629-6290
FAX (303) 629-6230

Fig. 8.7 A basic company letterhead designed with Excel.

Figure 8.8 uses the reverse text and background capabilities of Excel to emphasize the company name. This sample also uses the Symbol font to create the diamond design below the company name. To create the white text on black background as shown in figures 8.8 and 8.9, follow these steps:

1. To create the diamonds, type **Rept(Char(0168),11)** in cell J6. Choose Forma**t** Font and select 12 pt Symbol font.

2. Highlight the range I2:M7.

3. Set text to white by selecting Forma**t** Font Color White.

4. Set background to black by selecting Forma**t** **P**atterns Foreground and the solid black choice.

In order to get the logo and address to print closer to the top and bottom of the paper, select File Page Setup and type **.25** for the bottom and top margins.

Developing Company Logos with the Insert Object Command

If your company has a logo that you want to include in the letterhead or memo template, or if you want to include a custom-drawn graphic or a graphic taken from a library of graphic art, you can use Excel's **E**dit **I**nsert **O**bject command to add the graphic to your letterhead or memo design. The design shown in figures 8.10 and 8.11 contain graphics from clip-art packages.

To produce more sophisticated graphics, you must use a presentation graphics program, such as Harvard Graphics, Freelance Plus, or CorelDRAW!.

If you want to use a custom-drawn graphic, you have a couple of options for creating the graphic. If you purchased Microsoft Word for Windows, you may have the Microsoft Draw program that enables you to manipulate and import graphics. If you have other graphics applications, the application used to create a graphic will come up when you double-click the embedded object. You can, for example, draw the graphic directly with the freehand drawing tools available with the program that comes up when you insert an object. Be aware, however, that the drawing capabilities in Microsoft Draw are limited, and are best used for simple, uncomplicated graphics. To produce more sophisticated graphics that you can save in file formats that Excel can read, you must use a presentation graphics program, like Harvard Graphics, Freelance Plus, or CorelDRAW!. Once you have the graphic file, importing the graphic into your page design is very easy.

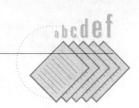

STANDARD
INTERNATIONAL
CORPORATION
◆◆◆◆◆◆◆◆◆◆◆◆

1714 Market Street, Denver, CO 80221, (303) 629-6290, FAX (303) 629-6230

Fig. 8.8 A letterhead using Excel's reverse text and background feature, with the Symbol font.

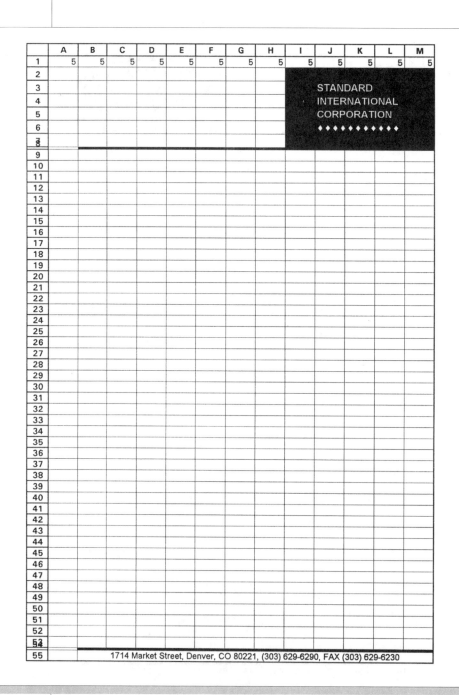

Fig. 8.9 The letterhead for figure 8.8 with column and row headings.

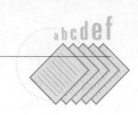

STANDARD

INTERNATIONAL

1714 Market Street
Denver, CO 80221
(303) 629-6290
FAX (303) 629-6230

Fig. 8.10 A letterhead with a map graphic as part of a company logo.

To add a graphic like the capitol in the letterhead in figure 8.11, you begin by determining the layout of the letterhead, including text, graphic, and any other format elements such as the solid black rule running across the page in figure 8.11. Next, determine the font and font sizes you want to use for the text in the letterhead. The text in figure 8.11, for example, uses 20-point Times New Roman for the company name *Capital City Printing* and 12-point Times New Roman for the address and phone number information. Before adding the graphic to your letterhead, add any lines or rules that will appear near the graphic. The solid black rule in figure 8.11 was created by changing the row height of row 8 to 3 and filling in from column B to column N with the Format Patterns command.

After you enter the text and other format elements to the letterhead, you are ready to place the graphic. To use the Clipboard, follow these steps:

1. Display and select the graphic in the presentation program.

2. Select Edit Copy to copy the graphic to the Clipboard.

3. Return to Excel by clicking the Excel program or minimized icon. Or, press Ctrl+Esc and select Excel.

4. Move the cell pointer to the first cell in the range.

5. Select Edit Paste.

You can move the object by clicking and dragging it to the location you want. If you want to change the size, click and drag one of the handles (small dark squares) surrounding the object. You can resize to scale by pressing Shift while you resize. Otherwise, your graphic will become distorted.

If you cannot display the graphic in a Windows program, you may be able to convert it through Microsoft Draw, a program available with Microsoft Word for Windows. To use Microsoft Draw, follow these steps:

1. Select Edit Insert Object.

2. Select the object type. To enter Microsoft Draw, select Microsoft Drawing (see fig. 8.12).

3. You can create or edit graphics in this program or import a graphic. To import, select File Import Picture.

4. Select the drive, directory, and file where the graphic is located. Microsoft Draw will show the available graphic files.

5. After you select the file, you will return to the Microsoft Draw program, where you can edit the graphic.

6. To insert the graphic into Excel, select Exit and return to your worksheet.

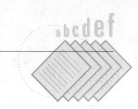

 Capital City
Printing

876 Connecticut Avenue ♦ Washington, DC 50034 ♦ (202) 745-3433

Fig. 8.11 A letterhead with a capitol dome graphic as part of a company logo.

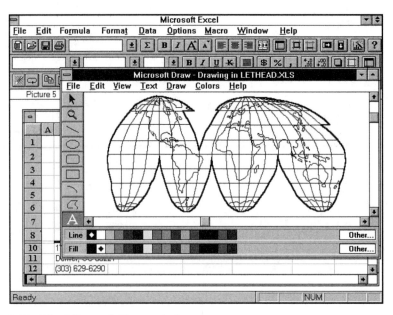

Fig. 8.12   The Microsoft Draw window.

You can use Excel to create a report that requires many different fonts, different types of lines and boxes, graphics, and columnar worksheet data.

Use Excel to add charts and worksheets to your correspondence.

The Times New Roman font, because it is a serif font, is easier to read whenever there are large blocks of text.

You can move the object by clicking and dragging it to the location you want. If you want to change the size, click and drag one of the handles (small dark squares) surrounding the object. You can resize to scale by pressing Shift while you resize. Otherwise, your graphic will become distorted.

Entering Text into a Letter or Memo Template

After you have created a template to use for your company's memos and letters, you can retrieve the template to enter text or any numeric information into the document. The great advantage to using Excel for correspondence is that you can create a worksheet or graph directly within the document or copy from another file a worksheet or file that already exists. Figures 8.1 and 8.13 show samples of correspondence created with Excel using the memo template shown in figure 8.4 and the letterhead template shown in figure 8.11.

The body of the customer letter in figure 8.1 contains all text. When creating a letter similar to this letter, you should plan to use a font that will be the most readable, yet conveys the professional tone you want. The letter in figure 8.1 uses the 12-point Times New Roman font. If you are using other fonts, select a serif font similar to the Times New Roman font.

Although Times New Roman is not available with some printers using Excel in Windows 3.0, the screen font, MS Serif, is. If you select MS Serif, Excel tries to find the closest font your printer has available. This font probably will be similar to Times New Roman.

Creating a memo like the memo shown in figure 8.13 requires using both a text box and normal worksheet mode. You enter the paragraph text by using the Text Box tool. (See Chapter 2 for more information on using a text box.) As recommended in "Understanding Word Processing with Excel," earlier in this chapter, you should indicate page breaks with the **O**ptions **D**isplay Automatic Page **B**reaks command. Save the template file with the **F**ile Save **A**s command. In the dialog box, select Save File as Type Template.

With Excel you can enter a table into your memo like the table listing salespeople and their sales in figure 8.13, and create the bullets and the itemized text that follows. To create the bullets, set the column width of the columns containing the bullets to 3 and enter the formula **=CHAR(183)** into the cell containing the first bullet. Format the cell with the Symbol font.

Creating Reports with Excel

You can create professional-looking reports by applying the techniques covered throughout this book for designing spreadsheet and text layouts. Think of reports as a combination of the design features discussed in Chapter 7, "Enhancing Excel Worksheets," and in this chapter. This section shows you how to produce high-quality reports. With Excel you may find that your company can achieve the same quality or better as achieved by outside agencies now producing your reports.

Following some basic design principles and using the desktop-publishing capabilities available in Excel, you can develop simple reports used to run your business day by day, as well as professional-looking reports that may be distributed to customers or other businesses. Excel, for example, gives you the ability to create a high-quality annual report. Even a report that requires many different fonts, different types of lines and boxes, graphics, and columnar worksheet data is easy to create.

MEMO TO: Rob Michaels

FROM: Frank O'Conner

DATE: 11-Feb-93

STANDARD

INTERNATIONAL

SUBJECT: **November Sales**

The November sales figures for your division just arrived. Because of a new Excel networked application, we are now able to process month end sales figures in record time! It looks like more of the sales people in your division had a good month. Even though Goldman's sales were down for October, he still met his quota for the month. After such spectacular results in October ($125,000), it would have been difficult for Goldman to achieve the same level in November. I am worried, however, about Smith. His sales have been steadily decreasing over the past year. Please call to schedule an appointment to discuss this issue.

Here is a summary of the November sales figures for the sales people in your division:.

Jones	$75,000
Smith	36,000
Black	68,000
Johnson	77,000
Goldman	85,000
	$341,000

Remind your sales people about the following items as soon as possible:

- The retail price of product line A will increase by 10%. All other prices will remain the same until further notice.

- Beginning in January, quotas will increase by 15% over this year's quotas.

- Because of cash flow problems, no bonuses will be given this year.

Keep up the good work, Rob. Please remember to call about the meeting to talk about Smith's performance.

Fig. 8.13 A memo created with a memo template.

The sample pages shown in figures 8.14 through 8.17 are from an annual report developed with Excel. Figure 8.14 shows the report's title page created by incorporating graphics in WPG format. Figures 8.15 and 8.16 show opening pages to the report—the table of contents and opening comments. Special elements of these pages include a double line beside the text, italic font, and the special positioning of text on the page. Figure 8.17 shows a page from the report that summarizes the company's financial highlights. Notice that this page combines numerical worksheet data with four graphs. The following paragraphs describe more specifically the techniques used to create the special elements on each of the pages shown in figures 8.14 through 8.17.

To create any multiple-page report, you should begin by defining the worksheet area needed for the pages. If you want to use one worksheet, create a grid that shows the boundaries of the pages needed for the report. If you are developing a report containing a great deal of text and are working with a single worksheet, you should position your pages below one another rather than to the side of each other. Working downward rather than across your worksheet enables you to make insertions, deletions, and other changes to your multiple-page report much more easily than you can when pages are laid out across the worksheet. Locating one page below another will, in other words, make text and graphics flow automatically from one page to another when you make changes. The task of having to reposition text and graphics manually whenever you make changes should be minimal when pages flow down the rows of the worksheet rather than across the columns. However, you must keep the column widths the same for all pages and be careful not to delete columns.

If you are using Excel 4, you have the option of locating the pages of your report on one single worksheet and placing pages below one another or creating separate worksheets for each page and combining the worksheets into a *workbook*. Open or create a new worksheet for each page. When you are ready, save all open worksheets with the **File Save Workbook** command. You then can use workbook icons and paging buttons to page through the individual pages of your report. Figure 8.18 shows the Contents page of a workbook with the corresponding documents. Changes made to a report laid out in a workbook, however, can be tedious if you make many deletions or insertions. If you think that you will be making many changes to your report, the best page layout is on a single worksheet with one page below another.

U se Excel's workbook feature to create multiple-page reports.

STANDARD

INTERNATIONAL

1993

ANNUAL

REPORT

SI

Fig. 8.14   The title page from an annual report.

TABLE OF CONTENTS

Fig. 8.15   The table of contents from an annual report.

Since the acquisition of the Data Services

Group at Standard International, we have

dominated the market with new products

for improving the ability of organizations

to access and use the data they need to

accomplish their goals. This year

Standard International invested in new

technology to continue to be the leader in

data services. With this new technology,

Standard International grew the Data

Services business over one hundred and

sixteen percent. The addition of many

hospitals to the list of customers using the

services of DSG promises many years of

continued growth.

Fig. 8.16   Opening comments from an annual report.

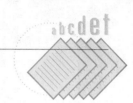

FINANCIAL HIGHLIGHTS   STANDARD INTERNATIONAL CORP.

(Dollars in millions except per share data.)

Year ended December 31,	1993	1992	1991	1990	1989
Sales of products and services	**$456.7**	$352.4	$382.3	$327.1	$270.8
Operating income	**$75.2**	$12.1	$53.8	$46.	$35.5
Net income	**$45.1**	$5.5	$28.3	$23.8	$18.2
Earnings per common share, before extraordinary items, assuming full dilution	**$4.01**	$0.54	$2.69	$2.31	$1.91
Average number of common shares, assuming full dilution (000)	**15,249**	13,154	11,276	10,466	9,646
Cash dividends per common share	**$0.95**	$0.72	$0.72	$0.60	$0.53
Depreciation and amortization	**$25.7**	$21.5	$17.2	$13.6	$10.1
Shareholder's equity	**$158.1**	$135.7	$137.3	$115.1	$98.4
Return on shareholders' equity	**35.0%**	5.0%	22.1%	21.9%	21.7%

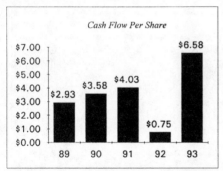

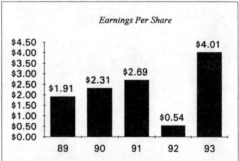

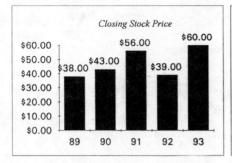

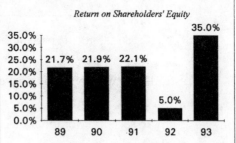

Fig. 8.17   The financial highlights page from an annual report.

To navigate and change a workbook, follow these steps:

1. To create a workbook, select File New from the New list box. Then select Workbook.

2. To add a worksheet to the workbook, select the Add button and choose the document you want to add from the dialog box.

3. To remove a worksheet from the workbook, select the worksheet in the Contents page and select the Remove button.

4. Click the document icon and name to move to a selected worksheet.

5. Click the Previous Document button or the Next Document button to scroll through the report.

① Workbook extension
② Worksheet document icon
③ Chart document icon
④ Add button
⑤ Remove button
⑥ Options button
⑦ Workbook contents icon
⑧ Previous document icon
⑨ Next document icon
⑩ Unbound icon
⑪ Bound icon

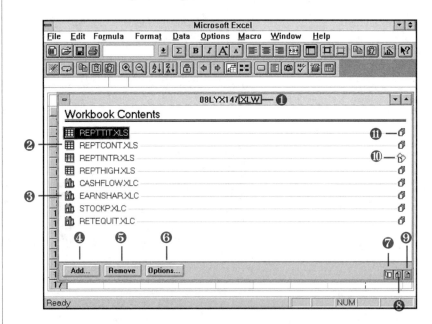

Fig. 8.18 The Contents page of the report workbook.

6. Click the Workbook Contents button to list all worksheets in the workbook.

7. To save the workbook, select File Save Workbook.

A second advantage of using a workbook for a multiple-page report is being able to adjust column widths whenever you need to due to different elements on different pages. If one page, for example, contains a worksheet requiring column widths of 9 and another page contains a worksheet containing column widths of 6, you can vary the column

widths without worrying about the changes affecting other pages. A third advantage of using workbooks is that you can use long names for the worksheets by selecting Options and renaming the sheet.

A fourth advantage to using the Excel 4 workbook (multiple worksheet) capability is that you easily can page through the report by selecting the buttons at the bottom of the screen or icons on the Contents page. A fifth advantage is that it is easier to organize and keep together the worksheets and charts necessary for a presentation. The annual report from which the sample pages in figures 8.14 through 8.17 were taken was developed with Excel 4 in a workbook because few major deletions and additions had to be made to the pages.

Creating a Report Title Page

To create a title page like the annual report title page shown in figure 8.14, you determine the elements you want to include in the title page design, the size of each element, and their positions on the page. After you use the Format Options Automatic Page Breaks command to show the boundaries of your report pages, you can lay out each page according to these boundaries. The page boundaries of the title page in figure 8.19, for example, cover the range A1:M40. You can use your page boundary range to determine how to position all the elements on your title page. If you use a box to surround all text and graphics on your title page, such as the double line box used in figure 8.14, you can position elements in reference to the boundaries of the box.

As shown in figure 8.19, one type of font, the Times New Roman font, is used for text on the title page, in three sizes. The name of the company, STANDARD INTERNATIONAL, surrounding the world graphic uses a point size of 28; the title, 1993 ANNUAL REPORT, uses a point size of 16; and the company initials at the bottom of the page, SI, use a point size of 36. Overall, the report uses the Times New Roman font consistently. The font is changed to bold and italic in some places to give emphasis to certain headings or pieces of information, or to create a special look for a section of text.

With the double line box as a boundary, the text and graphic elements in the title page are centered between the left and right lines. As figure 8.19 shows, the globe is located in the range D7:J14. You place a graphic like the world in figure 8.19 onto the page by using the Edit Insert Object command. You then can place text outside the graph range, as the text is placed in figure 8.19, or inside the range by using the Microsoft Draw program. Whenever you place text inside a graph or graphic you have added to your worksheet with Microsoft Draw, you are

Use the Zoom feature from the Windows menu for viewing the layout of the sheet. If you set magnification to 50 percent, you can get an overview of the sheet's layout.

limited by the amount of space available within the object range. The space available in the object range of the globe in figure 8.19 is too small, for example for the 28-point font used for the STANDARD INTER-NATIONAL name. STANDARD and INTERNATIONAL are centered within the range from columns D to J.

Other text on the title page also is centered within a range of columns. The title, 1993 ANNUAL REPORT, is centered between columns C and K, and the SI initials at the bottom of the page are centered directly within the central column of the page, column G.

The simple layout and design of the title page shown in figure 8.19 allows for one consistent column width on the title page—a column width of 5 (with the exception of the left and right margin columns A and M). The size of the rows, however, vary because of the size of the type appearing within the rows and because of the narrow solid black lines used at the bottom of the page with the initials SI. To create these solid black lines, you change the height of the rows directly above and below the SI to a height of 3. You then use the Format Patterns command to create the heavy black lines.

Developing Front Matter Pages of a Report

U se italic type sparingly. Italic type adds a distinct effect when used on pages where there is a small amount of text.

The sample pages of the annual report shown in figures 8.15 and 8.16 illustrate how you can use italic type, position, and lines to create a unique look for the opening pages of a report.

The position of front matter such as the table of contents and the opening comments pages shown in figures 8.15 and 8.16 can vary depending on the amount of the text, and on whether the text will appear on a left- or right-hand page. The table of contents page in figure 8.15 is a left-hand page, so a double line and text are aligned along the left column. On the right-hand page, directly opposite the table of contents, the opening comments page is aligned to the right. To increase white space and add balance to both figures, the row height of all rows was increased to 30.

Creating a Report Page with Worksheet Data and Graphs

The FINANCIAL HIGHLIGHTS page shown in figure 8.17 is an example of the techniques presented throughout this book for combining worksheet data and graphs. A few points are worth noting about the special format and layout elements of the page shown in figure 8.17.

Fig. 8.19 The annual report title page defining type sizes.

First, the FINANCIAL HIGHLIGHTS page uses the same font consistently throughout the report—the Times New Roman font. Font sizes, however, vary as shown in figure 8.20. Italicized text appears in 10 point rather than the default 12 point used for the labels and numbers in the section comparing financial data for years 1989 through 1993. The numbers appearing in the graphs use a sans serif font. The only other variation in font is the use of bold for the column showing the financial data for 1993, the year of the annual report.

Chapter Summary

In addition to using Excel to create professional-looking reports, you can use the program for creating your business correspondence. From creating simple memos to creating quality annual reports, Excel provides the text editing, formatting, and layout capabilities you need to produce the same quality available with some word processing programs and desktop publishing programs.

You also can use Excel to add graphics to memos and letters to create company stationery. Microsoft Word for Windows' built-in Draw program enables you to import many common graphics file formats or to draw your own graphics. Excel can become the program used to create most, if not all, of the documents you need to communicate inside and outside your company. Following the techniques presented in this chapter will enable you to create professional, high-quality documents.

Besides memos, letters, and reports, you can create many other types of business forms in Excel. The next chapter discusses how to create invoices, data-entry forms, travel expense forms, organizational charts, and other kinds of forms.

FINANCIAL HIGHLIGHTS ——— ❶   ❸ ——STANDARD INTERNATIONAL CORP.

(Dollars in millions except per share data.) —— ❷

Year ended December 31,	1993	1992 —— ❹
Sales of products and services	**$456.7**	$352.4
Operating income	**$75.2**	$12.1
Net income	**$45.1**	$5.5 —— ❺
Earnings per common share, before extraordinary items, assuming full dilution	**$4.01**	$0.54 —— ❻
Average number of common shares, assuming full dilution (000)	**15,249**	13,154 ❼
Cash dividends per common share	**$0.95**	$0.72
Depreciation and amortization	**$25.7**	$21.5
Shareholder's equity	**$158.3**	$135.2
Return on shareholders' equity	**35.0%**	5.0%

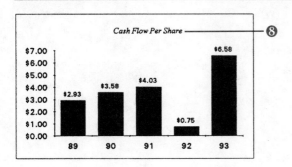

Cash Flow Per Share ——— ❽

❶ Times New Roman 12 Bold

❷ Times New Roman 10 Italic

❸ Times New Roman 10

❹ Times New Roman 10 Italic

❺ Times New Roman 12

❻ Times New Roman 12

❼ Bold used for 1993 data

❽ Times New Roman 10 Italic

Fig. 8.20 The FINANCIAL HIGHLIGHTS page showing font sizes.

9

Creating Business Forms

Many programs are available to produce high-quality business forms. Word processing programs such as Ami Pro, WordPerfect, Microsoft Word, and Microsoft Word for Windows enable users to create business forms. Most desktop publishing programs have features that make creating business forms easy. Other programs are designed for creating business forms, including those programs that combine database capabilities with desktop publishing capabilities. Excel provides all the form-creation capabilities available in word processing, desktop publishing, and business form programs.

xcel gives users the capability to produce high-quality, desktop-published business forms without requiring users to learn new commands and key functions to produce these forms.

E xcel gives users and businesses numerous advantages over businesses that use other programs for creating business forms. First, Excel gives users the same capability to produce high-quality, desktop-published business forms available in other programs without requiring users to learn new commands and functions of keys to produce these forms. Second, and probably the greatest advantage, is the capability of making business forms part of Excel spreadsheet and database applications. Unless they contain database capabilities in addition to form creation, other programs enable users to create good-looking paper forms, but cannot automate the process of entering data into forms and storing that data in a worksheet or database that can be used to run a company's business.

The real benefits of using Excel result from creating forms as part of the Excel applications you already have, or will develop, for running your business. This chapter begins by discussing how you can integrate the creation of forms with actual Excel applications, and then focuses on the techniques for producing good-looking, professionally designed forms.

Specifically, this chapter covers designing business forms for data-management applications, techniques for creating business forms, and creating sample business forms.

Designing Business Forms for Database Applications

Business forms created with Excel can be part of the overall design of an Excel database application, or developed for databases that already exist and are currently in use. This section discusses how to design business forms by keeping in mind how they fit your database application.

You can design Excel business forms so that they fit easily into a database application used to run your business. Suppose that your business uses an Excel application for processing customer orders. Such an application may contain various input screens for entering information about a customer order. Figures 9.1, 9.2, and 9.3 show three input screens used to enter customer order information. Screen I contains the cells for entering invoice, salesperson, customer account number, and customer and shipping information for an order. Screen II shows the cells used for entering payment and more shipping information. Screen III enables the user to enter the actual product order information. This screen also calculates the total sales amounts, shipping costs, and tax.

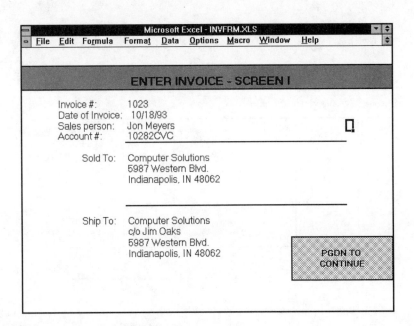

Fig. 9.1 Input screen for customer information.

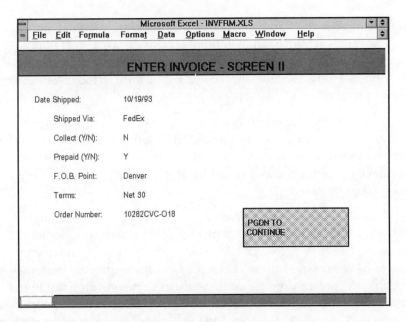

Fig. 9.2 Input screen for payment and shipping information.

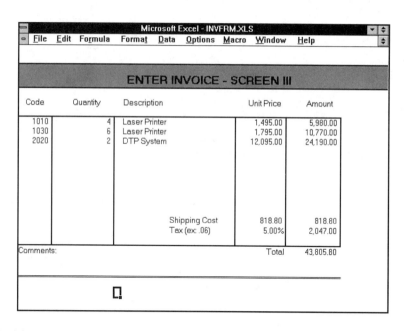

Fig. 9.3 Input screen for product order information.

Creating your own input screens gives you flexibility in placing data, the ability to control form design, and the ability to make your design look like existing forms.

You also can use the **Data Form** command to have Excel quickly create input screens. Creating your own input screens can be a good idea, however. First, you have much more flexibility in placing data and how the form will look. Second, you can design the form to look like existing forms in your office.

The three screens in figures 9.1, 9.2, and 9.3 are linked to a database containing customer account information. Information entered into the three screens is stored automatically in the database. Some businesses may have multiple databases where the information entered into the three screens is stored.

The Excel data commands, macros, and advanced macro commands make it possible to produce a complete data management system for managing customer accounts. With such systems, data input screens such as those shown in these figures are not only sources for customer, account, and order information; they also can retrieve information from an existing database. This capability saves users from having to retype information, such as a customer's address, special discount terms given to a customer, or shipping charges. For more information on developing such data-management applications with Excel, see Que's *Using Excel 4 for Windows*, Special Edition.

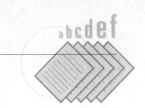

The data input screens shown in figures 9.1 through 9.3 were created to correspond with the design of an invoice form that is completed automatically and printed when a user enters information into these screens. Figure 9.4 shows a blank printed invoice form. This invoice form was generated from an area of the same worksheet containing the data input forms in figures 9.1 through 9.3. Figure 9.5 illustrates the worksheet area where the invoice form is stored.

In an automated database application, users responsible for entering customer order information should not need to view the parts of the worksheets containing the invoice form and the actual databases where customer and order information is stored. All information for the invoice shown in figure 9.4, for example, is entered automatically into the invoice form area through formulas. Figure 9.6 shows the formulas used for the information in the top section of the invoice form.

The formula to the right of INVOICE NUMBER will display any information entered into the cell in screen I, where the actual invoice number is entered. The following IF function in the invoice form keeps the cell in the invoice form blank if nothing is stored in the input screen cell (otherwise, a 0 would appear):

=IF(E24="","",E24)

In other words, the formula states *if cell E24 in screen I is empty, keep this cell empty—otherwise display the data in cell E24 in this cell*. Throughout the invoice form, similar formulas are used to display data from the input screens shown in figures 9.1 through 9.3 to the invoice form. Some formulas contain additional elements in the IF formula. String functions (such as the LEFT formulas shown in figure 9.6) are used to control the length of text entries displayed in the invoice form.

If you compare the invoice shown in figure 9.4 with the input screens shown in figures 9.1 through 9.3, you will notice that the order of information is the same. The input screens and invoice form are laid out differently, however, to make them easy to use. The input screens are organized to make data entry as simple (and error-proof) as possible; the invoice is laid out to make reading and verifying the information as clear as possible.

Do not make your business form also serve as a data input screen if the layout required for the form will make data entry more difficult than having separate input screens. If your business form requires using a small font and organizing data into complex grids, consider developing separate data input screens that use a large, easy-to-read font. Also, organize your data input screens to make data entry fast and error-proof.

U se =IF (cell="", "",cell) to display information from another part of the worksheet.

L ay out your input screens for quick and easy data input.

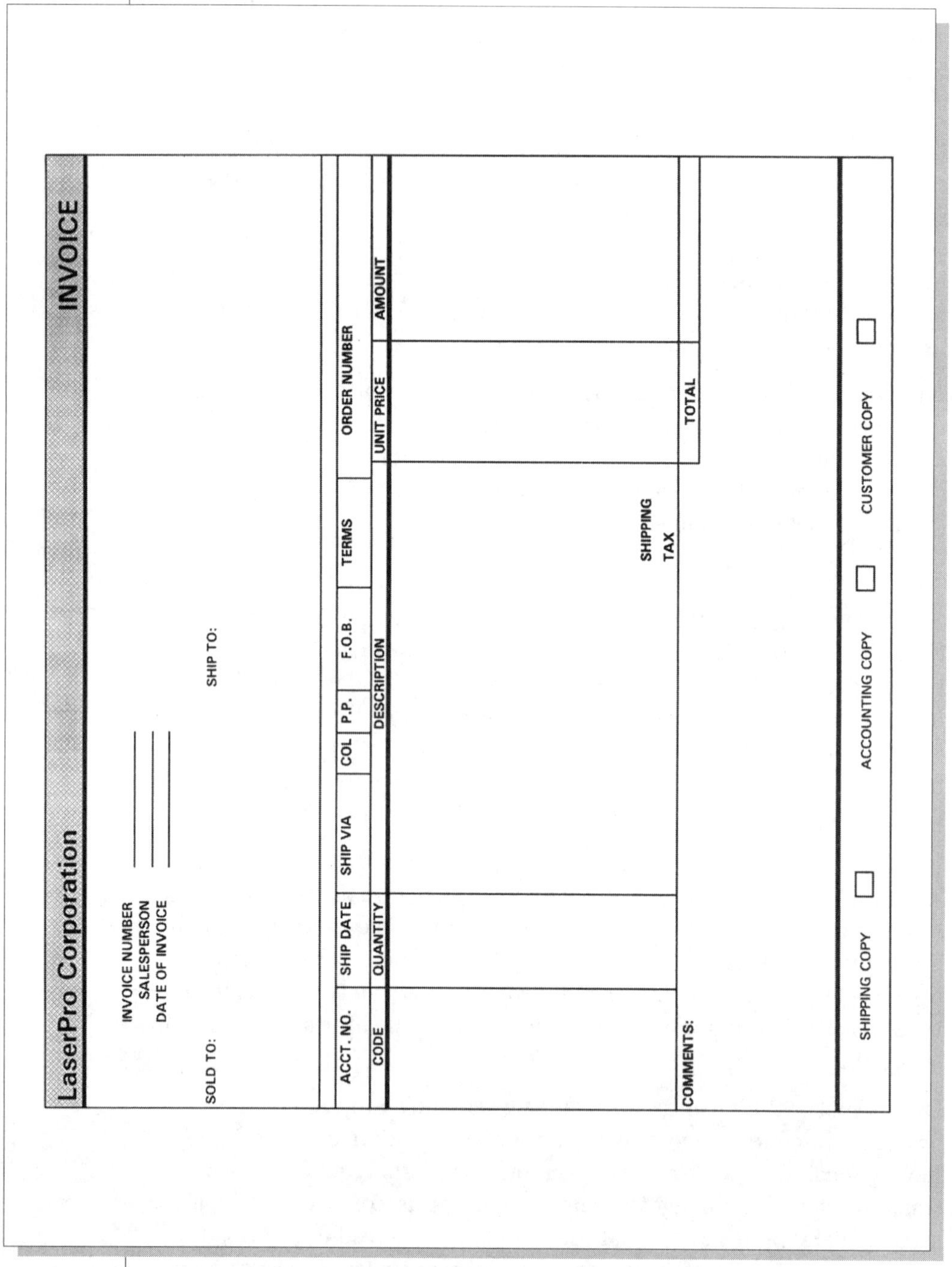

LaserPro Corporation INVOICE

INVOICE NUMBER
SALESPERSON
DATE OF INVOICE

SOLD TO:
SHIP TO:

ACCT. NO.	SHIP DATE	SHIP VIA	COL	P.P.	F.O.B.	TERMS	ORDER NUMBER

CODE	QUANTITY	DESCRIPTION	UNIT PRICE	AMOUNT
		SHIPPING		
		TAX		
			TOTAL	

COMMENTS:

SHIPPING COPY ☐ ACCOUNTING COPY ☐ CUSTOMER COPY ☐

Fig. 9.4 A printed invoice form for the customer database application.

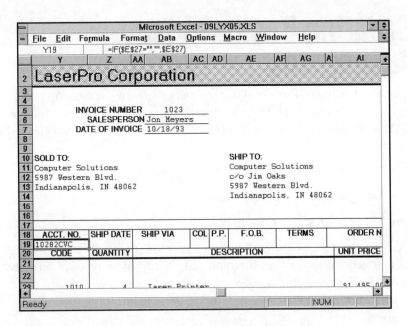

Fig. 9.5 The worksheet area containing the invoice form.

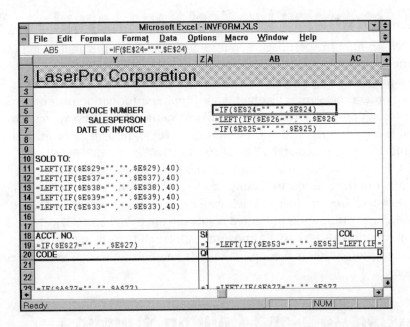

Fig. 9.6 Invoice form screen showing formulas used to reference data from input screens.

The following sections describe how to design professional business forms like the invoice form shown in figure 9.4. Your forms should be easy to read, emphasize the most important information, and easy to use for collecting handwritten data.

Creating Business Forms: Techniques

The sample invoice form in figure 9.4 uses many of the desktop publishing capabilities of Excel. Specifically, the most commonly used features for the invoice form and many other types of business forms include the following:

- Using the column and row format of Excel
- Using different font styles and sizes
- Using boldface, italic, and borders

Using the invoice example shown in figure 9.4, the next few sections present general techniques that you can use for many types of business forms. Following sections show examples of other types of forms, with instructions for creating and modifying these forms for your own business.

Determining the Best Page Layout

Analyze your business form to determine what information should be emphasized.

Determining the best page layout for your form requires analyzing how the form will be used and determining what information should be emphasized or de-emphasized. The invoice form in figure 9.4 emphasizes the order processing, customer, and shipping information over other information. The form is clearly laid out so that those who are responsible for getting an order to a customer have no difficulty viewing that information immediately. The INVOICE NUMBER, SALESPERSON, and DATE OF INVOICE information is given prominence in the upper left corner of the invoice, to ensure that readers find the information easily when tracking an order or solving an order problem. The account and shipping information presented below the SOLD TO: and SHIP TO: information also is easy to find and read. Finally, the actual product order information makes up the middle and bottom part of the invoice form.

Using Row-and-Column Structure To Design Your Form

Use the Format Border command to separate sections of the invoice.

Excel is one of the easiest programs to use when creating desktop-published documents that contain many columns. The column/row format of the worksheet and the way Excel works with cells and ranges

makes laying out and formatting columnar information very easy. The invoice form shown in the printout in figure 9.4 and shown on-screen in figure 9.5, for example, was created using the Format Border command to separate columns and rows of the invoice. Once you determine the maximum number of columns and rows, the column widths, and the row heights you need for your form, you can use the Options Display Automatic Page Breaks command to mark the boundaries of your page and then use Format Border to define the horizontal and vertical blocks of the form.

The steps for creating most business forms (like the invoice form in figure 9.4) follow:

1. Determine the maximum number of columns (and corresponding column widths) needed in the form.

2. Determine the number of rows (and corresponding row heights) needed in the form.

3. Determine where text or numbers should appear in larger or smaller fonts than the default font used for most of the form.

4. Use the Options Display Automatic Page Breaks command to mark the page boundaries of your form.

5. Adjust margin settings, column widths, and row heights to fit the form on the marked page(s).

6. Use the Format Border command to mark the different blocks of your form.

7. Enter headings and formulas.

8. Format the form with font, line drawing, shading, and other features.

The following sections describe these steps in detail.

Determining the Number of Columns and Column Widths

As mentioned previously, you must determine the maximum number of columns and their column widths needed in the form. The invoice form, shown with columns and column widths marked at the top of figure 9.7, contains 14 columns, including a column used for left margin space. If you look at the middle part of the invoice form in figure 9.7, you will notice that the row beginning with ACCT. NO. contains the most column entries. Also, notice that the last row of text in the form, beginning with SHIPPING COPY, uses the narrowest columns in the form (for

To determine the maximum number of columns, find the row with the most number of entries.

the check boxes). In this example, the ACCT. NO. and SHIPPING COPY rows determine the number of columns and column widths for the form. Table 9.1 lists the columns and column widths for the form in figure 9.7. The *invoice item* determines how wide each column will be.

Table 9.1   Layout of LaserPro Invoice Form

Column	Column Width	Invoice Item
Y	13	ACCT. NO.
Z	10	SHIP DATE
AA	2	Box to right of SHIPPING COPY
AB	10	SHIP VIA
AC	4	COL
AD	4	P.P.
AE	11	F.O.B.
AF	2	Box to right of ACCOUNTING COPY
AG	9	TERMS
AH	1	Left border for UNIT PRICE
AI	13	UNIT PRICE
AJ	2	Box to right of CUSTOMER COPY
AK	18	AMOUNT

Determining the Number of Rows and Row Heights

Drawing a rough draft of the layout of your form before determining the number of rows and columns will help you use space efficiently in your form.

After determining the number of columns and the widths for each column, next determine the approximate number of rows you need for the form. The number of rows will, of course, depend on how you lay out the form. When determining the number of rows and columns, remember to consider how much information will be copied from input forms, databases, and worksheets directly to your form—this allows for information that is automatically transferred to the form. The invoice form in figure 9.7, for example, contains 45 rows to hold all the data entered into the input screens shown in figures 9.1 through 9.3 at the beginning of this chapter. Rows also are included in the invoice form for white space and for headings.

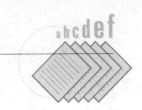

X	Y	Z	AA	AB	AC	AD	AE	AF	AG	AH	AI	AJ	AK
7	13	10	2	10	4	4	11	2	9	1	13	2	18

LaserPro Corporation   **INVOICE**

INVOICE NUMBER   1023
SALESPERSON   Jon Meyers
DATE OF INVOICE   10/18/93

SOLD TO:
Computer Solutions
5987 Western Blvd.
Indianapolis, IN 48062

SHIP TO:
Computer Solutions
c/o Jim Oaks
5987 Western Blvd.
Indianapolis, IN 48062

ORDER NUMBER

ACCT. NO.   10282CVC

SHIP DATE	SHIP VIA	COL	P.P.	F.O.B.	TERMS

CODE	QUANTITY	DESCRIPTION	UNIT PRICE	AMOUNT
1010	4	Laser Printer	$1,495.00	5,980.00
1030	6	Laser Printer	$1,795.00	10,770.00
2020	2	DTP System	$12,095.00	24,190.00
			SHIPPING 818.80	818.80
			TAX 5.00%	2,047.00
			TOTAL	$43,805.80

COMMENTS:
Include five extra copies of service manual with
shipment of the Model 1010.

SHIPPING COPY ☐   ACCOUNTING COPY ☐   CUSTOMER COPY ☐

Fig. 9.7 An invoice form with columns and column widths marked.

To accurately determine whether all the rows you need in your form will fit onto the page, you should make certain that the row heights reflect the font sizes you will use throughout the form. If the default font and font size in the Format Font menu need to be changed, change them. Also, try to determine where your form will contain font sizes larger or smaller than the default size used throughout the form. Forgetting to set the heading of your form to 20-point Arial (or another sans serif font), for example, until you are ready to print could cause problems with fitting everything in your form onto one page. Likewise, if you determine at the beginning of designing your form where it will contain small font sizes, you will know how much extra room is available from the reduction in row height and column width allotted by small font sizes.

Marking Page Boundaries of a Form

After you determine the number of columns and rows and the corresponding column widths and row heights for your form, use the Options Display Automatic Page Breaks command to mark the page boundaries of the form. Setting the print range to mark your page may require resetting margins in the File Page Setup dialog box, or may require changing column widths until you get the form to fit on the page. Frequently, you will want to limit your form to one page. The examples of business forms shown in this chapter are designed for one-page layouts. Limiting your form to one page requires that you determine the right layout, choose the right font sizes, and abbreviate text and headings. If your form doesn't quite fit on one page, you can mark the Fit option in the Scaling area in the Page Setup dialog box.

Also, fitting your form on one page may require that you choose a horizontal (landscape) rather than a vertical (portrait) layout. The invoice form in figure 9.7 is designed for landscape layout. Whenever you use landscape layout, you must change the orientation of the page by selecting Landscape in the Page Setup dialog box.

Using Format Border To Create a Form Grid

Use the Format Border command to mark the primary divisions of your form.

After you determine the number of columns and rows for your form, determine column widths and special row heights, and mark your page boundaries by using the Options Display Automatic Page Breaks command, you can use the Format Border command to mark the primary divisions of your form. Marking a form this way provides a grid, which enables you to see immediately the space for major sections of your form. The invoice form in figure 9.7, for example, is divided into five

major sections: the main heading, the sales information and customer and shipping address section, accounting and shipping information, the order information, and the copy information at the bottom. Figure 9.8 shows the invoice form with lines marking the divisions of its main sections.

With the form marked for overall layout, you can begin to enter headings and formulas and format the form with fonts, borders, patterns, and other capabilities. The following sections present general techniques for choosing fonts and using lines, boxes, and shading in business forms.

Selecting Fonts and Font Sizes for Business Forms

The guidelines presented throughout this book for choosing fonts and font sizes apply to business forms as well as other types of documents designed using the WYSIWYG capabilities of Excel. These guidelines include avoiding the use of too many fonts or font sizes in a document, choosing fonts that will be the most readable, and using fonts to help communicate the information to the reader. Using the invoice form example shown in figure 9.9, this section explains how to make the right decisions when selecting fonts for your business forms.

The invoice form in figure 9.9 uses only two styles of fonts. Arial (or another sans serif font) is the predominant font used for everything in the form except the data copied into the form from information entered into the input screens. The Courier font is used for data copied from the input screens. Because the Arial font is a sans serif font and Courier is a serif font, the Courier font helps the reader quickly distinguish order, customer, shipping, and other information from the headings in the form. Arial is the only other font used because white space, the layout of the form, use of lines, and boldface help to distinguish different headings from each other.

Use the Courier font to give the impression of fill-in on a form.

The invoice form uses only three font sizes:

Font	Element
20-point Arial	Heading at top of form
12-point Arial	Headings in body of form
10-point Courier	Data copied from input screens

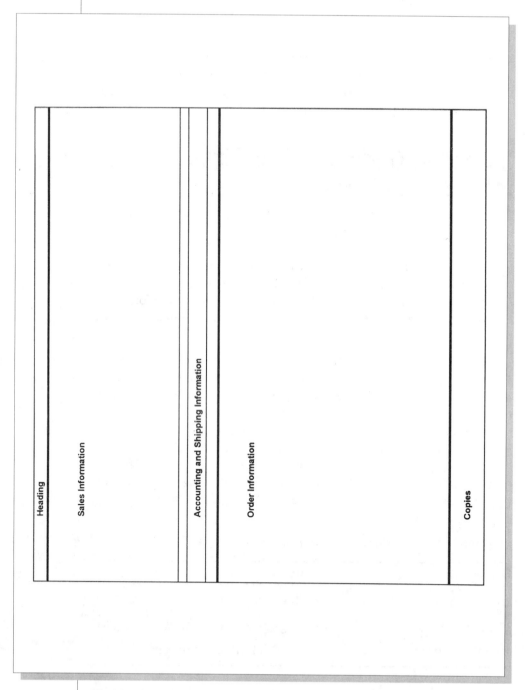

Fig. 9.8 The invoice form in figure 9.7 with sectional dividing lines.

LaserPro Corporation   **INVOICE**

INVOICE NUMBER   1023
SALESPERSON   Jon Meyers
DATE OF INVOICE   10/18/93

SOLD TO:
Computer Solutions
5987 Western Blvd.
Indianapolis, IN 48062

SHIP TO:
Computer Solutions
c/o Jim Oaks
5987 Western Blvd.
Indianapolis, IN 48062

ACCT. NO. 10282CVC	SHIP DATE	SHIP VIA	COL	P.P.	F.O.B.	TERMS	ORDER NUMBER	
CODE	QUANTITY	DESCRIPTION					UNIT PRICE	AMOUNT
1010	4	Laser Printer					$1,495.00	5,980.00
1030	6	Laser Printer					$1,795.00	10,770.00
2020	2	DTP System					$12,095.00	24,190.00
						SHIPPING	818.80	818.80
						TAX	5.00%	2,047.00
							TOTAL	$43,805.80

COMMENTS:
Include five extra copies of service manual with
shipment of the Model 1010.

SHIPPING COPY ☐   ACCOUNTING COPY ☐   CUSTOMER COPY ☐

Fig. 9.9 The invoice form with data, displaying font styles and sizes.

The 10-point Courier font provides the room needed for data in the invoice form, but is also very readable. A Courier font smaller than 9 point would be more difficult to read (see fig. 9.10). Courier also gives the impression of typing information on the form.

10 Point Courier	9 Point Courier	8 Point Courier
Computer Solutions c/o Ron Meyers 5987 Western Blvd. Indianapolis, IN 48062	Computer Solutions c/o Ron Meyers 5987 Western Blvd. Indianapolis, IN 48062	Computer Solutions c/o Ron Meyers 5987 Western Blvd. Indianapolis, IN 48062

Fig. 9.10   The Courier font in 10-, 9-, and 8-point sizes.

Using Underlining, Boldface, and Italics in Business Forms

Underlining, boldface, and italics are effective when used for a consistent, specific function in a business form. Use these elements to make it easy to find and understand information. Boldface and underlining are used in the invoice form example in figure 9.9 for very specific purposes. First, boldface is used to make headings more distinct. Notice the difference between headings in bold and not in bold. Compare figure 9.9 with figure 9.11 to see the difference the use or absence of boldface has on the invoice form. Boldface headings particularly stand out when other text is very close to the heading. Boldface calls attention to the INVOICE NUMBER, SALESPERSON, and DATE OF INVOICE information at the top of the page.

Using Borders and Patterns in Business Forms

Borders and patterns communicate the logic of the form quickly ensure that the form is completed correctly, and make forms easy to use.

As shown in all the examples presented in this chapter, borders and patterns play a very important part in the design of business forms. These elements communicate the logic of the form quickly to those using the form, contribute to ensuring that the form is completed correctly, and contribute to making forms easy to use once information

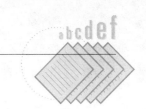

is put into them. Using lines, boxes, and shading is important particularly when information will be entered by hand. The travel expense form in figure 9.12, for example, uses lines, boxes, and shading to ensure that those using the form can easily fill out the form completely and accurately.

The invoice form referred to throughout this chapter uses borders and patterns to show the organization of the form and to help readers use the completed forms. Lines segment the main parts of the form; the lines shown in figure 9.8 separate the sales, customer, shipping, and order data. Customer and shipping address information is boxed at the top of the form, and specific order information is boxed in the bottom half of the form. A light pattern is used to highlight the company name and form heading at the top of the invoice.

Creating Sample Business Forms

This section explains how to create with Excel two types of purchase requisition forms, a travel expense form, and an organizational chart. Each example is explained by showing the layout of the example on the Excel worksheet and describing the format features used in each example, including the font, boldface, italic, and borders used in each example.

Purchase Requisition Forms

Figures 9.13 and 9.14 show two purchase requisition forms created with Excel. The purchase requisition form in figure 9.13 was designed for office employees who need to fill in purchase requisition forms by hand—writing or typing the information. The purchase requisition form in figure 9.14, on the other hand, was designed for a Excel application that automatically fills data into the form and prints the form for those who need to process the requisition and have a printed copy of the requisition to file. Notice that the purchase requisition form in figure 9.13 uses Excel to create a grid—enabling employees to easily fill in the information required for the requisition. The following sections describe the layout and format of each purchase requisition.

U se the Options
Protect Document and Format Cell Protection commands to protect your form from mistakes and make data entry easier.

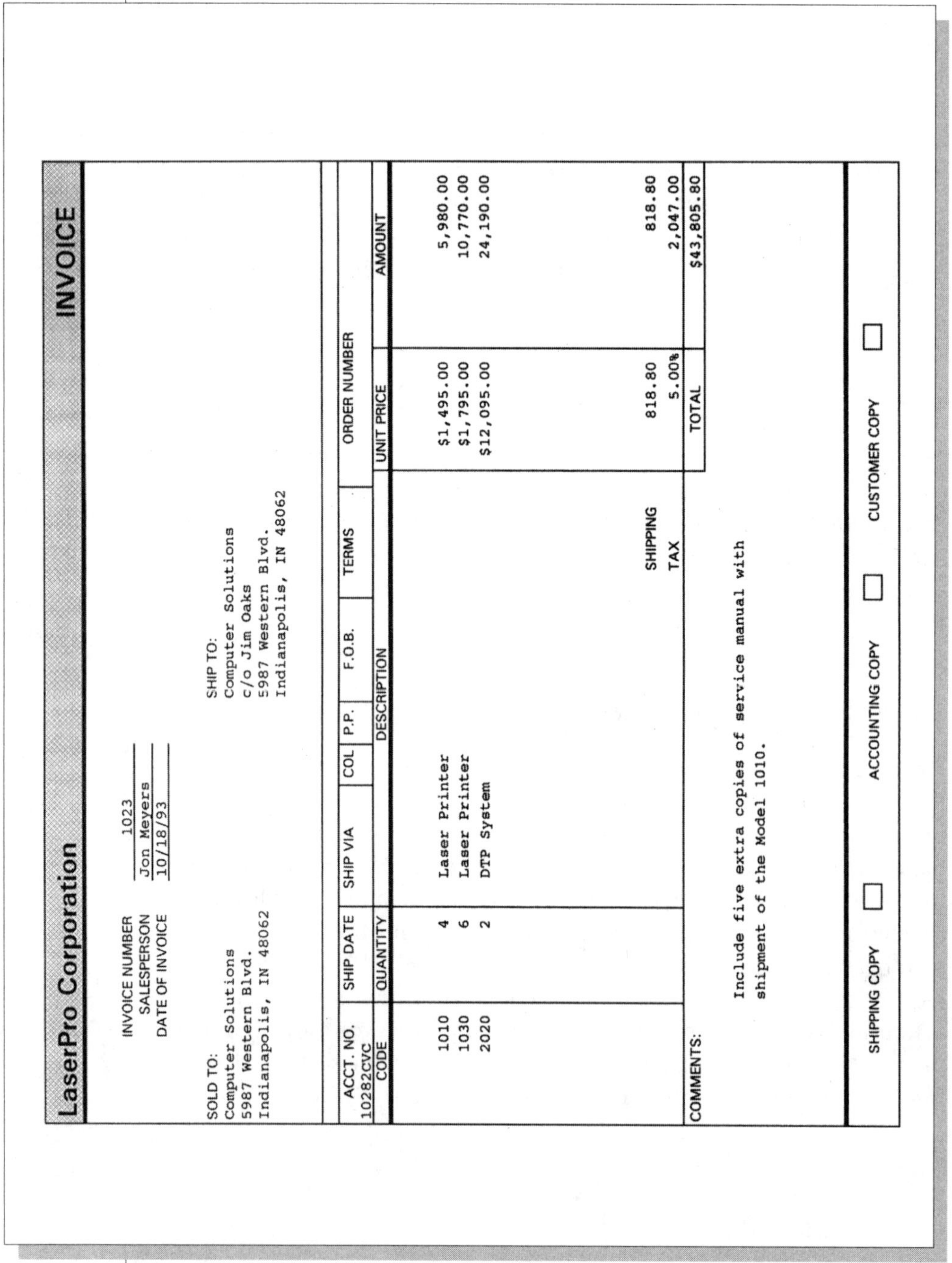

LaserPro Corporation   **INVOICE**

INVOICE NUMBER   1023
SALESPERSON   Jon Meyers
DATE OF INVOICE   10/18/93

SOLD TO:
Computer Solutions
5987 Western Blvd.
Indianapolis, IN 48062

SHIP TO:
Computer Solutions
c/o Jim Oaks
5987 Western Blvd.
Indianapolis, IN 48062

ORDER NUMBER

ACCT. NO. 10282CVC CODE	SHIP DATE QUANTITY	SHIP VIA	COL	P.P.	F.O.B.	TERMS	DESCRIPTION	UNIT PRICE	AMOUNT
1010	4						Laser Printer	$1,495.00	5,980.00
1030	6						Laser Printer	$1,795.00	10,770.00
2020	2						DTP System	$12,095.00	24,190.00
						SHIPPING		818.80	818.80
						TAX		5.00%	2,047.00
								TOTAL	$43,805.80

COMMENTS:

Include five extra copies of service manual with
shipment of the Model 1010.

SHIPPING COPY ☐   ACCOUNTING COPY ☐   CUSTOMER COPY ☐

Fig. 9.11   An invoice form without boldface used for body headings.

Travel Expense Report								
Dates			**Purpose**					
Date								Totals
Airplane/Train/Bus								
Hotel								
Driving Miles								
@								
Rental - Car								
Meals — Breakfast								
Meals — Lunch								
Meals — Dinner								
Taxi/Tips								
Parking/Tolls								
Phone								
Supplies								
Entertainment								
Daily Totals								

Detail of Entertainment Expenses Above

Date	Place and City	Amount	Guest and Company

Accounting	Total Expenses
Received Date _____	Total Paid by Employee _____
	Less Cash Advance _____
Paid Date _____	Total Due Employee _____

Signature _____ Date _____

Signature _____ Date _____

Accounting Copy

Fig. 9.12 A travel expense form illustrating the use of borders and patterns.

You may want to protect your form by allowing only the data entry person to add data or change cells that need input. To do this, unlock (unprotect) the cells in the form where entry is expected by selecting those cells and then choosing Format Cell Protection and unchecking the Locked box. Then protect the sheet by selecting Options Protect Document (with or without a password). Cell editing will be limited to those cells that were unprotected to help preserve the template. You can use the Tab key to move the selection among unprotected cells.

Developing a form that employees will complete manually, like the purchase requisition form in figure 9.13, is easy with Excel because of the ease of drawing the lines and boxes—where employees will write information needed to process the requisition. You can create a purchase requisition form like that in figure 9.13 by determining how to use columns, rows, widths, and heights to structure the boxes and grids you need for the form. Figure 9.15, for example, shows that the first purchase requisition form (for manual data entry) contains nine columns, including two used for left and right margins. The form contains 51 rows, including rows used for top and bottom margin space (in addition to the margin space automatically added by Excel).

You can determine the number of columns and the column widths for a form like the purchase requisition form in figure 9.13 by determining which part of the form will require the most columns and the narrowest columns. The center section of the form in figure 9.15 contains six columns for purchase information. Notice that except for columns A, E, and I, the columns in figure 9.15 define the structure of the center part of the form: column B is used for Item information; column C for Quantity Ordered information; column D for Description; column F for Unit of Purchase; column G for Unit Price; and column H for Estimated Cost. The other parts of the form are organized according to the boundaries of these columns.

Except for the row containing the PURCHASE REQUISITION title in the upper right corner, all rows of the purchase requisition form use the default row height of 14. The form is laid out according to the number of default-sized rows in the worksheet needed for the information required.

PURCHASE REQUISITION

LaserPro Corporation
4938 West 18th St.
Suite 32
Indianapolis, IN 46022

Date _____

Primary Vendor:	Secondary Vendor:

Date Requested	Charge to	Job No.	Ship via
Purpose		Purchase Required	Stock Transfer
		Material Required	Other

Item	Quantity Ordered	Description	Unit of Purchase	Unit Price	Estimated Cost
				Subtotal	

Requested by		Date	Tax
			Shipping
Requested by		Date	Total
Requested by		Date	

Purchase Order No.	Purchase Order Date	Date Ordered	Date Received

Fig. 9.13 A purchase requisition form designed for handwritten or typed data.

PURCHASE REQUISITION

FROM: _____ DEPT: _____ DATE: _____

PURPOSE:
(of requested items)

#	Item	Model	Qty	Description	Date Required	Est. Cost
1						
2						
3						
4						

Manufacturer Name and Address (if known):

Contact Person:
Phone #:

Recommended Supplier (Person / Company):   Phone #:

Special Instructions:

Approved By:

For Accounting Use Only

#	Equipment	Make/Model	Serial #	Use	%
1					
2					
3					

For Accounting Use Only

#	Date Acquired	Cost
1		
2		
3		
4		

For Purchasing Use Only

#	Order Date	Receive Date	PO.#	Quoted Cost
1				
2				
3				
4				

Fig. 9.14 A purchase requisition form designed for automated data entry.

	A	B	C	D	E	F	G	H
1	2	8	9	18	3	9	9	9

2			PURCHASE REQUISITION
3	LaserPro Corporation		
4	4938 West 18th St.		
5	Suite 32		
6	Indianapolis, IN 46022		Date _____
7			
8	Primary Vendor:		Secondary Vendor:
9			
10			
11			
12			
13			

14	Date Requested	Charge to	Job No.	Ship via
15				
16	Purpose		Purchase Required	Stock Transfer
17			Material Required	Other
18				

	Item	Quantity Ordered	Description	Unit of Purchase	Unit Price	Estimated Cost
19						
20						
21						
22						
23						
24						
25						
26						
27						
28						
29						
30						
31						
32						
33						
34						
35						
36						
37						
38						
39						

40				Subtotal
41	Requested by		Date	Tax
42				Shipping
43	Requested by		Date	Total
44				
45	Requested by		Date	
46				
47				
48	Purchase Order No.	Purchase Order Date	Date Ordered	Date Received
49				
50				
51				

Fig. 9.15 The manual purchase requisition form showing column and row positions and column widths.

If you have many boxes and grids on your form, limit your changes in type and shading.

Because the number of boxes and grids in the form make it complex, the purchase requisition form in figure 9.13 requires the simplest combination of other formatting elements. The form uses, therefore, only one type of font—the Arial (or another sans serif) font. Also, because the boxes and the white space around sections of the form delineate the structure of the form, no special formatting attributes such as boldface, italics, or patterns are used to segment one section of information from another. The purchase requisition form uses four sizes of fonts to emphasize or deemphasize certain information as necessary: 8, 10, 12, and 14 point. Most of the text is printed in the default 10-point Arial font.

Because the information is entered automatically into the form in figure 9.14, it does not use as many borders as used in the form in figure 9.13. The form in figure 9.14 uses boxes to enclose different categories of information with spacing left within each box for Excel to enter data in the same way that data is entered into the Customer Order form described earlier in the chapter. The form shown in figure 9.14 was created as part of an Excel database application containing data forms, a database where data is stored, and the form.

As shown in figure 9.16, the second purchase requisition form contains 13 columns, including columns used for additional left and right margin space (column Z and AL). You can determine the number of columns to use and the corresponding column widths by determining the needed information in the first box (containing Item information), and the last three boxes at the bottom of the form (Equipment, Date Acquired, and Order Date information).

The format of the purchase requisition form includes the use of patterns and heavy black borders to delineate one section from another. Notice in figure 9.14 that light shading is used in five of the information boxes in the form. The heavy black rule at the top of the form highlights the heading, while a second rule separates the bottom three boxes from the rest of the form.

Use shading and thick black rules to separate parts of your form.

The automated purchase requisition form uses only one type of font—Arial—although three sizes appear in the form. The form contains the following font specifications:

Main heading	Arial 20 point, bold
All other headings	Arial 10 point, bold
Parenthetical note	Arial 8 point

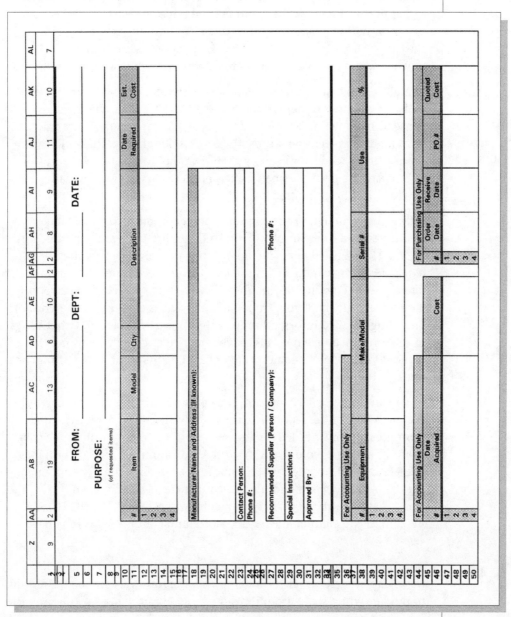

Fig. 9.16 The automated purchase requisition form with column and row indicators.

Travel Expense Report

The travel expense report shown in figure 9.12 was designed as part of a database application similar to the customer order application described earlier in the chapter. When printed, the travel expense report contains any information a user enters into a series of input screens. Like the Customer Order form, the travel expense report uses formulas that transfer to the report any data entered into the input screens.

In addition to being part of an automated Excel application that maintains a company's or department's travel expense data, the travel expense form shown in figure 9.12 is easy to use for entering data into the form manually. In other words, the form is designed so that employees can use blank forms for keeping their own day-to-day travel records or for preparing a draft of expenses before these expenses are actually entered into the computer.

Although the design of the form may look complicated, Excel makes creating such a form simple. If you study figure 9.17, you will notice that the travel expense report, like other forms described in this chapter, is a block of columns and rows in the Excel worksheet. Using 13 columns ranging from column V through column AH, the travel expense report includes a grid where you can record one week's expenses and a grid for providing detailed information for entertainment expenses. Other boxes in the form include a header (travel expense report), a footer (Accounting Copy), Accounting, Total Expenses, and two Signature lines.

As shown in figure 9.17, most of the columns provide the structure for the main part of the report—the listing of daily travel expenses. Apart from the columns needed for this section of the report, only three other columns are used; columns V, Y, and AH. Columns V and AH provide the left and right border, while column Y is used for the hyphen separating the beginning and ending dates of the travel period. Columns V, Y, and AH are one character in width; columns W, X, Z, AA, AB, AC, AD, AE, and AF are eight characters in width, and column AG is ten characters.

Row heights vary much more than column widths in the design of the travel expense report. First, notice that some rows vary in height in order to provide white space around headings, such as the rows containing the following headings:

```
Travel Expense Report
Detail of Entertainment Expenses Above
Accounting
Total Expenses
```

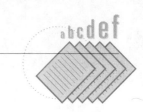

	V	W	X	Y	Z	AA	AB	AC	AD	AE	AF	AG	A
1	1	8	8	1	8	8	8	8	8	8	8	10	1

Travel Expense Report

Dates	-	**Purpose**		

	Date											Totals
Airplane/Train/Bus												
Hotel												
Driving Miles												
@												
Rental - Car												
Meals — Breakfast												
Meals — Lunch												
Meals — Dinner												
Taxi/Tips												
Parking/Tolls												
Phone												
Supplies												
Entertainment												
Daily Totals												

Detail of Entertainment Expenses Above

Date	Place and City	Amount	Guest and Company

Accounting	Total Expenses	
Received Date _____	Total Paid by Employee	_____
	Less Cash Advance	_____
Paid Date _____	Total Due Employee	_____

Signature _____ Date _____

Signature _____ Date _____

Accounting Copy

Fig. 9.17 The travel expense report form showing column and row indicators.

Some rows provide the spacing needed between boxes of information. These include rows 2, 5, 7, 26, 37, 48, 54, and 56. Rows 2 and 56 are used for the top and bottom borders. Other rows provide spacing between the information in the `Accounting`, `Total Expenses`, and `Signature` boxes. Notice also that some rows enable the headings to float within a boxed area; rows 4, 28, and 40 add spacing below headings. Row 41 is narrow in order to add space below the lines under `Accounting` and `Total Expenses`.

Vary your patterns on a form for organization as well as appearance.

Because the form contains many grids and boxes, few other formatting elements are used in the travel expense report. The report uses two types of fonts. The Times New Roman (or another serif font) font is used for all headings throughout the report—14 point is used for the headings `Travel Expense Report`, `Dates`, and `Purpose`, and 12 point is used for all other headings. All data entered into the report by being transferred through formulas appears in the Courier font, 10-point size. Bold type is used for all headings except the three headings in the column following the heading `Meals`. The most predominant formatting element used in the travel expense report is the use of patterns. A light pattern provides a border around the whole report and helps to separate grids and boxes of information. A dark pattern highlights the box where accounting dates are displayed.

Organizational Chart

Years ago, creating an organizational chart with a word processing program or even a desktop publishing program was very difficult, if not impossible. To create an organizational chart with your computer, you had to purchase programs developed specifically for this task or use a drawing program that made drawing lines and boxes fairly easy. Today, drawing lines and boxes with word processing programs and desktop publishing programs is much easier, but it is still not as easy as using Excel's line- and box-drawing capabilities. Creating an organizational chart with Excel is a matter of determining the page boundaries for your chart on the worksheet, determining the correct size for boxes, and positioning boxes evenly on the page.

To create an organizational chart like the chart shown in figure 9.18, you begin by setting all column widths to five characters; select the Standard Width text box after choosing Format Column Width. After you change column widths, you then define the page boundary for your organizational chart by using the Options Display Automatic Page Breaks command. The organizational chart in figure 9.18 fits on the page in regular Portrait mode; however, some charts may require Landscape mode. If so, select Landscape after choosing File Page Setup.

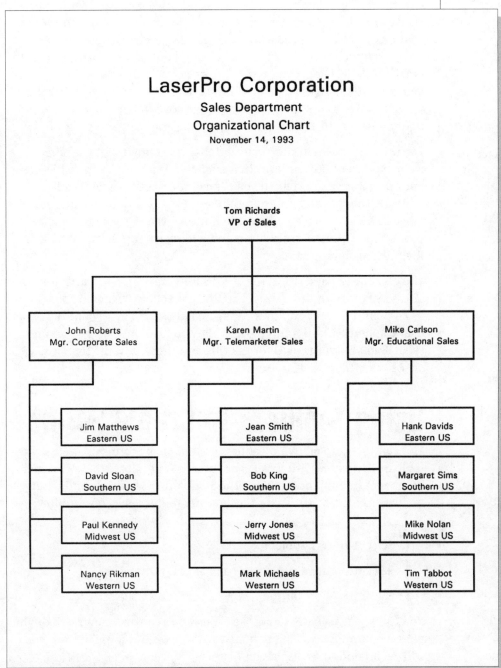

Fig. 9.18 An organizational chart created with Excel.

Once you have defined the page boundaries, you can determine the sizes of the boxes displaying staff positions and employee names. The organizational chart in figure 9.18 contains three box sizes: six columns by four rows, four columns by four rows, and three columns by three rows. Figure 9.19 shows how the boxes are positioned in reference to specific columns and rows on the worksheet. The largest box, the VP of Sales box, is centered between the left and right boundaries of the page, in the range F11:K14. The second tier of boxes, showing the sales managers, is laid out in the ranges B21:E24, G21:J24, and L21:024. Notice that the smallest boxes—containing sales staff employees—are aligned with the right border of the boxes containing manager names and positions.

To create the boxes in the organizational chart, highlight the ranges where you want boxes drawn (remember you can press Ctrl to highlight multiple ranges) and click the Outline Border tool (on the Standard toolbar). The first box, for example, VP of Sales, is drawn around the range F11:K14. To create connecting lines in the organizational chart, you use the Format Border command and select Top, Bottom, Left, or Right where appropriate.

The organizational chart in figure 9.18 uses one font—the Arial (or other sans serif) font—in three sizes. The title LaserPro Corporation appears in 24-point type; the subtitles Sales Department and Organizational Chart appear in 14-point type, and all other text appears in 10-point type. Boldface type is used for the title and the text in the first box (VP of Sales). All other text uses regular type.

U se the Outline Border tool to create organizational chart boxes.

Using Toolbars To Create Forms

You can speed up many procedures used to create forms if you use the toolbars that come with Excel. The three main toolbars that contain a number of helpful tools include the Standard, Formatting, and Utility toolbars (see fig. 9.20). To display another toolbar on-screen, follow these steps:

1. Select Options Toolbar.

2. Select from the list box the toolbar you want to use.

3. Select the Show button.

You can select as many toolbars as you want. You also can use the right mouse button. By clicking a toolbar with the right mouse button, you will get an option to display toolbars.

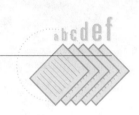

	A	B	C	D	E	F	G	H	I	J	K	L	M	N	O	P
1	1	6	6	6	6	6	6	6	6	6	6	6	6	6	6	1

LaserPro Corporation

Sales Department

Organizational Chart

November 14, 1993

Tom Richards
VP of Sales

John Roberts	Karen Martin	Mike Carlson
Mgr. Corporate Sales	Mgr. Telemarketer Sales	Mgr. Educational Sales

Jim Matthews	Jean Smith	Hank Davids
Eastern US	Eastern US	Eastern US

David Sloan	Bob King	Margaret Sims
Southern US	Southern US	Southern US

Paul Kennedy	Jerry Jones	Mike Nolan
Midwest US	Midwest US	Midwest US

Nancy Rikman	Mark Michaels	Tim Tabbot
Western US	Western US	Western US

Fig. 9.19 The organizational chart showing column and row indicators.

When you select a tool (or any formatting command), remember that you can highlight a series of ranges by pressing the Ctrl key as you highlight multiple ranges. Highlighting many ranges and using the tools on the toolbar or the right mouse button can speed up your formatting tremendously. The following are useful tools on the toolbars for creating applications described in this chapter. See Chapter 3 for descriptions of all the tools on these toolbars.

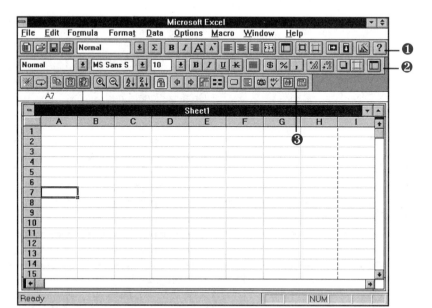

❶ Standard toolbar

❷ Formatting toolbar

❸ Utility toolbar

Fig. 9.20 The Excel window with the Standard, Formatting, and Utility toolbars.

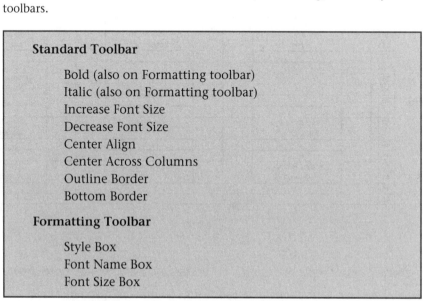

Standard Toolbar

> Bold (also on Formatting toolbar)
> Italic (also on Formatting toolbar)
> Increase Font Size
> Decrease Font Size
> Center Align
> Center Across Columns
> Outline Border
> Bottom Border

Formatting Toolbar

> Style Box
> Font Name Box
> Font Size Box

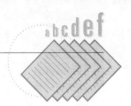

Justify Align
Light Shading
AutoFormat

Utility Toolbar

Paste Formats
Zoom In
Zoom Out
Text Box
Check Spelling
Set Print Area

Chapter Summary

If you are an experienced Excel user and have used the desktop-publishing capabilities of Excel for creating professional-looking worksheets, you easily can create professionally designed business forms for your office. With the ease of using the Format Border command to draw boxes and grids, you can apply your Excel skills to laying out and formatting the business forms needed for your business.

Using Excel to create professional business forms is not only an advantage because you can use the familiar commands, but you can connect business forms to the Excel database applications you presently use to run your business. This chapter showed you how to develop professional forms that you and your staff can create without learning other software programs or depending on outside production services.

The next chapter shows you how to use Excel to create computer, slide, and overhead presentations.

Excel Business Presentations and Promotional Pieces

News from the Breadbasket

Agricultural Products Quarterly Newsletter

Second Quarter	Volume 24

Sales are up!

This year has been our best yet. Sales are up, and things have never looked better! Let's keep up the good work and keep on going into the future. We've got a lot of potential for success in the years to come. Let's make sure we'll be taking advantage of it.

The most important news is that wheat has finally overtaken corn as our leading product. It shows what a little diversification can really do when you put your mind to it.

I'd like to recognize our key performers this period: Erin Mike Wolf, Smith, Stephen Tonkin, Al Ruiz and Marilyn Mills. They've been the key to our success in the second quarter. Next quarter it could be you! So, let's get out there and sell, sell, sell!!

Financial Results

Once again, revenues are higher than ever before. This is the best quarter in our short, but great, history as a company. As you can imagine, there have been a lot of pressures on the harvest and on prices. But we're holding our own and will continue to succeed.

In the coming years, we'll have even greater pressures on revenues and expenses, but I have no doubt that we'll

keep growing as we move into the future. Thanks again for your continued help and support, and thanks in advance for the next quarter.

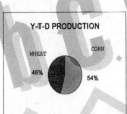

Y-T-D PRODUCTION

WHEAT 46%   CORN 54%

Wheat	Second Quarter	Year to Date	One Year Ago
Bushels	315,160	542,540	412,654
$ per bu.	3.24	3.49	3.31
Revenue	$1,021,118	$1,871,520	$1,365,885
Corn			
Bushels	273,610	457,350	442,674
$ per bu.	2.67	2.81	2.54
Revenue	$730,539	$1,270,734	$1,124,392
Total $	$1,751,657	$3,142,254	$2,490,277

Includes

Creating Computer, Slide, and Overhead Presentations

As discussed in previous chapters, Excel provides a wide array of spreadsheet publishing options for formatting worksheets. These capabilities can add emphasis to text and graphs used in slides and overheads, making their content more persuasive and easier to read.

This chapter shows you how to use Excel's formatting options to create effective, high quality, visually appealing presentation slides and overheads in black and white and a variety of colors.

This chapter also discusses how to convert your files to a presentation medium. As you will see, you easily can print your files and transfer them to transparencies or convert them to 35mm slides with the help of a professional graphics shop that has special equipment.

This chapter also tells you how to use the Excel Slide Show Manager. With a computer and relatively inexpensive projection equipment, you can create your own customized slide show that includes special features not available in a 35mm presentation.

Using Excel To Help Convey Your Message

Planning is critical in creating an effective presentation. With all the formatting and screen layout options available in Excel, it is very easy to get carried away and make your presentation too complicated and confusing. It is especially important that your slides and overheads be clear and readable. In many cases, the audience will be reading the information from a distance.

Reviewing Guidelines for Presenting Text

In this section, you examine several guidelines that will help you create presentation-quality slides and overheads. Specifically, the section looks at the effective use of different fonts and point sizes, enhancing text with bold and underlining, and using bullets. Figure 10.1 shows how you can use a variety of formatting techniques to create a professional-looking slide.

Use Large Point Type Sizes for Text

Slides and overheads often can be difficult to read during a presentation, so it is important that you use fonts that can be read from a distance. Titles should be a 24-point font or larger. Text should never be smaller than 14 point.

If the audience is to understand the message, your slides must be clear, in large type, and contain as few words as possible.

Key Title Text
Subtitle for additional information

⇒ **Supporting Bullet Point**
Explanatory text if necessary

⇒ **Supporting Bullet Point**
Explanatory text if necessary

⇒ **Supporting Bullet Point**
Explanatory text if necessary

Fig. 10.1   A common slide or overhead layout.

Limit the Number of Fonts and Use a Sans Serif Typeface

Excel can use up to 256 fonts in a worksheet. Although you may be tempted to use many fonts, keep your slide easy to read by not using more than two fonts and two or three point sizes. Figure 10.1 uses the sans serif font Helvetica with three point sizes. Helvetica is a font commonly recommended for titles and subtitles because it looks good and is easy to read in large point sizes. Helvetica also appears larger than other fonts because its x-character axis is larger than other fonts. Helvetica is an excellent font for slides because point sizes are always large and it is easy to read when projected. If you use other typefaces, be sure that they are readable when transferred to a slide or overhead and projected.

Reduce Point Size for Subtitles and Bullets

Use the largest text for a title to draw attention to the slide's key message. Choose smaller typefaces for subtitles and bullets. A subtitle usually is detailed, supporting information for the main message of the slide. Differentiate this information with a smaller type size and possibly italics. Do not complicate your slide with too many subtitles and bullets of different styles and text size.

Type size is important in setting the priority of your text.

Use Italics to Differentiate a Slide

Italics help separate the parts of a slide and position the text in different ways. Italics are effective for emphasizing direct or indirect quotes. In most cases, italics should be combined with boldface. Italic text tends to be lighter than even plain text and disappears into the slide.

Figure 10.2 shows how bold and italics are used to add emphasis and clarity to slides.

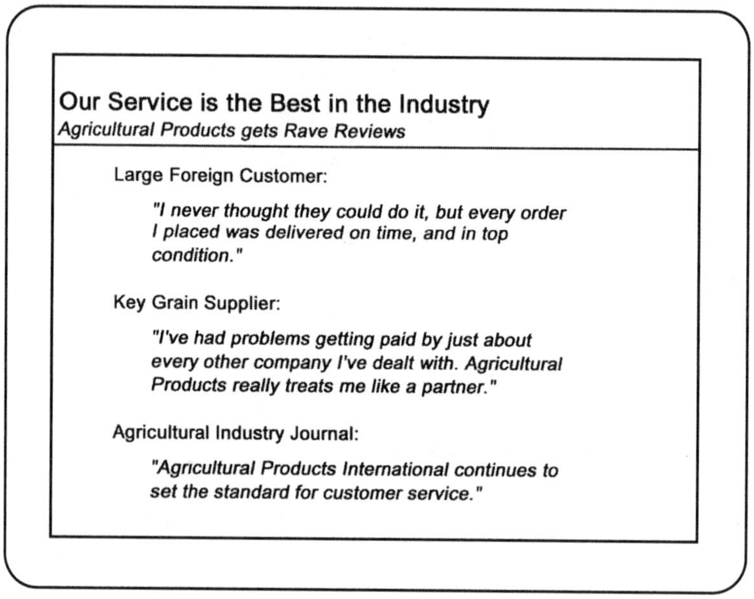

*I*talics should be combined with boldface. Italic text tends to be lighter than even plain text and disappears into the slide.

Our Service is the Best in the Industry
Agricultural Products gets Rave Reviews

Large Foreign Customer:

> *"I never thought they could do it, but every order I placed was delivered on time, and in top condition."*

Key Grain Supplier:

> *"I've had problems getting paid by just about every other company I've dealt with. Agricultural Products really treats me like a partner."*

Agricultural Industry Journal:

> *"Agricultural Products International continues to set the standard for customer service."*

Fig. 10.2   Using bold italics for quotes.

Use Bold for All Titles and Bullets

Slides usually are viewed from some distance, and most plain type tends to fade into the screen and become unreadable. Boldfaced text makes overheads and slides much easier to read. Use boldface for all titles, subtitles, and bullets. Be sure to apply boldface consistently.

Use Negative Leading for Multiple-Line Titles

Chapter 2 discusses negative and positive leading. The standard leading ratio used by Excel spaces most multiple-line text too far apart. The title block will look better if you use negative leading to bring the title lines closer together. The Format **R**ow Height command controls the row spacing, which affects the text leading.

Keep Slide Text to a Minimum

Slides should have a title and no more than four or five bullets or sub-bullets. Slides should not be narratives of the entire presentation. Use slides to emphasize main points and summarize concepts. Rely on your presentation and discussion to explain and elaborate.

Use Parallel Grammatical Structure

Grammatical consistency is very important in a professional presentation. All text should use the same grammatical structure. Bullets can start with a noun or a verb of any tense, but all bullets should use the same structure. Figure 10.3 shows a slide with nonparallel construction, and figure 10.4 shows a much more effective slide with parallel construction.

Agricultural Products Internation
Another great year for growing

⇒ **Sales are up in all categories**

⇒ **Working to expand on past successes**

⇒ **Develop plans for new products**

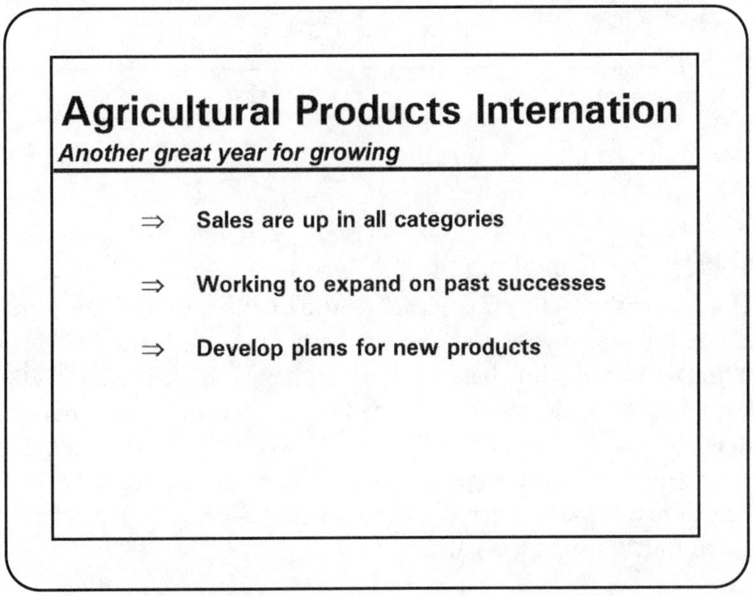

Fig. 10.3 Nonparallel bullet construction.

Reviewing Guidelines for Using Lines, Boxes, and Shading

Lines, boxes, and shading are essential to clear, organized slides. You should not overuse these elements, but they do add greatly to the effectiveness of any presentation. Lines, boxes, and shading offer an effective way to add structure and emphasis to a slide.

You can set off important text from other text or emphasize text with lines, boxes, and shading.

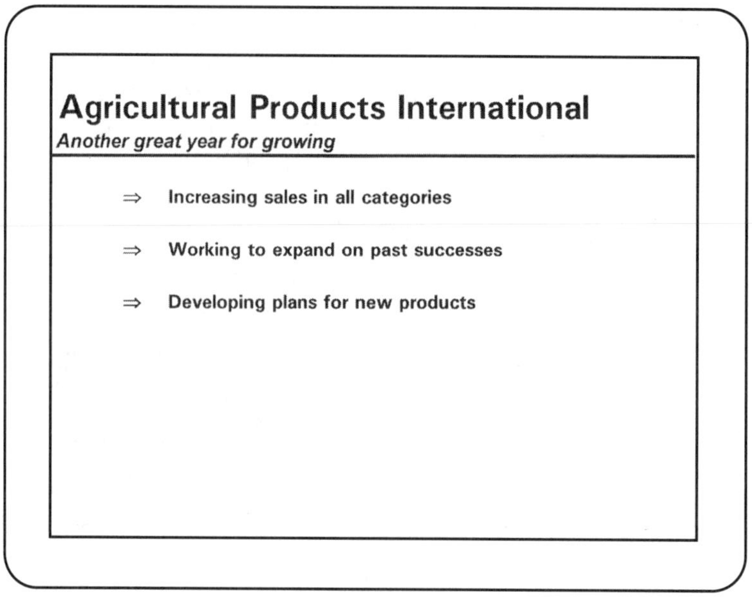

Agricultural Products International
Another great year for growing

⇒   Increasing sales in all categories

⇒   Working to expand on past successes

⇒   Developing plans for new products

Fig. 10.4   Parallel bullet construction.

Emphasize the Title of the Slides

Slides convey information better when the title is easy to locate and read. You can set off the title from the body of the slide with a box or a solid line or a dotted line below the title (see figs. 10.5, 10.6, and 10.7). You can add the solid lines and shaded boxes by using the Format Borders command discussed in Chapter 3. To create a dotted line, use a series of periods, each separated by a space. You need roughly 36 combinations of periods and spaces formatted with 24-point Arial (or another sans serif font) to span the page.

Use Text Boxes To Emphasize Important Text

Figure 10.8 shows a corporate mission statement in a text box for clarity and emphasis. This box was created using the Format Border command discussed in Chapter 3.

Use a Table To Emphasize Key Slide Text

The row and column structure of the Excel worksheet enables you to include tables in presentations. Simple rows and columns of numbers and labels, however, can be very hard to read. Adding lines, borders, and shading can greatly increase the clarity. You easily can create tables in Excel by using the AutoFormat feature discussed in Chapter 3. Figure 10.9 shows an example of an unformatted table, and figure 10.10 shows a formatted table created with the AutoFormat feature.

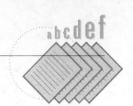

Key Title Text
Subtitle for additional information

⟹ **Supporting Bullet Point**
Explanatory text if necessary

⟹ **Supporting Bullet Point**
Explanatory text if necessary

⟹ **Supporting Bullet Point**
Explanatory text if necessary

Fig. 10.5 A dotted leader.

Key Title Text
Subtitle for additional information

⟹ **Supporting Bullet Point**
Explanatory text if necessary

⟹ **Supporting Bullet Point**
Explanatory text if necessary

⟹ **Supporting Bullet Point**
Explanatory text if necessary

Fig. 10.6 A wide leader running under the title.

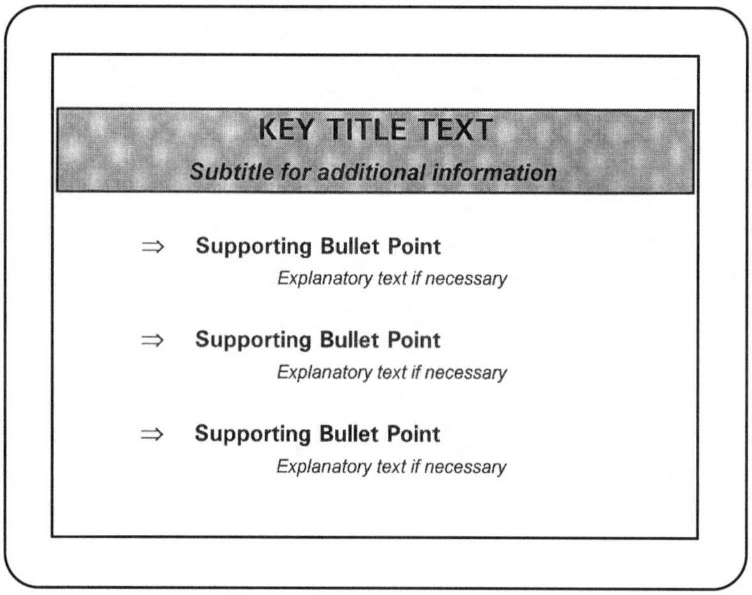

Fig. 10.7   A text box used for title text.

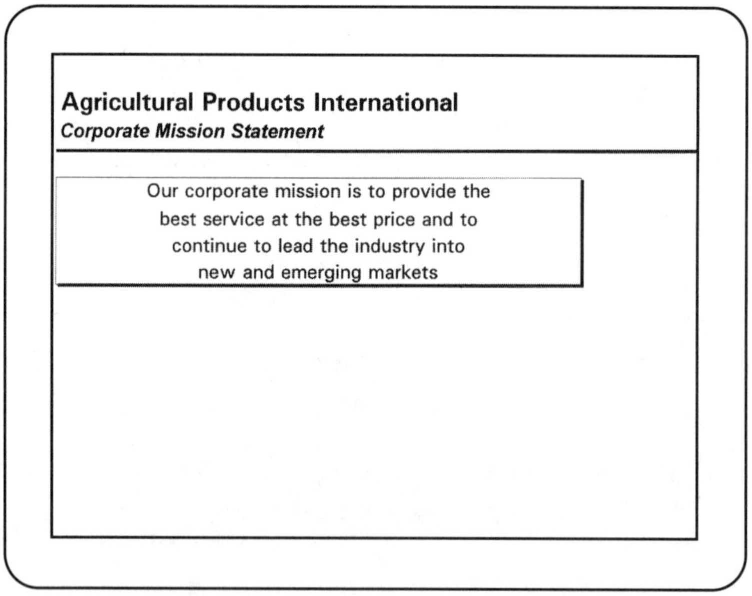

Fig. 10.8   A text box used for a corporate mission statement.

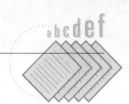

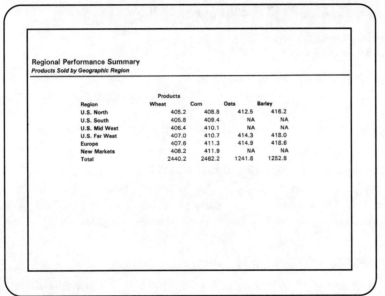

Fig. 10.9   A table with only basic formatting.

Fig. 10.10   A table organized with lines and shading.

Reviewing Guidelines for Presenting Graphics

Often, a well-designed graph can eliminate the need for lengthy text.

The saying *A picture is worth a thousand words* is especially true when dealing with slides or overheads. With the limited amount of text you can put on a slide, effective graphs become very important. Like text, graphics are most effective when used within certain guidelines.

Use Graphics To Explain the Key Point

The graphic should focus on the key point of the slide. You should not try to cover too many thoughts or points. The best graphics are clear, easy-to-read presentations of a single key point.

Use Text To Introduce and Explain the Graphic

A graphic should not be left to stand on its own. Use titles to introduce the key messages and to establish the context for the graphic. A graphic is more effective when its purpose is clear. You can use graphics with bullets to clarify or emphasize the points made by the text. Do not overload the page with too much information, however.

Position the Graphic To Balance the Page

Graphics, if not positioned carefully, will unbalance a slide and reduce its effectiveness. Position the graphic so that the overall page is balanced. Center the graphic if the slide contains little text. Position the graphic to the right or left to offset the weight of the remaining slide. Try changing the size of the graphic so that it is in proportion with the rest of the slide.

Use a Single Graphic per Slide

In most cases, a slide or overhead should contain only one graphic. The graphic may contain a chart that compares more than one set of data; do not include several charts, however. It is important to keep your slide from getting too cluttered and your audience confused and overwhelmed.

Add Visual Interest with Clip Art

Commercially available clip art can significantly improve a presentation. The numerous images available in these programs can be very useful in helping you develop a professional slide or overhead. The images in these programs cover a variety of subjects and you should be able to find

Commercially available clip art can significantly improve a presentation. The images in clip art programs cover a variety of subjects and you should be able to find a relevant graphic that will enhance your slide.

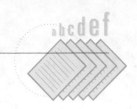

a relevant graphic that will enhance your slide. Again, don't get carried away by all that is available. Use these images sparingly and appropriately. Figure 10.11 illustrates how you can use clip art on slides. Chapter 6 discusses how to incorporate clip art by using the Windows Clipboard.

Agricultural Products International
Starting the New Year with a Bang

Fig. 10.11 A clip-art image.

Represent Concepts Visually with Diagrams

Presentations often introduce concepts to the audience. Graphics can convey these new ideas in a visual manner by using common objects to present the information. Look to your environment for metaphors that can effectively communicate your message. Building blocks can show the addition of new products over time. A person climbing stairs can characterize striving for a goal. A bridge can represent the joining of two separate entities.

Present Key Trends or Relationships

With Excel, you can create charts and graphs from data in worksheets that compare information or track trends. Often, it is easier to understand information presented in a chart than in a spreadsheet format. Be sure to limit the amount of information in order to keep the graphs simple. Figure 10.12 shows the effective use of a graph to present data.

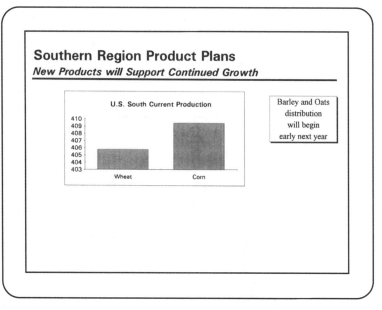

Fig. 10.12 Effective presentation of data using a graph.

Using Excel Color Capabilities

Excel enables you to format the worksheet with up to 16 colors for the foreground or background. Excel has 16 standard colors, or you can create your own colors. You can combine these capabilities to create an array of colorful presentations.

Creating Alternate Color Schemes

If the standard Excel colors do not meet your needs, you can replace any of the 16 standard colors with your own colors.

To choose your own colors, follow these steps:

1. Select **Options Color Palette** for worksheets or **Chart Color Palette** for charts (see fig. 10.13).

2. Click on the color you want to replace.

3. Choose **Edit** (this is not available on monochrome monitors).

4. Click in any area of the large colored box to select the color you want. To change the luminance, drag the pointer up or down the right column (see fig. 10.14).

xcel has a large se-
lection of sample
orksheets that have
stom color palettes
eady set up, which
can copy. You can
ss these sample
sheets from the
L\EXAMPLES di-
y.

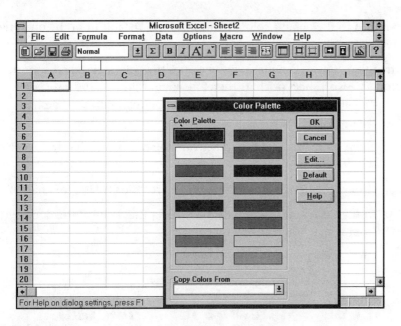

Fig. 10.13 The Color Palette dialog box.

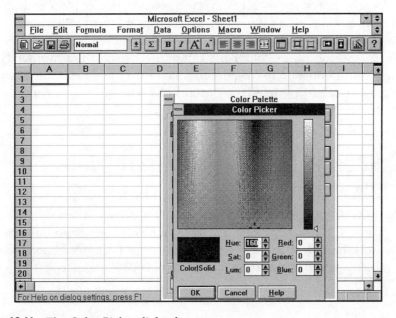

Fig. 10.14 The Color Picker dialog box.

5. Select OK to return to Color Palette. The color you created now is an option.

6. Select OK to leave Color Palette.

To return to the default color settings, choose Default from the opening screen (step 1).

When you copy a document, Excel carries the palette number—not the color. The worksheet or chart therefore assumes the colors associated with the target worksheet. To ensure that you maintain your desired color, follow these steps:

1. Open both documents and activate the document that will receive the palette.

2. Choose Options Color Palette (or Chart Color Palette for charts).

3. In the Copy Colors From list box, select the name of the document from which you are copying colors.

4. Choose OK.

Selecting Schemes for Black and White Printing

Color schemes can be useful even if you plan to produce black and white presentations. With most printers, Excel prints different colors in different shades of gray. If you use a black and white Postscript printer, you should choose the color Postscript printer driver. This driver sends the color information to the printer, which then translates it into shades of gray. Figure 10.14 shows the custom color scheme in approximate shades of gray.

Selecting Color and Patterns for Background, Text, and Graphics

With Excel, you can set the color of the cell background and the cell contents. This capability enables you to emphasize text or portions of the worksheet, or to add excitement to the worksheet. In addition, you can pick a pattern for your cell background. Follow these steps:

1. Select Format Patterns (see fig. 10.15). The Patterns dialog box appears.

2. To select a pattern, click Pattern.

   A pattern pull-down menu appears (see fig. 10.16). Click the down arrow in the pull-down menu to see more choices.

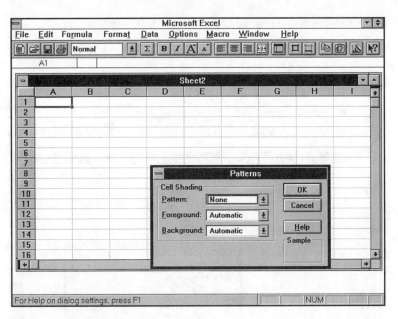

Fig 10.15 The Patterns dialog box.

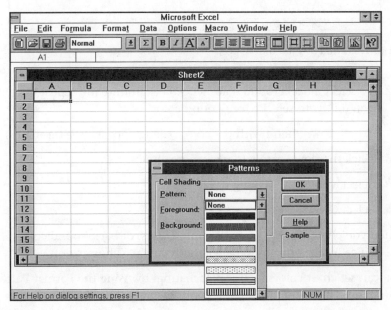

Fig. 10.16 Viewing cell patterns.

3. Make your selection by clicking it.

4. Click OK.

To select foreground or background colors, follow these steps:

1. To select a foreground color, click Foreground while in the Patterns dialog box (see fig. 10.17).

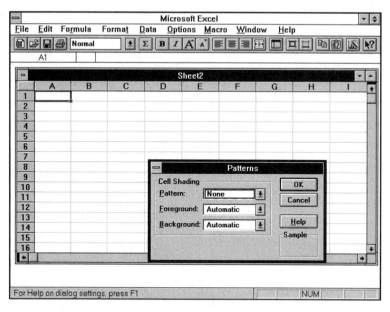

Fig. 10.17   The Patterns dialog box.

2. To select a background color, click Background and repeat the steps you follow to select a foreground color.

A pull-down menu with the color palette appears (see fig. 10.18).

3. Click the down arrow to view more choices.

4. Select a color by clicking it.

5. Select OK.

When you change patterns, foreground colors, or background colors, selected cells take on the characteristics you have chosen.

You can set chart colors in a similar manner by using the Format Pattern command. This command enables you to change chart colors and patterns rather than cell colors and patterns. If a graph is selected when you choose Format Pattern, a box appears from which you can change the border colors, graph colors, and patterns. The Automatic option returns your graph to Excel's defaults. Use the same steps you used to select patterns and colors for cells.

Some effective uses of these features are discussed in the next sections.

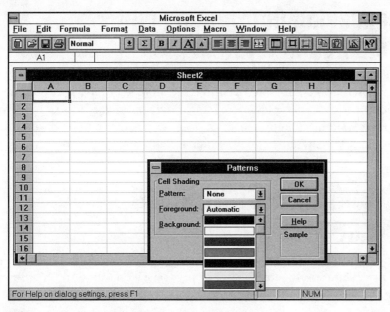

Fig. 10.18 Setting foreground and background colors.

Highlighting Elements with Color

You can use colors in many ways in a presentation. The most obvious is to use a different color for the key point in the presentation. You can implement color in several other ways, however.

Color can add to the organizational structure of your presentation. Choose consistent colors for different regions of the slide. Use blue text, for example, for the titles, red for the bullet symbols, and black for the bullet text. Or use different background colors for different sections of the slide. Using a standard color layout makes the slides easier to understand and more interesting to read. Be careful when selecting colors for a slide or overhead. Colors that look good on your screen may not look as good when projected. Yellow, for example, looks faded when projected. Remember that projected colors appear differently when shown in a dark room. If your presentation will take place in a dark room, use dark background colors and light-colored lettering. If you will be showing Overheads in normal light, you should use a light background and dark text.

B e careful when selecting colors for a slide or overhead. Colors that look good on-screen may not look as good when projected.

Conveying Information with Selected Colors

Color can add significantly to a presentation by adding information to the presentation. Standard meanings are attached to many common colors. The best examples are red, meaning a monetary loss or negative number, and black, representing a profit or positive number. You can use green to represent money or blue to represent gallons of water.

Creating a Structured Presentation

Most presentations start with an agenda of the topics to follow. You can tie a presentation together by repeating the agenda slide and highlighting the next item to be covered using a different color (see fig. 10.19).

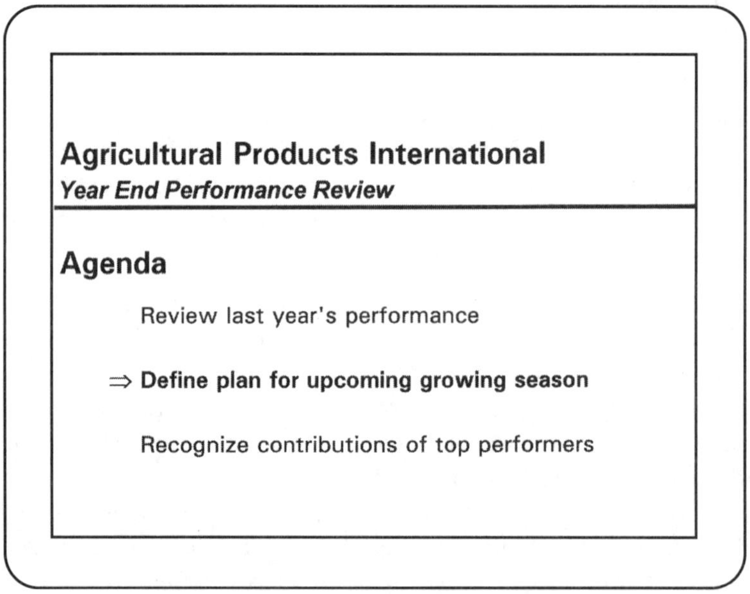

Agricultural Products International
Year End Performance Review

Agenda

      Review last year's performance

   ⇒ **Define plan for upcoming growing season**

      Recognize contributions of top performers

Fig. 10.19   Introducing the next topic on an agenda slide.

Setting Up Your Worksheet Area

Whether you plan to print your presentation or project it directly from the computer, setting up the work area is an important first step. The following sections provide many tips for creating a presentation in Excel.

When you prepare a presentation, the first step is to arrange the worksheet area to build the presentation. Then, if you are planning to project the presentation from the computer, you must modify the screen appearance so that Excel can display the slides without looking like a spreadsheet. The following sections tell you how to accomplish this.

If you are planning to project the presentation from the computer, you must modify the screen appearance so that Excel can display the slides without looking like a spreadsheet.

Using the Row and Column Structure To Assist with Layout

Creating a presentation in Excel is much easier with the row and column structure inherent to all spreadsheets. You can change the column widths and row heights as well as the row and column grid to customize your presentations. Row heights automatically change to fit the largest font in the row; occasionally, you may need to manually adjust these heights for a better appearance. The key to creating the slide layout is setting up the appropriate column widths for text, bullets, and graphics. Figure 10.20 shows a slide with the columns displayed in the worksheet frame.

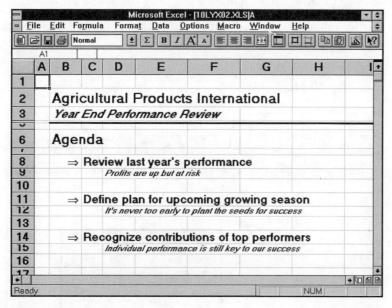

Fig. 10.20   A sample slide layout.

In this layout, the first few columns are critical to the overall layout. Table 10.1 contains the cell widths (the number of spaces in the cell) and descriptions of these columns.

Table 10.1   Slide Specifications

Column	Cell Width	Description
A	2	Space to separate the overall slide contents from the page frame
B	5	Space for the bullet symbols
C	3	Indentation for text below bullets

Modifying the Excel Display for On-Screen Presentations

You must modify the standard Excel screen to give it the look of a presentation graphics screen. The screen must be blank, except for the information you want to display. You can make the screen blank by hiding gridlines and column and row indicators, hiding toolbars, and modifying the workspace. You perform these modifications by using the Options command; these changes affect only the active worksheet.

To remove gridlines, row and column headings, and outline symbols, for example, follow these steps:

1. Select Options Display. The Display Options dialog box appears (see fig. 10.21).

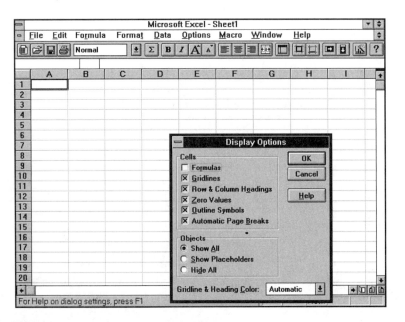

Fig. 10.21   The Display Options dialog box.

Any selections marked with an X will be displayed. If you click a marked box, the X disappears. If you click an empty box, the X appears, indicating that the option has been selected. The changes are for that spreadsheet only.

2. Click marked boxes to remove or add the various displays.

3. Choose OK.

The worksheet reflects your changes.

The following is a brief description of each option shown in figure 10.21:

Formulas	Enables you to display the formula in a cell, rather than the result when selected.
Gridlines	Enables you to display or suppress the spreadsheet gridlines.
Row & Column Headings	Enables you to display or suppress the spreadsheet column headings (A, B, and so on) and row numbers.
Zero Values	Displays blanks instead of zeros if it is not selected.
Outline Symbols	Displays outline symbols if selected.
Automatic Page Breaks	Displays page breaks if selected.
Show All	Displays all charts, drawings, and other graphical images if selected.
Show Placeholders	Displays charts and pictures as gray boxes.
Hide All	Hides all graphical images.
Gridline and Heading Color	Enables you to select a color other than black for row and column headings and gridline display.

To remove the toolbars, follow these steps:

1. Select Options Toolbars. The Toolbars dialog box appears (see fig. 10.22).

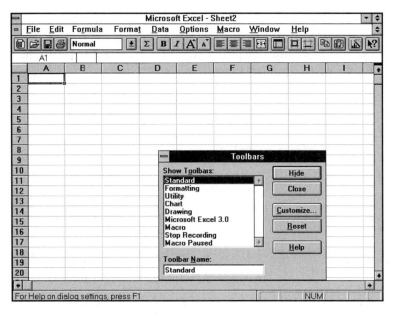

Fig. 10.22 The Toolbars dialog box.

2. Scroll through the toolbar list by clicking the down arrow. When you highlight a toolbar, select Hide to suppress the toolbar or Show Toolbars to display the toolbar in the Excel worksheet. You also can suppress toolbars by clicking the box in the upper left corner of the toolbar.

3. Choose Close.

The toolbar then is displayed, or it disappears, depending on what you selected in step 2.

To hide row and column information, the status bar, the information window, the scroll bars, the formula bars, and the note indicator, follow these steps:

1. Select Options Workspace. The Workspace Options dialog box appears (see fig. 10.23).

2. Click any Workspace items currently marked with an X under Display to remove them from the screen.

3. Choose OK.

The screen reflects your changes.

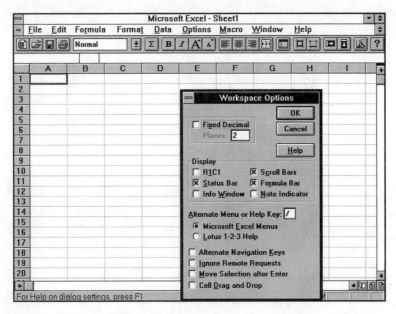

Fig. 10.23 The Workspace Options dialog box.

Selecting the Appropriate Font

Several factors affect your choice of fonts for presentations, including whether the presentation is for screen display or printing. If you plan to print only the presentation and have a PostScript printer, for example, you may want to choose from the PostScript printer fonts. If you will be presenting from the worksheet screen, you must limit your choices to fonts with screen images available in Excel.

The beginning of this chapter discusses several guidelines for choosing fonts. Although these guidelines are not hard-and-fast rules, they are important to consider when designing a slide page. Overall, it is important to use point sizes that are readable from a distance, as well as typefaces that work together and match the entire set for balance on-screen. Figure 10.24 shows a slide with font selections that work together on the page, while figure 10.25 shows a slide with fonts that do not follow the guidelines.

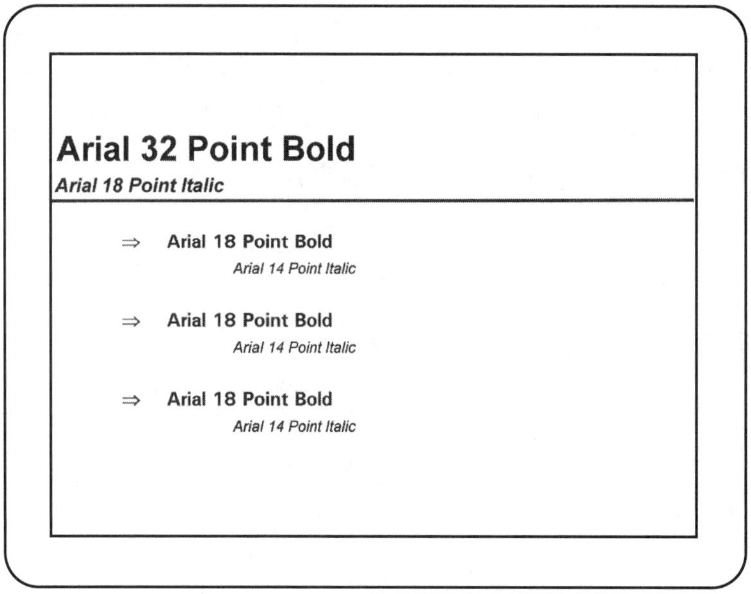

Fig. 10.24   A slide with fonts that work together for clarity of presentation.

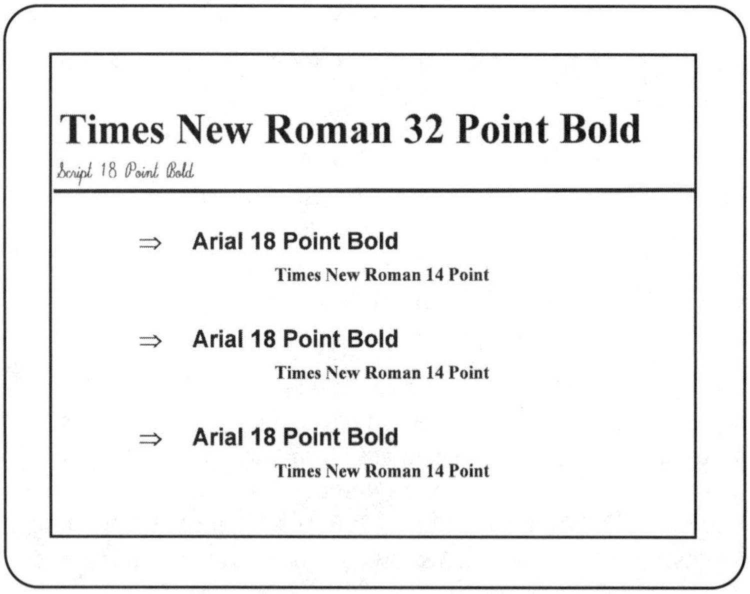

Fig. 10.25   A slide with fonts that make the slide hard to follow and understand.

Selecting Symbols

Text items often are preceded with a special symbol such as a diamond or an arrow. These symbols and many more are available in Excel (see fig. 10.26). The symbols font point size should correspond to the adjacent text.

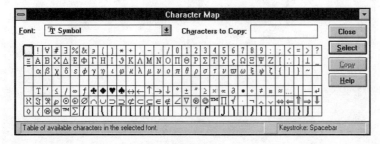

Fig. 10.26   Symbols available for Excel.

If you are using Windows 3.1 with Excel, you have two options for inserting symbols. If you are using Windows 3 you have only one option.

To select a symbol, follow these steps:

1. Select the cell where you want to display the symbol.

2. Format the cell with the Symbol format.

   Select Forma**t** **F**ont. Click the down arrow in the Font box until you see T Symbol (see fig. 10.27). Select this font.

3. Select any other attributes, such as bold, size, and so on.

4. Click OK.

   There will be no visible change in the cell appearance.

5. Press Alt while entering the symbol code (see Appendix B). Use the number keys on the 10-key pad. Numbers across the top of the keyboard will not work.

Pressing Alt while typing **0222**, for example, inserts the arrows seen in many of the figures used in this chapter.

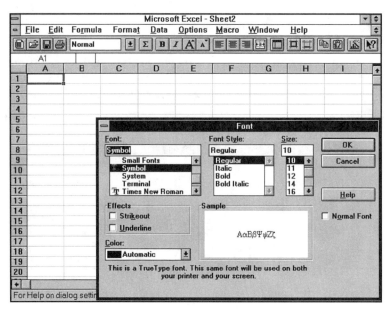

Fig. 10.27 Accessing the Symbol font.

To use an alternate method for selecting symbols in Excel 4 (with Windows 3.1), follow these steps:

1. Activate the Windows Accessories menu.

2. Click the Character Map icon twice.

   You can select the Windows Program Manager by pressing Alt+Tab. (You may have to press Alt+Tab a few times to reach the Program Manager.) Select Window from the Top Line menu. Select 1 Accessories.

3. Select the symbol you want by double-clicking it or by choosing Select.

4. Select Copy. This option places the symbol in the Clipboard.

5. Select Close to return to the Excel worksheet. You may have to press Alt+Tab to display and return to the active spreadsheet.

6. Select a cell and paste the symbol with the Edit Paste command.

Using the Graph Commands To Add Impact

Slide presentations come alive when they include graphic images. The Excel Graph commands discussed in Chapters 5 and 6 provide a vast

array of capabilities for adding graphs, clip art, and freehand drawings to presentations. Graphs and graphic images can make slides easier to understand by presenting the information in pictures, relating the text to common images, or providing visually interesting breaks in the presentation.

An effective slide to present worksheet data may include the key conclusions drawn from the data and a graph that supports these conclusions. Figure 10.28 shows just such a graph.

Tables of data seldom are effective in slide presentations, and in most cases should be supplemented or replaced by graphs and charts.

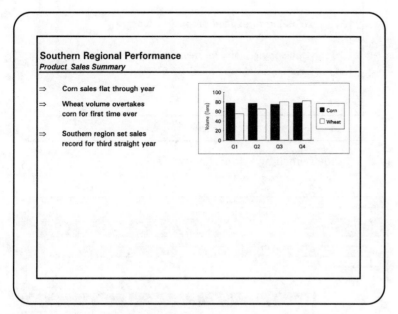

Fig. 10.28 An Excel chart added to a slide.

Page borders can help to frame a slide on the page. Figure 10.29 was created using the Format Border command discussed in Chapter 3.

Printing Slides from Excel

Most presentations are printed for distribution or for duplication onto overheads or slides. After you create the screens, you easily can format them for printing by using the File Page Setup command to access the Page Setup dialog box (see fig. 10.30).

Fig. 10.29 A slide framed by a drop shadow.

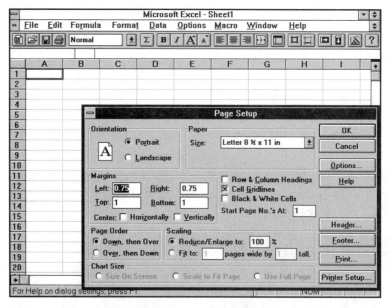

Fig. 10.30 The Page Setup dialog box.

B efore printing, view the slide by using the File Print Preview command to make sure that the slide meets your specifications.

Slides and overheads usually are designed to fit a Landscape orientation. Mark the Landscape option in the Page Setup box. To center your slide, be sure to select Horizontally and Vertically. A slide formatted to fit the screen area will not fill a printed page, because the screen is smaller than

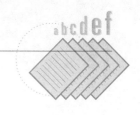

the printed page. To ensure that your slide will fill the page completely, try increasing the default size from 100% to 125% or selecting Fit to Page.

If you will be printing your work to files for later conversion to 35mm slides, be sure to contact the graphics shop you will be using to find out which file format you should use when saving your work.

Using the Excel 4 Slide Show

Excel 4 comes with a very powerful, easy-to-use slide show template that enables you to build an entire show that can be run manually or automatically.

This template enables you to control how slides are opened and closed with a variety of fade-in transitions. The template has a built-in timer to control how long a slide is displayed, it facilitates easy editing of slide order, and it even enables you to add sound to your program.

Using the Slide Show Template

You can create a slide show by using the slide show template, which you access from the EXCEL\LIBRARY\SLIDES directory. Follow these steps:

1. Select File Open. The Open dialog box appears (see fig. 10.31).

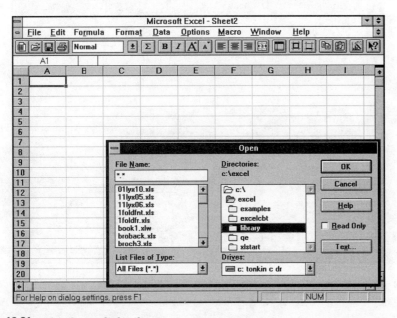

Fig. 10.31   The Open dialog box.

2. Double-click Library (see fig. 10.32).

3. Double-click Slides (see fig. 10.33).

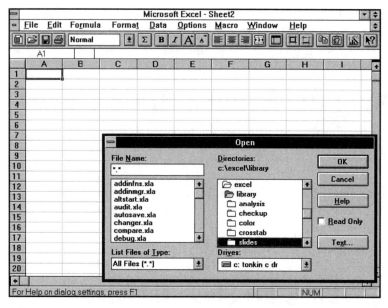

Fig. 10.32   The Library files.

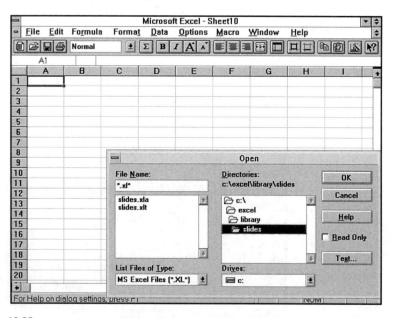

Fig. 10.33   Accessing the Slides directory and *.XLT files.

4. In the List Files of Type field, click the arrow to the right and display MS Excel Templates (*.XLT).

5. Select SLIDES.XLT by clicking it.

6. Select OK.

The screen in figure 10.34 appears for you to set up your slides.

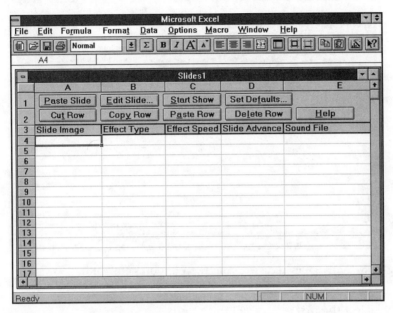

Fig. 10.34 The slide show template.

Creating Slides

You create slides by copying information from worksheets, charts, or other files to the slide show screen. To add a slide, follow these steps:

1. Open the file that contains the information you want in the slide by choosing File Open. Double-click the Excel folder in the Directories area to get a list of your spreadsheets. If you do not save your spreadsheets in the Excel directory, you will have to change to the directory where you keep your files.

2. Select the file to be included by highlighting it and double-clicking it.

3. Select the range you want to include in the slide. If you want the entire spreadsheet, you must highlight (select) the entire spreadsheet.

4. Select Edit Copy.

5. Select the **Window** command from the main menu; then select the slide show file (see fig. 10.35).

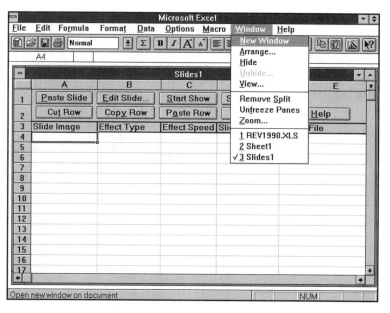

Fig. 10.35 Active files accessed from the Window command.

6. Select the first empty cell in column A.

7. Select **Paste Slide** from the Slide Show menu. The Edit Slide box with several presentation options appears (see fig. 10.36).

The Effect options enable you to control how slides will fade in. You have several options. Click the down arrow in the Effect box to see your options. You can see the effects in the test box when you select **Test**.

The **S**peed option controls how long the fade-in should last. The higher the number, the faster the transition. Click the right arrow to increase the speed and the left arrow to decrease the speed.

The Advance options control how slides are displayed. If you select **Manual**, you will advance slides by pressing the space bar on your keyboard. If you select Time**d**, you should enter how long you want Excel to display each slide before moving to the next slide.

You can add sound files to a slide by selecting Choose from the Sound box. The sound plays during the transition. You can purchase sound files, or you can create sound files on your computer with various sound software packages and the necessary hardware. The Test Sound option enables you to play the sound you included. Clear removes the sound.

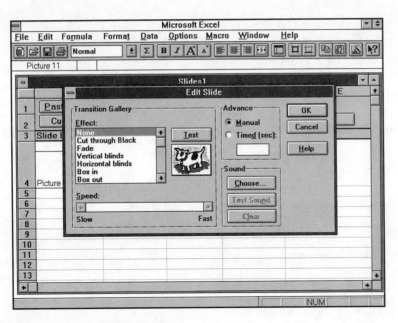

Fig. 10.36 The Edit Slide dialog box.

Editing Slides

After creating and viewing a slide show, you may want to make changes in a particular slide or change the order of presentation. You can do this easily with the Slide Show Edit feature.

You can edit a slide by selecting its row in the slide show worksheet and choosing Edit Slide. The Edit Slide dialog box appears, enabling you to make any necessary changes.

At this point, you can change the way slides fade in or out by selecting a new effect. You also can change transition speed or any of the other options described earlier.

Moving, Copying, and Deleting Slides

To move or copy a slide, follow these steps:

1. Select the slide you want to move or copy by selecting a cell in the row the slide is in. The Edit Slide box appears.

2. Choose Cut Row to move the slide or Copy Row to duplicate the slide.

If you choose Cut Row, the slide is removed from that row. If you select Copy Row, the slide remains in that row because it is being duplicated.

3. Move your cursor to the location where you want to move or copy the slide and activate that row.

4. Choose Paste Row.

The slide appears in the row.

To delete a slide, follow these steps:

1. Select the row containing the slide to delete.

2. Choose the Delete Row icon.

The slide is removed.

Setting Defaults

You can change the slide show defaults by choosing the Set Defaults command. The Edit Slide screen appears, but any changes made will be default changes.

Starting and Running a Slide Show

You can start the slide show by opening the file with File Open, selecting the file by double-clicking it, and then choosing Start Show after the file has been opened. If you have selected Manual advance for the slides, you will have to press the space bar to advance the slide. If you selected Timed advance, the slides will advance automatically, based on the time you selected for each slide duration.

To stop a slide show, press Esc.

Saving a Slide Show

You must save a slide show, just as you must save any other file.

Excel saves a slide show as a normal worksheet file. You should also save all files used to create the slide show if you want to use them later to update your slides.

If you make any changes to files used to create slides, the changes can be reflected in the slide. When you open a slide show, Excel asks you to update references. If you choose Yes, Excel prompts you to open any files related to the worksheet. This process updates the slides.

If you save the slide show as a workbook, Excel automatically retrieves and updates all slides.

Chapter Summary

This chapter discussed how to use fonts, background and foreground colors, shading, and other formatting features to create effective slides and overheads. You also learned how to use bullets, boxes, and other methods of highlighting text, along with guidelines for the effective use of charts and clip art.

You also learned how to transform your material into presentation form. After you complete your material, you can have a professional shop convert it to slides, and you can produce overheads on a copying machine.

The Excel 4 slide show template and presentation-quality projection equipment eliminate the need for slides or overheads. With the slide show template, you can create interactive presentations with features not achievable in a regular slide show.

The next chapter "Creating Brochures, Newsletters, and Other Promotional Pieces," tells you how to use different fonts, point sizes, and other formatting features to create professional-looking printed promotional pieces.

Creating Brochures, Newsletters, and Other Promotional Pieces

This chapter discusses how to combine Excel's row-and-column format with its powerful graphics capabilities to create effective, eye-catching brochures, promotional pieces, and newsletters.

Excel supports many of the desktop-publishing features found in dedicated publishing-software packages. Excel supports numerous publishing fonts and TrueType fonts. You can choose different borders for boxes, tables, and underlining. Excel also enables you to select different shading patterns and colors to use in your presentation material. Excel's powerful chart-generating capabilities exceed most desktop-publishing programs and can be used to drastically improve the quality and clarity of your material.

This chapter uses several examples to show you how to effectively use Excel's desktop-publishing features to create professional-looking promotional pieces.

Planning Your Promotional Pieces

I t is important to carefully plan your promotional pieces so that they will be as effective as possible.

Planning is critical to an effective announcement or newsletter, just as it was with the slides and overheads discussed in Chapter 10. In Chapter 10, you learned that your audience may have difficulty in analyzing and understanding slides, because your review of the data is limited to the time the slide is projected. Your audience also may find it difficult to read projected information. For these reasons, it is very important to select large fonts and limit the amount of information on each slide; this keeps projected material easy to read and understand.

The promotional material discussed in this chapter will be distributed on paper, so your audience will have more time to review the information and absorb the detail. You still may find it difficult to keep your information organized and easy to read, but you can include more detail in this type of presentation.

Figure 11.1 is an example of a promotional newsletter that contains a great deal of information. Figure 11.2 is the same newsletter, but it includes several of the desktop-publishing features present in Excel. Notice that in figure 11.1, your audience may find it hard to determine the purpose of the newsletter, find major points, and read the financial data. Figure 11.2, on the other hand, uses larger fonts and bolding to emphasize important information. The financial information is displayed in a table in a graph, which makes it easier to read and understand.

The following sections give you guidelines for achieving the professional look you want in your promotional materials.

News from the Breadbasket

Agricultural Products Quarterly
Newsletter

Second Quarter

Sales are up!

This year has been our best yet. Sales are up, and things have never
looked better! Let's keep up the good work and keep on going into the
future. We've got a lot of potential for success in the years to come.
Let's make sure we'll be taking advantage of it.

The most important news is that wheat has finally over taken corn as our
leading product. It shows what a little diversification can really do
when you put your mind to it.

I'd like to recognize our key performers this period: Dylan Jones,
Richard Pasternak, and Frank Franklin. They've been the key to our
success in the second quarter. Next quarter it could be you! So, let's
get out there and sell, sell, sell!!

Financial Results

Once again, revenues are higher than ever before. This is the best
quarter in our short, but great, history as a company.

As you can imagine, there have been a lot of pressures on the
harvest and on prices. But we're holding our own and will continue
to succeed In the coming years, we'll have even greater pressures
on revenues and expenses, but I have no doubt that we'll keep
growing as we move into the future.

Thanks again for your continued help and support, and thanks in advance
for the next quarter.

	Second Quarter	Year to Date	One Year Ago
Wheat			
Bushels	315160	542540	412654
$ per bu.	$3.24	$3.49	$3.31
Revenue	1,021,118.40	1,893,464.60	1,365,884.74

Fig. 11.1 An unformatted document that may be difficult to read.

News from the Breadbasket

Agricultural Products Quarterly Newsletter

Second Quarter

Sales are up!

This year has been our best yet. Sales are up, and things have never looked better! Let's keep up the good work and keep on going into the future. We've got a lot of potential for success in the years to come. Let's make sure we'll be taking advantage of it.

The most important news is that wheat has finally over-taken corn as our leading product. It shows what a little diversification can really do when you put your mind to it.

I'd like to recognize our key performers this period: Erin Smith, Mike Wolf, Stephen Tonkin, Al Ruiz, and Marilyn Mills. They've been the key to our success in the second quarter. Next quarter it could be you! So, let's get out there and sell, sell, sell!!

Financial Results

Once again, revenues are higher than ever before. This is the best quarter in our short, but great, history as a company. As you can imagine, there have been a lot of pressures on the harvest and on prices. But we're holding our own and will continue to succeed.

In the coming years, we'll have even greater pressures on revenues and expenses, but I have no doubt that we'll

keep growing as we move into the future. Thanks again for your continued help and support, and thanks in advance for the next quarter.

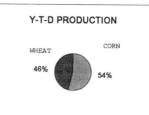

Wheat	Second Quarter	Year to Date	One Year Ago
Bushels	315,160	542,540	412,654
$ per bu.	3.24	3.49	3.31
Revenue	$1,021,118	$1,871,520	$1,365,885
Corn			
Bushels	273,610	457,350	442,674
$ per bu.	2.67	2.81	2.54
Revenue	$730,539	$1,270,734	$1,124,392
Total $	$1,751,657	$3,142,254	$2,490,277

Fig. 11.2 The document in figure 11.1, with several formatting features added.

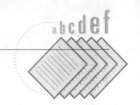

Avoiding Distractions with Simple Designs

With all the fonts, letter sizes, shading, borders, and other formatting options available, you may be tempted to overcomplicate your material. Remember to keep your material pleasing to the eye, easy to read, to the point, and not confusing.

The reader should be able to determine your message and key points quickly. Your announcements and promotional pieces should have one message only, and readers should not have to search for information.

Newsletters may contain more than one article, but each article should have one clear message. If you have more than one article, keep your titles consistent and use the same font and letter size.

Use the following guidelines to help create printed promotional material:

- Avoid widows and orphans in all your professional documents. A *widow* is the last line of a paragraph that appears alone at the top of a new column or page. An *orphan* is the first line of a paragraph that appears alone at the bottom of a page.

- Use only one banner for brochures and announcements. A *banner* is a title, which is the primary way you display the theme of your brochure, flier, or newsletter. It is important that each promotional piece have a single purpose or theme, and a banner should focus on that theme. More than one theme will confuse and clutter your material.

- Use larger type sizes and weighting to emphasize the title and subtitles.

- Keep your most important information near the top of your document. Readers tend to lose interest as they move down a page.

- Use a sans serif font for titles, subtitles, and headings. Sans serif fonts are harder to read than serif fonts, but they have a classic look that looks nice in titles or headings. Sans serif fonts also set the titles and headings apart from the text of the document, which you should put in a serif font.

Keep your material easy to read, concise, and uncluttered.

Avoid widows and orphans in all your professional documents.

- Use a serif font, such as Times Roman or Courier, for the body of text. Serif fonts are easier to read than sans serif fonts. It is especially important to use a serif font in the text of newsletters, which contain a lot of printed matter. A sans serif text will make the text difficult to read.

- Never print the body of text in all uppercase. This distracts the reader and is hard to read.

- Use different typefaces and emphasis to affect perception. If something is important, emphasize it with bold and possibly a larger font. Use italics to add a different effect. Be careful, however—too many fonts, type sizes, and styles will clutter a document and make it hard to read.

- Avoid underlining; it clutters the text and makes it hard to read.

Y ou should limit the number of fonts you use to a maximum of two or three.

Good balance makes a document easier to read and more effective. Keep your text columns generally the same width. If you include graphs or art, keep the size proportional to your typed text. Do not let your text overwhelm your figures, and do not let your figures overwhelm your text.

Add a professional touch to your work with clip art. Clip-art software packages contain pre-designed graphical images. These programs are relatively inexpensive, and you can use them in your Excel spreadsheets. A clip-art image probably is available for every need you can imagine. Chapter 12 discusses the addition of clip art to a document.

Color adds a professional, highly effective touch to your document. Color complements your shading and boldfacing. Select different colors or shades to differentiate titles, subtitles, and headings. Boxes and outlines also can be effective.

Be careful that you do not get carried away with colors. Too many colors can complicate a document. Printing costs also increase dramatically with each color. Chapter 10 discusses how to add color to a document.

F or one-page announcements and promotional materials, do not try to extend much beyond the limits of what you see on a full screen.

Organizing Your Message

If you use too much of the worksheet, you must use the File Page Setup command to condense the material to fit on one page (see Chapter 4 for more information). This makes the material cluttered and difficult to read. Don't be afraid of using white space. When used effectively, it makes your material more readable.

The File Page Setup command enables you to expand or compress your work to make it fit on one page (see fig. 11.3). You also can use the File Page Setup command to center your work horizontally and vertically and to suppress the gridlines in your worksheet.

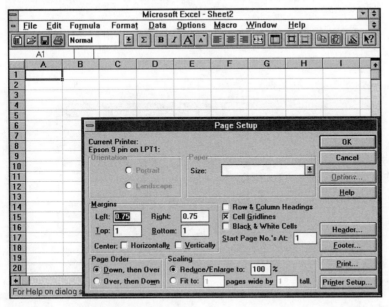

Fig. 11.3   The Page Setup dialog box.

The gridlines automatically displayed in Excel can be a very powerful tool in helping to create a balance and proportional document. By widening or narrowing rows and columns, you can balance and strategically place information in the worksheet.

You also can separate text columns in documents by including blank columns. Later, you can adjust the width of these columns to create the best possible spacing and look.

Excel does not print the grid unless you tell it to by choosing the File Page Setup command. For on-screen presentations, you can suppress the grid and row and column headings by using the Options Display command.

Proper alignment of text and titles is very important in creating a well-balanced professional document. Excel's Alignment command is easy to use and will be very helpful in this process. Use Excel's Format Alignment command to align titles and text in your document. With this command, you can control the horizontal position of text in a cell or range of cells. You also can control the vertical position of text in a cell. Because cell centering does not work on large titles, the Center across selection command probably is the most useful. It enables you to highlight a range and then center your text in that range (see fig. 11.4).

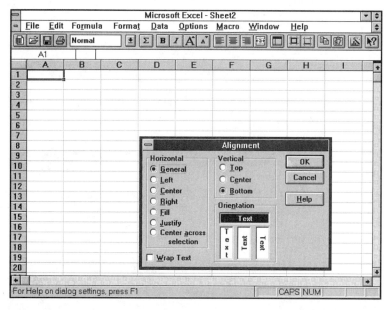

Fig. 11.4 The Alignment dialog box.

You also can use the Format Alignment command to turn on the word wrap feature in Excel (with the Wrap Text option). With word wrap, you can type information in a cell and have it wrap automatically to the next line.

The Format Alignment Justify option enables you to create justified text, generally making most documents look neater and more formal. You may want to leave your document unjustified if it looks better without even justification, or if it is harder to read when justified. Figure 11.5 shows a column of word-wrapped text that is not justified. Figure 11.6 shows the same column with even justification.

The biggest problem with cell word wrap is that the entire row height changes when text wraps to the next line of the cell. This may cause problems with row spacing in adjoining columns. A text box enables you to word wrap without changing row heights (see Chapter 3 for more information). Excel does not enable you to have full justification in a text box, however.

Emphasizing Important Information

Use the Format command to emphasize text in your document. The Format Font command enables you to change fonts, text size, and

weighting. The Forma**t B**order command enables you to draw boxes, underline, and shade areas. The Forma**t P**atterns command enables you to add different patterns or colors to cells (see figs. 11.7, 11.8, and 11.9). These commands are explained in Chapter 3.

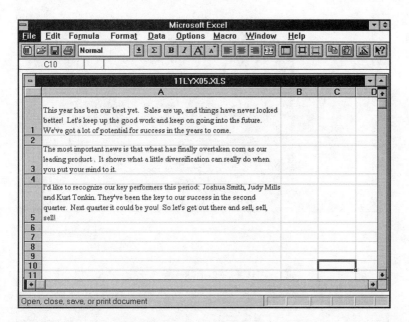

Fig. 11.5 Word-wrapped text with no justification.

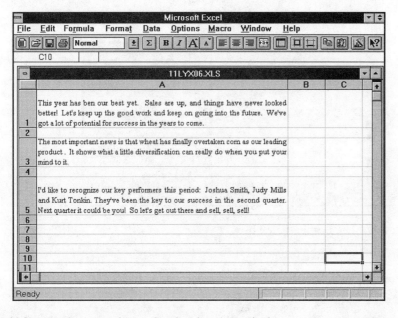

Fig. 11.6 Word-wrapped text that has been justified.

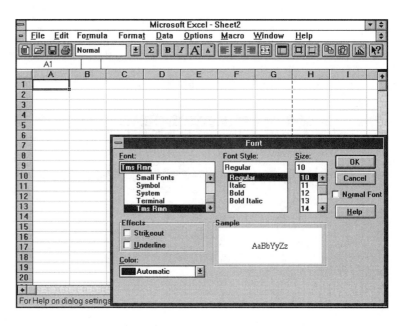

Fig. 11.7 The Font dialog box.

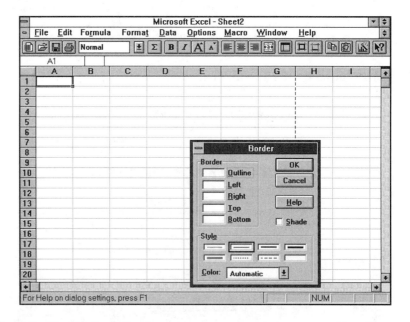

Fig. 11.8 The Border dialog box.

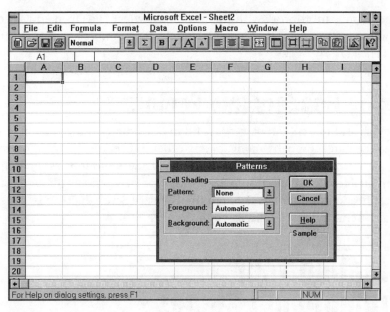

Fig. 11.9 The Patterns dialog box.

The newsletter in figure 11.2 was created using the Format commands. The fonts and text sizes were selected using the Format Font command. The boxes were created using the Format Border command, and the shading was done with the Format Patterns command.

Using One or Multiple Worksheets To Create Documents

You can create an entire document with one worksheet or multiple worksheets. You use page breaks to create multiple-page promotional pieces in one worksheet.

Because newspapers typically carry the same format from page to page, it is easiest to type the entire document in one worksheet. If the format of the pages will vary considerably from page to page, however, it is easier to create each page in a different worksheet and print each worksheet separately.

You can create a workbook by selecting File Save Workbook and naming the workbook. From the Workbook screen, click the Add tool and select Open to list all existing worksheets. Select the worksheets you want to include in the workbook, and they will be added.

When you use multiple files to create newsletters or promotional pieces, consider using the workbook feature of Excel 4. This feature enables you to save related files in one workbook file.

When you want to work with the workbook, select File Open and select Workbook Files from Files Types. Highlight the workbook to retrieve it and click OK.

Using Headers and Footers

Headers and footers can be very useful in documents you create. If you need the date, company name, or any other information printed on the top or bottom of every page, for example, headers and footers can help. Both enable you to select different fonts, type sizes, and attributes. You select headers and footers through the File Page Setup dialog box. Headers and footers are discussed in Chapter 4.

Creating Your Promotional Pieces

In this section, you learn the various approaches you can take in creating your promotional materials. You will review several layouts: two- and three-column newsletters, two- and three-fold brochures, and some basic fliers. These types of promotional materials are fairly representative of the type of material that you can create in Excel.

Determining the Layout

Layouts will change with the different promotional pieces you create. The layout you choose will depend on the amount of material you have to present and an analysis of the most effective way of presenting your information. A discussion of various layouts follows, along with samples of newsletters, brochures, and other promotional pieces.

- *Newspapers* typically have considerably more text than other documents and should be laid out in a word-wrapped column format.

- *Brochures* also use a column format, but they normally have less text than newspapers. They have more bullets, boxes, graphics, and highlights. Brochures also must be designed to be folded for mailings.

- *One-page announcements or fliers* should be laid out in a balanced pattern with many bullets, boxes, and highlights.

The following sections discuss some general guidelines to follow when developing a layout for brochures, promotional pieces, and newsletters.

Creating Effective Newsletters

Figures 11.10 and 11.11 show examples of two newsletters. A newspaper should have a large opening banner with the name of the publication. This title should cover the entire top of the first page and have the largest text in the publication (usually 24 point). A creative font often is used, and the information usually is boldfaced. A smaller subtitle frequently is included to give information on who is publishing the paper and how often it is published. The title may be outlined with a box or underlined.

If you have a central theme to the publication, include a smaller subtitle (18 point). You can use italics to offset article or topic headings, which also should be boldfaced like all titles.

Most newsletters are two or three columns of 10 or 12 point text. Figure 11.10 shows an example of a three-column format, and figure 11.11 shows an example of a two-column format. Before typing your columns, create either two columns or three columns, with a small column (gutter) between each column of text to separate the text.

If you plan to use graphics, tables, or boxes in your newsletter, be sure to allocate space for the graphic as you set up your document.

Fig. 11.12 shows how the newsletter in figure 11.2 looks on-screen.

Creating Effective Brochures and Other Promotional Pieces

A one- or two-fold brochure is a common promotional piece. Brochures are set up in a columnar format similar to a newspaper, but brochures must be folded. A two-fold brochure will have three columns of text with a gutter between each text column for folding. These brochures usually are printed on 8 1/2-by-11-inch paper in Landscape mode. Figures 11.13 and 11.14 show the front and back of a two-fold brochure; figures 11.15 and 11.16 show the front and back of a one-fold brochure.

Newsletters usally are set up in a three-column format. However, two-column formats also are common. A three-column format usually looks better, but often is harder to set up and edit. If you don't have a lot of text, a two-column newsletter with a slightly larger than normal font will look good.

News from the Breadbasket

Agricultural Products Quarterly Newsletter

Second Quarter   Volume 24

Sales are up!

This year has been our best yet. Sales are up, and things have never looked better! Let's keep up the good work and keep on going into the future. We've got a lot of potential for success in the years to come. Let's make sure we'll be taking advantage of it.

The most important news is that wheat has finally over-taken corn as our leading product. It shows what a little diversification can really do when you put your mind to it.

I'd like to recognize our key performers this period: Erin Mike Wolf, Smith, Stephen Tonkin, Al Ruiz and Marilyn Mills. They've been the key to our success in the second quarter. Next quarter it could be you! So, let's get out there and sell, sell, sell!!

Financial Results

Once again, revenues are higher than ever before. This is the best quarter in our short, but great, history as a company. As you can imagine, there have been a lot of pressures on the harvest and on prices. But we're holding our own and will continue to succeed.

In the coming years, we'll have even greater pressures on revenues and expenses, but I have no doubt that we'll keep growing as we move into the future. Thanks again for your continued help and support, and thanks in advance for the next quarter.

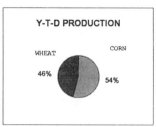

	Second Quarter	Year to Date	One Year Ago
Wheat			
Bushels	315,160	542,540	412,654
$ per bu.	3.24	3.49	3.31
Revenue	$1,021,118	$1,871,520	$1,365,885
Corn			
Bushels	273,610	457,350	442,674
$ per bu.	2.67	2.81	2.54
Revenue	$730,539	$1,270,734	$1,124,392
Total $	$1,751,657	$3,142,254	$2,490,277

Fig. 11.10   A three-column layout.

The Little Valley Quarterly

Volume V   **5th Edition**   **Fall 1992**

900 W. Littlewood Drive   Little Town, CO 80011   (303)555-5555

Produced quarterly for the residents of Little Valley Townhomes

What's New in the Valley

November!! Where has 1992 gone ??? We are entering the official Holiday Season, and we hope that all of you will have a great one!

Be sure and mark several dates on your calendar now! On December 1st we will have our annual Holiday Decorating party, and on December 14th we will have our annual Holiday Open House. Do plan to participate.

Thank you for helping and cooperating with the Halloween party. And thanks for giving treats to the tricksters. Hope everyone had fun!

We welcome those of you who are new to our community, and we hope that you can participate in our community activities so that you may meet your neighbors.

We thank again our maintenacne staff for helping things to run smoothly around here! If you have anything that you would like to have taken care of in your townhome, please call the office, and we will try and take care of it as soon as possible.

Have a great Thanksgiving and an extra special Holiday Season!

Agenda and Social Calendar

Nov. 1 -- Rent is due

Nov. 3, 10, 17 & 24 -- Office is closed, but clubhouse open for all residents

Nov. 9 -- Clubhouse reserved for a private party

Nov. 28th -- Office and Clubhouse closed Happy Thanksgiving!

Dec. 1-- Rent is due

Dec. 1 1:00 p. m. -- Holiday Decorating Party for all residents

Dec. 14th -- Holiday Open House from 11:00 to 3:00

Dec. 24th -- Office and Clubhouse close at noon and will be closed until 9:00 a. m. on Dec. 26th

HAPPY HOLIDAYS

Fig 11.11   A two-column layout.

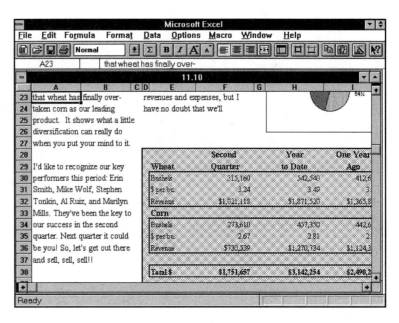

Fig. 11.12 A newsletter screen showing column width and row heights used to build the table and graphic.

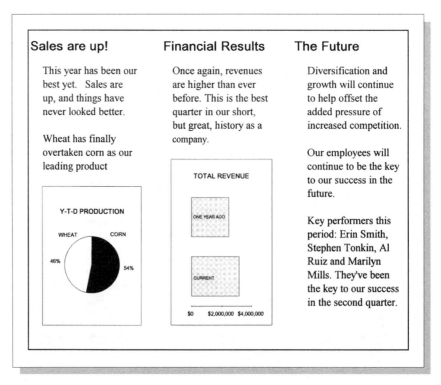

Fig. 11.13 The front cover of a two-fold brochure.

Performance

Second Quarter	Year To Date	One Year Ago
1,751,657	3,178,618	2,490,277

AGRICULTURAL PROD.
1000 MAIN STREET
DENVER , CO. 80000

NEWS FROM THE
BREADBASKET

Fig. 11.14 The back cover of a 2-fold brochure.

A one-fold brochure can have as many columns as you want, but it must be a length of one-half page only. These brochures are printed on 8 1/2-by-11-inch paper, but usually in Portrait mode (see figs. 11.15 and 11.16). Each page is made up of two half-pages with enough space between for folding. A one-fold brochure can be done in Landscape mode for a book-like appearance.

Figure 11.17 shows how row height, column width, and text typed vertically appear on-screen for the brochure in figure 11.14. You can set up the vertical text by selecting text orientation in the Format Alignment dialog box.

Like newspapers, a brochure must be planned. When setting up the worksheet, be sure to leave room for any graphics, boxes, or lines.

One-page announcements and brochures are the easiest to set up. Keep your design to approximately one page so that you do not have to shrink your text when you print.

To create a shaded box appearance, select the range you want for the box and then select the Format Border command. Choose Outline, the style of border you want, and mark the box for shading, if it is not already selected.

To create the shadow effect, use the Drop Shadow tool on the Drawing toolbar. Highlight the text you want to shadow, and then click the Drop Shadow tool.

Keep your design for announcements and brochures to one page.

AGRICULTURAL PRODUCTS

QUARTERLY HIGHLIGHTS

Published Quarterly by Robert Mills Company
The Agricultural Consultants

Wheat	Second Quarter	Year to Date	One Year Ago
Bushels	315,160	542,540	412,654
$ per bu	3.24	3.49	3.31
Revenue	$1,021,118	$1,893,465	$1,365,885
Corn			
Bushels	273,610	457,350	442,674
$ per bu	2.67	2.81	2.54
Revenue	$730,539	$1,285,154	$1,124,392
Total $	$1,751,657	$3,178,618	$2,490,277

Fig. 11.15   The front cover of a one-fold brochure.

SALES ARE UP !

This year has been our best yet.   Sales are up, and things have never looked better.

Wheat has finally overtaken corn as our leading product.

Once again, revenues are higher than ever before. This is the best quarter in our short, but great, history as a company.

THE FUTURE

Diversification and growth will continue to help offset the added pressure of increased competition.

Our employees will continue to be the key to our success in the future.

Erin Smith, Stephen Tonkin, Al Ruiz and Marilyn Mills. They've been the key to our success in the second quarter.

Fig. 11.16   The back cover of a one-fold brochure.

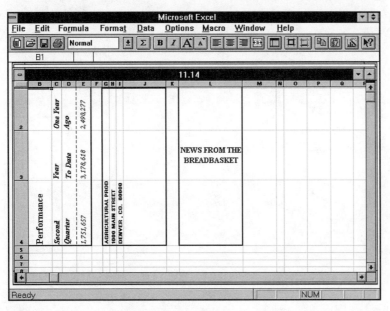

Fig. 11.17 Vertical text layout, column width, and row height for a two-fold brochure.

Chapter Summary

Excel is an excellent tool for creating newsletters and promotional materials. Its column-and-row format enables easy positioning of text and graphics. Its very powerful formatting capabilities enable you to use a variety of fonts and text sizes. In addition, you can emphasize text with highlighting, boxes, and shading. Excel's limitless color capabilities enable you to create very professional-looking color materials.

The next chapter discusses importing and exporting text and graphics from other programs. Excel enables you to import formatted text, data, graphics, and other information so that you can enhance your work and avoid re-creating data.

Importing and Exporting Text and Graphics

Windows applications have greatly enhanced the capability to import and export text and graphics from other programs. In some DOS applications you have the ability to import other program files if you can figure out complicated user manuals. For example, 1-2-3 enables you to import files with a PRN extension. If you don't know how to create that type of file, you must use the manual to figure it out. WordPerfect Corporation made conversion easier by including a conversion program with the DOS version of WordPerfect. The only problem with this approach is that you need to know how to run the conversion program.

icrosoft has made the import and export features of Windows applications much easier. Now you can much more easily take advantage of sharing information between applications. With Excel, you have five choices for transferring information between applications:

- If the file is in the correct format, you can open the entire file.

- You can copy a static picture of data, text, or graphics from one application and paste it into another. If the data changes in the source application, the client application (target application) will not change.

- You can link two applications. In this case, when the data is changed in the source application, it is updated in the client application.

- You can embed an object in an application. An embedded object retains all the information necessary to update the object from within the document in which it is pasted.

- You can use another program to translate the data and bring it into Excel.

With Excel, you easily can import an entire file or cut and paste pictures or text. If you want a bigger challenge, you can link your worksheet or chart to a word processing document.

Exchanging Documents with Other Applications

In some spreadsheet programs you can import files from other applications. In Excel you can accomplish the same thing by exchanging documents with other applications. All you have to do is open the document into Excel.

When you are working with text files, you can choose a character to delimit fields or columns of text, or you can separate (parse) the data later. A *text file* is a file consisting of nothing but the standard ASCII characters with no control characters or formatting.

To open a text file from another application, follow these steps in Excel:

1. Select File Open.

2. Choose the Text button on the bottom right of the dialog box (see fig. 12.1).

When you create a document in the word processor, make sure that you save it as a text file.

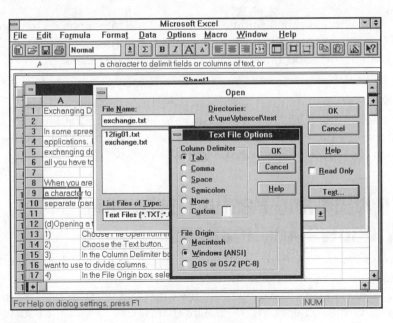

Fig. 12.1   Opening a text file in Excel.

3. In the Column Delimiter box, select the character you want to use to divide columns. You can choose from Tab, Comma, Space, Semicolon, None, or Custom.

4. In the File Origin box, select the environment the file came from. You can choose from Macintosh, Windows, and DOS or OS/2.

5. Choose OK.

6. Select the name of the file you want to open in the list files box. Or, type the file name and path in the File Name box, if necessary.

7. A message screen appears. Choose OK to open the file as text.

Using the Windows Clipboard

Using the Windows Clipboard enables you to copy data, charts, or objects from Excel to other applications. You also can copy data, charts, or objects into your Excel worksheets from other applications.

When you select data and then cut or copy it, Windows temporarily stores the data on the Clipboard. You then can paste the data into another document or into another location in the same document.

In some Windows applications, you also can use the Clipboard to paste links to documents. When you change the spreadsheet, it updates all the links to the other documents. This process is called *Dynamic Data Exchange (DDE).*

In Windows 3.1 and Excel 4, you can paste the worksheet and the instructions for updating the worksheet to another application. From the other application, you can launch Excel to make changes. This process is called *Object Linking and Embedding (OLE).*

Copying and Pasting between Windows Applications

If you want to copy from one Windows application to another, you can simply use the Clipboard as the intermediate location for the copy. The next step is to paste the contents of the Clipboard into the application to receive the contents. The document that is the source of the data is called the *server* or *source document.* The document receiving the data is the *client* or *target document.*

When you use the Copy and Paste commands, a static or unchanging picture of the document goes into the client document. When the data changes in the original server document, it will not change in the client document. Depending on the application and your copy procedure, fonts and formatting may or may not be copied.

To copy a static version of text, numbers, graphics, or other data from one Windows application to another, follow these steps:

1. Select the server application in one of the following ways:

   - Click the program icon.

   - Press Alt+Tab until the application title appears.

   - Press Ctrl+Esc and choose the application from the Task List box.

2. Open or move to the file containing the data you want to copy.

3. Select the text, numbers, or graphic you want to copy in one of the following ways:

   - Click the graphic or object.

   - Highlight the text or numbers by dragging the mouse or using Shift and your arrow keys.

W hen you use Copy and Paste, a static or unchanging picture of the document goes into the client document.

- Use menu choices to select the object or a portion of the object. Double-click an embedded chart, for example, to bring up the chart window. To select an entire Excel chart, choose Chart Select Chart.

- To copy a bitmap image of the entire screen, press the Print Screen key.

- To copy a bitmap image of only the active window, press Alt+Print Screen.

4. Switch to the application to receive the copy (the client) by one of the methods described in step 1.

5. Move to the area of the document where you want to paste the data.

6. Choose Edit Paste.

A copy of the source document appears in the client document (see fig. 12.2).

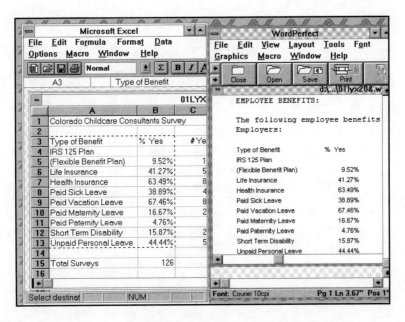

Fig. 12.2 Pasting Excel data into a WordPerfect for Windows document.

Copying and Pasting Notes for Excel

Each application may have additional enhancements or procedures for copying documents or portions of documents. In Excel, for example, you can copy the data or a picture of the data. If you copy the data, you can edit each portion of the data in the client document. If you copy a picture of the data, the entire portion of the worksheet is one unit. You cannot change the data, but you can manipulate the picture by using borders or moving and sizing the picture. Depending on the applications, the formatting (font and boldface, for example) of the server application may or may not appear in the client application.

When you copy a portion of the worksheet with the Edit Copy and Edit Paste commands, the resulting copy becomes a table in a word processing application such as Word for Windows or WordPerfect for Windows.

If you want a picture of an Excel worksheet, rather than the data, pasted into another application follow these steps:

1. When you are in Excel, select the range by highlighting the cells.

2. Press shift while selecting Edit.

   Notice that the menu choice for Copy now says Copy Picture rather than Copy.

3. Select Copy Picture.

4. The Copy Picture dialog box appears. Select from the following:

   - To copy the range as shown on-screen with raised column and row headers and the screen grid, select As Shown on Screen (see fig. 12.3).

   - To copy the range as it would print, select As Shown when Printed. The image will change depending on your printer setup options. You can show row and column headings and cell gridlines, for example (see fig. 12.3).

   - If you select As Shown on Screen, you also can select the format of the image. To copy the file in the Windows Metafile format, select Picture. Of the two formats, this is probably the better format, but see the client application documentation.

   - To copy the image as a bitmap image, select Bitmap.

5. Move to the application to receive the image by clicking the program icon, pressing Alt+Tab, or pressing Ctrl+Esc to bring up the task list.

6. Select Edit Paste.

When you copy a portion of the worksheet with Edit Copy and Edit Paste, the copy becomes a table in a word processing application.

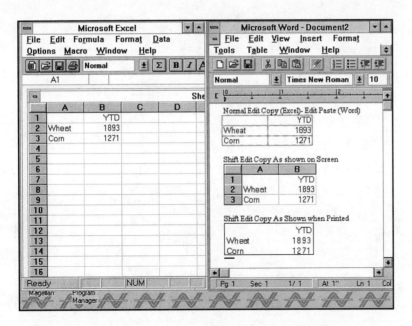

Fig. 12.3 Pasting a picture of an Excel worksheet into a word document using different options.

Some Windows programs (such as Microsoft Word, Excel, and Ami Pro) have an additional option on the Edit menu. You can use Edit Paste Special to tell the client document what kind of format to use for the source document as well as to link the documents. Identifying the format this way is another method of indicating whether the Excel worksheet is a picture or text.

Using Paste Link

If you paste data into a word processing document from a spreadsheet, you may want the spreadsheet data in the word processing document to be updated when you change the spreadsheet (see fig. 12.4). To accomplish this, you simply select the menu choice to link instead of paste.

To create links between applications, follow these steps:

1. Select the data you want to copy.

2. Choose Copy from the Edit menu.

3. Select the client application in one of the following ways:

- Click the program icon.

- Press Alt+Tab until the application title appears.

- Press Ctrl+Esc and choose the application from the list box.

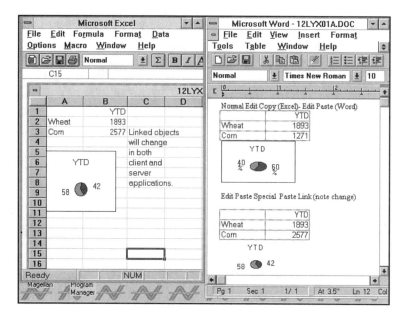

Fig. 12.4 Data in a Word document that is linked to Excel automatically updates when changes are made to the Excel worksheet.

4. Open or move to the file to receive the copy and move to the location on the document to receive the copy.

5. Perform the linking procedure in the client application. This procedure may be different than listed here, so check the application's documentation.

- For Excel, Ami Pro, Freelance, and other programs, select Edit Paste Link.

- For Excel, Ami Pro, and other programs, you have an option of identifying the server document type. Select Edit Paste Special, choose the document type in the list box, and select the link button.

Depending on the applications, you can double-click the linked portion of the client application and edit the document from the server application. In many client applications, this works when a portion of an Excel worksheet is the server. However, this does not work in many current applications when a word processing document is the server.

Depending on the client and server applications, you can double-click on the linked portion of the client application and edit the document from the server application. In many client applications, this works when a portion of an Excel workseet is the server. However, this does not work in many current applications when a word processing document is the server.

Using Object Linking and Embedding

Object Linking and Embedding (or OLE) is accomplished with the Edit, Paste Link, or Paste Special commands in Excel, and is available only if you are using Windows 3.1 or higher. Embedding is a way to directly access text, drawings, or presentations in another application without copying the information from one application to another. This exciting feature provides the flexibility to edit and format the information in the application you used to create it. If you embed an object in a document, you don't need to save the object as a separate file.

In addition to the capability of linking pictures and text, Windows 3.1 and Excel 4 enable you to link sound and videos to your Excel documents. This opens up all kinds of options for creating slide shows and presentations. To take advantage of the sound and video capabilities with Object Linking and Embedding, you must have a video card and a sound card. Some popular sound cards include Sound Blaster or Sound Blaster Pro, Media Vision's Thunderboard or ProAudio Spectrum, and IBM's Multimedia Audio Board.

To use OLE with Excel, you must be running both applications in Windows 3.1, and both applications must support Object Linking and Embedding.

Another way of linking an object is to embed the object with the instructions on changing the object directly in the client document. When you embed a document, you create a new document or *copy* information from an existing document. You cannot open a file once the embedded program appears.

Embedding an Excel Object in a Word for Windows Document

So that you can go to the Excel program directly from your Word document, you will want to embed the Excel object in your Word document. To embed an Excel object into a Word for Windows document, follow these steps:

> Embedding is a way to directly access text, drawings, or presentations in another application without copying the information from one application to another.

1. In Excel, select the range of cells or the chart you want to embed in the Word for Windows document.

2. Choose Copy from the Edit menu or the shortcut menu.

3. Access the document in Word for Windows.

4. Move the insertion point to the position where you want to embed the Excel object.

5. Choose Edit Paste Special.

   If you are embedding an Excel object in a different application, follow the procedures required in the application to embed an object. You use the Edit Paste Link command in Freelance, for example.

6. The Paste Special dialog box appears. Select the data type corresponding to the Excel object. In Word for Windows, for example, select the Microsoft Excel Worksheet object.

7. Choose the Paste button.

Embedding a Word for Windows Object in an Excel Worksheet

If you want to include a Word document within an Excel worksheet, you can embed the object. An embedded Word object appears as an icon with the Microsoft Word logo. You cannot see the embedded document on-screen or print it, but it may be helpful for references, notes, or a letter that should be attached to the document. To embed a Word for Windows object in an Excel worksheet, follow these steps:

1. Open the Excel worksheet to receive the document.

2. Open the Word for Windows document that contains the object you want to embed in an Excel document.

3. Select the information you want to embed.

4. Choose Edit Copy.

5. Access the Excel document by clicking the program icon, pressing Alt+Tab or Ctrl+Esc to see the task list, and selecting Excel.

6. Select the cell in the upper left of the range where you want to embed the new object.

7. Choose Edit Paste Special.

8. The Paste Special dialog box appears. Select Word Document Object.

9. Choose the Paste button.

The Word for Windows icon appears in your worksheet.

If you are embedding an object from a different application, follow that application's procedures for selecting and copying the information.

After you have embedded an object, you can view or edit that object by double-clicking it to open the source application and make any changes. Figure 12.5 shows some embedded objects.

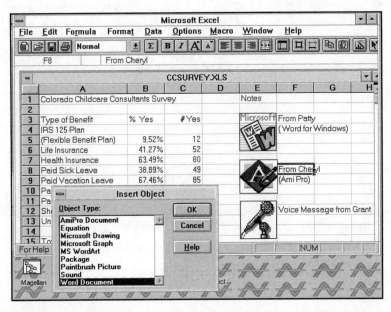

Fig. 12.5 Embedded objects from Word, Ami Pro, and Sound in an Excel worksheet.

Embedding Other Types of Information in an Excel Worksheet

Although you can embed certain types of objects by using the Edit Paste Special command, Excel 4 also offers the Edit Insert Object command to show you the list of server application types available. You can use this command if the document in the other application was not created yet. To embed new information in an Excel worksheet, follow these steps:

1. Move to the upper left cell where you want the embedded object to appear on the Excel worksheet.

2. Choose Edit Insert Object.

   A list of objects you can embed appears. This list is determined by the applications you have installed. The applications do not have to be active.

3. Select the Object Type you want to embed.

 In some programs, the Object Type command is on the Edit menu (Excel, Ami Pro). In other programs, this command is the Object item on the Insert menu (Word for Windows).

   Figure 12.5 shows object types available when you have installed Windows 3.1, Word for Windows, and Ami Pro.

4. Choose OK.

   The source application is started and a blank document window is displayed.

5. Create the information you want to embed in your Excel document.

6. From the source application in which you are creating the object, choose Close, Exit, or Exit and Return from the File menu (depending on your application). Or, click the OK button.

The object then appears in the Excel document.

WordArt is also useful for creating letterheads and logos.

The list of object types depends on the other applications you installed under Windows. The applications don't appear if you use File **Run** from the Program Manager to execute the program. The applications that come with Excel and Windows 3.1 are fairly limited. If you have installed Word for Windows, however, you can use some very helpful applications with Excel Word such as Microsoft Drawing, Equation, Microsoft Graph, and MS WordArt. Microsoft calls these programs *applets*. These applets are not stand-alone applications, but can be used only within an application such as Excel. You don't need Microsoft Graph because it is really a subset of Excel's Chart program. Microsoft Drawing, however, is a very useful tool and is explained in the following section. WordArt is also useful for creating letterheads and logos (see fig. 12.6).

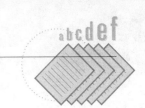

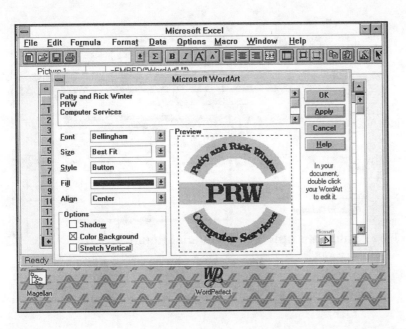

Fig. 12.6 MS WordArt enables you to manipulate text into interesting logos.

The type of objects you can embed depends on the applications you have installed on your computer. The applications that are shipped with Windows 3.1 or Excel 4 and installed through the setup routine follow:

> Microsoft Graph
> Package
> Paintbrush Picture
> Sound

If you use Word for Windows 2.0, you will see that Word Document is added to the Insert Object list (see fig. 12.7). The following applets also come with Microsoft Word: Equation, Microsoft Drawing, Microsoft Graph, and MS WordArt. Any other applications that support Object Linking and Embedding will be displayed on the same list.

Importing Graphics

When you are using Excel for desktop publishing, you may find instances where you would like to insert a graphic object into your Excel document.

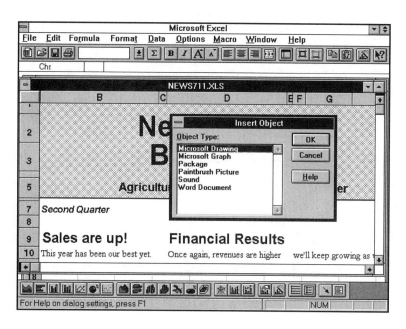

Fig. 12.7 List of available file types when you select Edit Insert Object within Excel.

If you are using other Windows applications, you can use the Clipboard to copy a graphic object into your Excel worksheet. You simply select the object in the other application and then paste it in the position you want it in your Excel worksheet. The Windows Clipboard translates only Windows Metafile (WMF) or Bitmap (BMP) formats.

Many clip-art packages are available on the market today. You can purchase one of these programs and then use the Object Linking and Embedding feature of Windows applications to insert the object into your worksheet. You also can create your own graphic objects using one of many graphics packages available. When considering what type of graphic file Excel can use, you need to understand graphic formats.

Three types of graphic files are available: raster, vector, and metafile. Even though there are three types of graphic files, you can create an image on a computer in only two ways. The metafile option combines the properties of the raster and vector files.

A *raster* file gives a description of the color of each possible dot in a picture. A raster file would be analogous to people in a stadium holding up different colored cards at predetermined intervals to create an image. When viewed from a distance, the pattern created by the cards gives the illusion of a picture.

Vector files are an assimilation of mathematically coded objects used to create a picture. It is up to the program that creates the vector picture to properly interpret the file and instruct the hardware how to display or print the picture.

Metafile files store everything in one file. These files can accommodate both raster and vector information, although software packages usually do not write both types of information to a metafile. Currently, most metafiles contain vector information only.

Using Microsoft Draw

If the application you have does not support Windows, or if you don't have the application installed under Windows, you may want to translate the file. You can do this through the Microsoft Drawing applet that comes with Word for Windows 2.0.

Table 12.1 shows the file formats that Microsoft Draw will import. Those files at the top of the list export better than those at the bottom of the list. Table 12.2 lists some of the programs that can export to these file formats. Any of the Microsoft Draw graphic filters listed will convert; however, the output may not be acceptable. If you choose a file with one of the following file formats, Microsoft Draw will import the file automatically. *Graphic filter* is another term for *graphics conversion*. A graphic filter enables you to translate a graphics file format to a file that Microsoft Draw can use.

Table 12.1   Microsoft Draw Graphic Filters

File Extension	File Format Name
WMF (preferred)	Windows Metafile
BMP (preferred)	Bitmap
PCX	PC Paintbrush
WPG	WordPerfect Graphic
TIFF	Tagged Image File Format
HPGL	HP Graphics Language Plotter File
CGM	Computer Graphics Metafile
EPS	Encapsulated Postscript
DXF	AutoCAD file format
DRW	Micrografx Draw format

Table 12.2 Acceptable Microsoft Drawing Formats for Exporting Graphics

Program	Export File Format
1-2-3 Release 2.x	PIC
1-2-3 Release 3.x	PIC or CGM
Arts & Letters	CGM
AutoCAD	DXF
DesignCAD	DXF
Designer 1.2	DRW
Designer 2.0	DRW
Diagram Master	HPGL
Dr. Halo II, III	WPG
DrawPerfect	WPG
Freelance Graphics	CGM
GEM Draw	TIFF
GEM Paint	TIFF
GEM Scan	HPGL
Harvard Graphics	CGM
Hijaak	WMF
HP Graphics Gallery	PCX
HP Scanning Gallery	PCX
PC Paintbrush	PCX
PicturePak	PCX
Windows (Clipboard)	WMF
Windows (Paintbrush)	BMP
WordPerfect	WPG

Follow the procedures for embedding new information in an Excel worksheet. Choose Microsoft Drawing as the data type. The Microsoft Draw application opens on top of the Excel window (see fig. 12.8). You then can choose the graphic file you want to embed in your document.

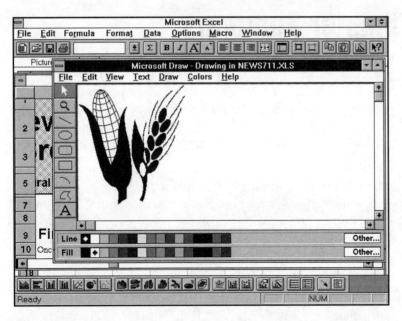

Fig. 12.8 A Microsoft Draw window open on top of an Excel worksheet.

To import a graphic file into Microsoft Draw, follow these steps:

1. Choose File Import Picture from within Microsoft Draw.

The Import Picture dialog box appears. The files you can import appear in the files box when you choose the directory where the graphic files are located.

2. To select a file, do one of the following:

- Type the complete path and file name in the File Name text box.

- Select the directory from the Directories list box and choose the file name from the Files list box.

3. Choose OK.

If the file is not formatted as a bitmap (BMP) or a Windows Metafile (WMF), Microsoft Draw will disassemble the image as it is imported. The disassembling process reduces the image to basic objects such as rectangles, lines, and ellipses. If Microsoft Draw does not recognize a feature, it will substitute the closest matching feature.

After you have imported the graphic file into Microsoft Draw, you can edit it using the features in Microsoft Draw.

To return to Excel, select File Exit and Return. When you return to Excel, you probably will have to resize the figure by dragging the small black rectangles around the edge of the diagram.

Sometimes, when reassembling the picture, Microsoft Draw will not make a very clear image of the original file. If that happens, try exporting your picture to another format or use the Clipboard feature.

Chapter Summary

When using Excel for desktop publishing documents, you have the opportunity to use some of the advanced features in the Windows environment. In this chapter, you learned how to open other document files while you are in Excel. In other programs, you must import a file to use it. In Excel, you can open the file directly from within the program. This capability makes it easier to convert data from other file formats.

A Windows feature that sometimes is overlooked involves the Edit Paste and Edit Paste Link commands. When you understand the benefits of sharing information between programs, you may realize the power of the Cut, Copy, and Paste options on the Edit menu of many Windows applications programs. Object Linking and Embedding (OLE) is a powerful tool that connects different types of information in your Excel worksheet and enables you to edit that information without exiting Excel.

The capability to import graphics directly into an Excel worksheet takes Excel past being a number-crunching program to being a spreadsheet, word processing, and desktop publishing program all rolled into one.

A

Glossary of Desktop Publishing Terms

alignment Definition of text edge: flush right, flush left, justified, or centered.

American Standard Code for Information Interchange (ASCII) See *ASCII*.

analytical graphics The preparation of charts and graphs to aid a professional in the interpretation of data.

area chart (or area graph) In presentation graphics, a line graph in which the area below the line is filled to emphasize the change in volume from one time period to the next. The x-axis is the horizontal axis, and the y-axis is the vertical axis.

ascender The portion of the lowercase letters b, d, f, h, k, l, and t that rises above the height of the letter x. The height of the ascender varies in different typefaces. See *descender*.

Arial A TrueType sans serif font. See *TrueType* and *sans serif*.

ASCII (American Standard Code for Information Interchange) A standard computer character set devised in 1968 to enable efficient data communication and achieve compatibility among different computer devices.

The standard ASCII code consists of 96 displayed upper- and lowercase letters, plus 32 nondisplayed control characters. Because ASCII code includes no graphics characters, most modern computers use an extended character set containing needed characters. See *extended character set.*

ASCII file A file that contains only characters drawn from the ASCII character set.

aspect ratio The ratio of the horizontal dimension of an image to the vertical dimension. In sizing a graphic, maintaining the height-to-width ratio is important in order to avoid distortion.

attached text In Excel charting, labels that connect from the worksheet to the chart. When the labels change in the worksheet, they also change on the chart. Text can attach to data points, the chart title, the x-axis, or y-axis.

attribute A character emphasis (such as boldface and italic) and other characteristics of character formatting (such as typeface and type size).

AutoFormat A new feature in Excel 4 that enables the user to format a highlighted range with built-in formats for titles, row and column headings, data, and summary data. The formats include a mixture of fonts, shading, colors, borders, and patterns.

automatic font downloading The transmission of disk-based, downloadable printer fonts to the printer, done by an application program as the fonts are needed in order to complete a printing job.

Avant Garde See *ITC Avant Garde.*

axis See *x-axis* and *y-axis.*

balance Effect achieved by positioning graphics, dark and light type, and other elements on a page relative to their weight. Do not put large bold type at the top of a page without something to counter it at the bottom. Heavy graphics often belong at the bottom, rather than the top of the page.

banner   A newsletter, newspaper, or periodical title, usually located in large type at the top of the first page.

bar chart (or bar graph)   A graph with horizontal bars, commonly used to show the values of independent items. The x-axis is the vertical axis, and the y-axis is the horizontal axis.

Properly, the term *bar graph* is used only for graphs with horizontal bars. If the bars are vertical, the graph is a *column graph*. In practice, however, the term *bar graph* is used for both. You should use bar graphs to display the values of discrete items (apples, oranges, grapefruit, and papaya, for example); use column graphs to show the changes in one or more items over time (for example, apples versus oranges in January, February, March, and so on). See *column chart, line chart, paired bar chart, x-axis*, and *y-axis*.

baseline   The lowest point that characters reach (excluding descenders). The baseline of a line of text is the lowermost point of letters such as a and x—not the lowest points of p and q.

bitform   A typeface, such as Peignot, that combines lowercase and small-cap characters to form the lowercase alphabet (see fig. A.1).

ABCDEFGHIJKLMNOPQRSTUVWXYZ
abcdefghijklmnopqrstuvwxyz 1234567890

Fig. A.1   The Peignot bitform typeface.

bit-mapped font   A screen or printer font in which each character is composed of a pattern of dots. Bit-mapped fonts represent characters with a matrix of dots. To display or print bit-mapped fonts, the computer or printer must keep a full representation of each character in memory.

Because the computer's or printer's memory must contain a complete set of characters for each font you use, bit-mapped fonts consume enormous amounts of disk and memory space. *Outline* fonts, however, are constructed from mathematical formulas and can be scaled up or down without distortion. Because outline fonts are considered technically superior, printers that can print outline fonts are more expensive.

bit-mapped graphic A graphic image formed by a pattern of pixels (screen dots) and limited in resolution to the maximum screen resolution of the device being used. Bit-mapped graphics are produced by paint programs, such as PC Paintbrush, MacPaint, SuperPaint, GEM Paint, and some scanners.

black letter A family of typefaces derived from German handwriting of the medieval era (see fig. A.2).

Black letter typefaces often are called *Fraktur* (after the Latin word *fractus*, meaning *broken*) because the medieval scribes who created this design lifted their pens from the line to form the next character—fracturing the continuous flow of handwriting.

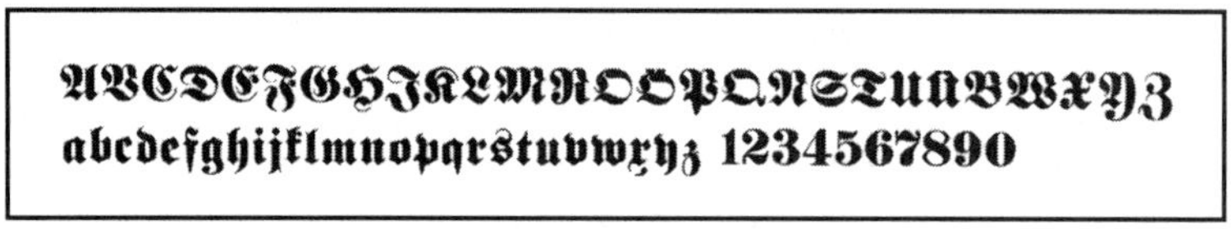

ABCDEFGHJKLMNOPQRSTUVWXYZ
abcdefghijklmnopqrstuvwxyz 1234567890

Fig. A.2 The black letter typeface.

bleed A photograph, shaded box, bar, or other element that extends to the edge of the page. Laser printed pages have a 0.3" margin and cannot have bleeds.

block graphics When working with IBM PC-compatible computers, graphics formed on-screen by graphics characters in the extended character set.

The graphics characters in the IBM extended character set are suitable for creating on-screen rectangles but not for fine detail. Because the block graphics characters are handled the same way as ordinary characters, the computer can display block graphics considerably faster than bit-mapped graphics. See *bit-mapped graphic* and *extended character set*.

body type The font (normally 8- to 12-point) used to set paragraphs of text (distinguished from the typefaces used to set headings, subheadings, captions, and other typographical elements).

Serif typefaces, such as Times Roman and Courier are preferred over sans serif typefaces for body type because they are more legible. See *display type*, *sans serif*, *serif*, and *Times Roman*.

boldface A character emphasis visibly darker and heavier in weight than normal type.

Bookman   See *ITC Bookman*.

brush style   A typeface design that simulates script drawn with a brush or broad-pointed pen (see fig. A.3).

ABCDEFGHIJKLMNOPQRSTUVWXYZ
abcdefghijklmnopqrstuvwxyz 1234567890

Fig. A.3   The brush style typeface.

build   In a slide or overhead presentation, when a series of slides combine to create the effect of adding points or parts. The first slide, for example, contains the first item of an agenda, the second slide contains both the first and second item of the agenda, and so on.

built-in font   A printer font encoded permanently in the printer's read-only memory (ROM).

bullet   An open or closed circle (•), about the height of a lowercase letter, used to set off items in a list. Bullets are effective for listing items with content roughly equal in emphasis or significance.

bulleted list chart   A text chart used to communicate a series of ideas or to enumerate items of equal weight.

camera-ready copy   A printed and finished manuscript or illustration ready to be photographed by the printer for reproduction.

cartridge   A removable module that expands a printer's memory or font capabilities.

cartridge font   A printer font supplied in the form of a read-only memory (ROM) cartridge that plugs into a receptacle on Hewlett-Packard LaserJet printers and clones.

Hewlett-Packard LaserJet printers rely heavily on cartridge fonts that have some merits over their chief competition, downloadable fonts. Unlike downloadable fonts, the ROM-based cartridge font is immediately available to the printer and does not consume space in the printer's random-access memory (RAM), which can be used up quickly when printing documents loaded with graphics.

CGA (Color Graphics Adapter)   A bit-mapped graphics display adapter for IBM PC-compatible computers. This adapter displays four colors simultaneously with a resolution of 200 pixels horizontally and 320 pixels vertically, or it displays one color with a resolution of 640 pixels horizontally and 200 vertically. The screen resolution produced by CGA adapters is inferior to *EGA*, *VGA (Video Graphics Array)*, and *Super VGA* adapters.

CGM (Computer Graphics Metafile)   An international graphics file format that stores object-oriented graphics in device-independent form so that you can exchange CGM files among users of different systems (and different programs).

Personal computer programs that can read and write to CGM file formats include Harvard Graphics, Lotus Freelance Graphics, and Ventura Publisher.

character   Any letter, number, punctuation mark, or symbol that can be produced on-screen by pressing a key.

character set   The fixed set of keyboard codes that a particular computer system uses. See *ASCII (American Standard Code for Information Interchange)*.

characters per inch (cpi)   The number of characters that fit within a linear inch in a given font. Standard units drawn from typewriting are pica (10 cpi) and elite (12 cpi).

chart   A drawing or picture produced from worksheet data.

chart type   The way data is represented in a chart. Excel has 14 chart types: area, bar, column, line, pie, radar, xy (scatter), combination, 3-D area, 3-D bar, 3-D column, 3-D line, 3-D pie, and 3-D surface.

ChartWizard   A new Excel 4 feature that provides a step-by-step approach to creating a chart.

check boxes   In a graphical user interface, a square option box that the user clicks to select or deselect an option from a group of options in a dialog box. See *dialog box* and *radio button*.

clip art   A collection of graphics images, stored on disk and available for use in a spreadsheet, page layout, or presentation graphics program.

clipboard   A temporary storage area used by Microsoft Windows compatible programs to copy or move text or images between areas of a document, between documents, or between programs.

column chart A chart with vertical columns. Column graphics commonly are used to show the values of items as they vary at precise intervals over a period of time. The x-axis is the horizontal axis, and the y-axis is the vertical axis.

combination column/line chart A chart that displays one data series using columns and another data series using lines.

compose sequence A series of keystrokes that enables you to enter a character not found on the computer's keyboard. In Excel, for example, pressing Alt and typing **0183** enters a bullet.

condensed type Type narrowed in width so that more characters will fit into a linear inch. In dot-matrix printers, condensed type usually is set to print at 17 characters per inch (cpi). See *characters per inch (cpi)*.

Courier A monospace typeface, commonly included as a built-in font in laser printers, that simulates the output of office typewriters (see fig. A.4).

```
ABCDEFGHIJKLMNOPQRSTUVWXYZ
abcdefghijklmnopqrstuvwxyz 1234567890
```

Fig. A.4 The Courier typeface.

crop marks Marks on a page or photograph that tell the printer how to trim the page or position the photograph. Some desktop publishing programs can print crop marks on the page automatically.

cropping Sizing a box to eliminate a portion of a photograph, image, chart, and so forth.

cross-hatching The black-and-white patterns added to areas within a pie, bar, or column graph to distinguish one data range from another. See *Moire distortion*.

cut and paste A fundamental editing technique in which a marked block of text, data, or graphic is cut from one location and inserted into another.

data point The intersection of an x- and y-value on a graph. The location of the intersected values determines the position for a bar, column, point on a line, or size of a pie slice.

data series (or data points) A set of data that becomes the basis for the points for one line, column, or bar series on a graph.

default font The font that the printer uses unless you instruct otherwise.

descender The portion of a lowercase letter that hangs below the baseline. Five letters of the alphabet have descenders: g, j, p, q, and y. See *ascender*.

desktop publishing (DTP) The use of a personal computer as an inexpensive production system for generating typeset-quality text and graphics. Desktop publishers often merge text and graphics on the same page and print pages on a high-resolution laser printer or typesetting machine.

DHP Dr. Halo PICT file format.

dialog box In a graphical user interface, an on-screen message box that conveys or requests information from the user. See *graphical user interface*.

dingbats Ornamental characters such as bullets, stars, and arrows used to decorate a page.

display type A typeface, usually 14 points or larger and differing in style from the body type, used for headings and subheadings. See *body type*.

dot leader A line of dots (periods) that leads the eye horizontally from one text element to another—for example, from a chapter title to a page number.

dot-matrix printer An impact printer that forms text and graphics images by pressing pins against a ribbon. Dot-matrix printers are fast, but their output is generally poor quality because the character is not fully formed. Some dot-matrix printers that use 24 pins rather than 9 pins have better quality output.

dot pitch The size of the smallest dot that a monitor can display on-screen. Dot pitch determines a monitor's maximum resolution.

dots per inch (dpi) A measure of screen and printer resolution that counts the dots that the device can produce per linear inch.

In expressing the resolution of display devices, the custom is to state the horizontal measurement before the vertical measurement. A Super-VGA monitor with a resolution of 1,024 dpi x 768 dpi, for example, can display 1,024 dots per inch horizontally and 768 dots per inch vertically.

downloadable font A printer font that must be transferred from the computer's (or the printer's) hard disk drive to the printer's random-access memory before the font can be used.

drop cap A large initial capital letter used to guide the reader's eye to the beginning of body text.

drop out type White characters printed on a black background.

drop shadow A shadow placed behind an image, slightly offset horizontally and vertically, that creates the illusion that the topmost image has been lifted off the surface of the page.

dual y-axis chart A line or column chart that uses two y-axes when comparing two data series with different measurement scales. Dual y-axis graphs are useful when you are comparing two different data series that must be measured with two different y-axes (dollars and volume, for example).

Dutch A serif typeface. See *serif*.

DXF AutoCAD file format.

EGA (Enhanced Graphics Adapter) A color bit-mapped graphics display adapter for IBM PC-compatible computers that displays up to 16 colors simultaneously with a resolution of 640 pixels horizontally by 350 pixels vertically.

elite A typeface that prints 12 characters per inch. See *pitch*.

encapsulated PostScript (EPS) file A high-resolution graphic image using instructions written in the PostScript page description language.

evocative typeface A display type design intended to evoke an era or place, such as the Bracelet typeface (see fig. A.5).

ABCDEFGHIJKLMNOPQRSTUVWXYZ
1234567890

Fig. A.5 The Bracelet evocative typeface.

exploded pie chart A pie chart in which one or more of the slices has been offset slightly from the others.

extended character set A character set that includes extra characters such as foreign language accent marks, in addition to the standard 256-character IBM character set.

facing pages The two pages of a bound document that face each other when the document is open.

flush left The alignment of text along the left margin, leaving a ragged-right margin. Flush-left alignment is easier to read than right-justified text.

flush right The alignment of text along the right margin, leaving a ragged-left margin. Flush-right alignment is seldom used, except for decorative effects or epigrams.

folio Printed next to a document title, the folio indicates issue date, volume, and number.

font One complete collection of letters, punctuation marks, numbers, and special characters with a consistent and identifiable typeface, weight (Times Roman or boldface), posture (upright or italic), and font size.

Technically, *font* still refers to one complete set of characters in a given typeface, weight, and size, such as Arial italic 12. *Font* often is used to refer to typefaces or font families, however.

Two kinds of fonts exist: bit-mapped fonts and outline fonts. Each comes in two versions: screen fonts and printer fonts. See *bit-mapped font, font family, outline font, screen font, typeface, type size,* and *weight.*

font family A set of fonts in several sizes and weights that share the same typeface.

The following list describes a font family in the Times Roman typeface:

Times Roman 10
Times Roman bold 10
Times Roman italic 10
Times Roman 12
Times Roman bold 12
Times Roman italic 12
Times Roman bold italic 12

font metric The width and height information for each character in a font. The font metric is stored in a width table.

footer   A short version of a document's title or other text positioned at the bottom of every page of the document. See *header*.

format   The style and physical arrangements of labels, values, and constants in a cell. Numeric formats include the display of decimal places, commas, and currency symbols. Alignment formats for labels include flush left, centered, flush right, and justified. Other formats include patterns and borders.

free-form text chart   A text chart used to handle information difficult to express in lists, such as directions, invitations, and certificates. See *text chart*.

GEM   GEM Draw file format.

global format   A numeric format or label alignment choice that applies to all cells in the worksheet. You can override the global format by defining a range format for certain cells.

graph   A drawing or picture produced from worksheet data. Also called *chart*.

graphic   A drawing or picture created or imported from another program and embedded in a graph or in the worksheet. Also called *object*.

graphical user interface (GUI)   A user interface that uses the mouse and a bit-mapped graphics display to make basic computer operations substantially easier for novices.

Standard features of the graphical user interface include alert boxes, a clipboard, desk accessories, the desktop metaphor, dialog boxes, scroll boxes, on-screen display of fonts, what-you-see-is-what-you-get (WYSIWYG) on-screen page representation, and multiple on-screen windows.

graphics mode   In IBM and IBM-compatible computers, a mode of graphics display adapters in which the computer can display bit-mapped graphics.

graphics monitor   A computer monitor that can display text and graphic images.

graphics scanner   A graphics input device that transforms a picture into an image you can display on-screen and print from various application programs.

gray scale   A series of shades from white to black.

grid, gridlines The series of lines that mark rows and columns on a worksheet. Another type of grid is a series of lines used to create a layout separating pages or portions of a page.

gutter The vertical space between text columns. Some designers use *gutter* to refer to the empty space in the middle of a two-page spread, and *alley* to refer to the space between columns.

halftone A copy of a photograph prepared for printing by breaking down the continuous gradations of tones into a series of discontinuous dots. Dark shades are produced by dense patterns of thick dots, and lighter shades are produced by less dense patterns of smaller dots.

handle In an object-oriented graphics program, the small black squares that surround a selected object, enabling you to drag, size, or scale the object.

hanging indent Paragraph formatting in which the first line extends into the left margin.

header Repeated text (such as a page number and a short version of a document's title) that appears at the top of each page in a document. See *footer*.

Helvetica A sans serif typeface frequently used for display type applications and occasionally for body type (see fig. A.6). One of the most widely used fonts in the world, Helvetica is included as a built-in font with many laser printers. See *sans serif*.

ABCDEFGHIJKLMNOPQRSTUVWXYZ
abcdefghijklmnopqrstuvwxyz 1234567890

Fig. A.6 The Helvetica typeface.

high-resolution output In typesetting, generally refers to a printing quality of 1,200 dots per inch or better.

histogram A stacked column graph in which the columns are brought together to emphasize variations in the distribution of data items with each stack.

HPGL Hewlett-Packard Graphics Language Plotter file format.

icon In a graphical user interface, an on-screen symbol that represents a computer function, a program file, or data file. Icons on the toolbars in Excel are called *tools*.

image recorder An output device that can capture images from the computer screen and record them on slides.

image scanner Hardware that converts photographs, drawings, or line images into computer-readable graphics files.

IMG GEM Paintbrush file format.

indentation The alignment of a paragraph to the right or left of the margins set for the entire document.

initial cap A large letter that indicates the beginning of body text. An initial cap can be dropped (inset) into the text, raised above the first line of text, or printed to the left of the body text.

italic A posture of a typeface that slants to the right and commonly is used for emphasis. See *oblique*.

ITC Avant Garde A sans serif typeface frequently used for display applications (see fig. A.7).

ABCDEFGHIJKLMNOPQRSTUVWXYZ
abcdefghijklmnopqrstuvwxyz
1234567890

Fig. A.7 The ITC Avant Garde typeface.

ITC Bookman A serif typeface frequently used for body type (see fig. A.8).

ABCDEFGHIJKLMNOPQRSTUVWXYZ
abcdefghijklmnopqrstuvwxyz
1234567890

Fig. A.8 The ITC Bookman typeface.

ITC Zapf Chancery An italic typeface that imitates calligraphy (see fig. A.9).

```
ABCDEFGHIJKLMNOPQRSTUVWXYZ
abcdefghijklmnopqrstuvwxyz
1234567890
```

Fig. A.9 The ITC Zapf Chancery typeface.

justification The alignment of multiple lines of text along the left margin, the right margin, or both margins. The term *justification* often is used to refer to full justification, or the alignment of text along both margins.

kerning The reduction of space between certain pairs of characters in display type, so that the characters print in an aesthetically pleasing manner.

label alignment See *alignment.*

label prefix A punctuation mark at the beginning of a cell entry that tells the program that the entry is a label and specifies that it should align the entry within the cell.

landscape orientation The rotation of a page design to print text and/or graphics horizontally across the longer axis of the page. See *portrait orientation.*

laser printer A high-resolution printer that uses a version of the electrostatic reproduction technology of copying machines to fuse text and graphic images to the page.

Alternative technologies include light-emitting diode (LED) imaging printers, which use a dense array of LEDs rather than a laser to generate the light that exposes the drum; and liquid crystal shutter (LCS) printers, which use a lattice-like array of liquid crystal gateways to block or transmit light as necessary. See *resolution.*

layout In desktop publishing, the process of arranging text and graphics on a page.

leading The space between lines of type, measured from baseline to baseline. Synonymous with *line spacing.*

The term originated from letterpress-printing technology, in which thin lead strips were inserted between lines of type to control the spacing between lines.

left justification   The alignment of text along the left margin only. Synonymous with *ragged-right alignment.*

legend   An area of a chart or graph that explains the meaning of the patterns or colors used in the presentation.

letter-quality printer   An impact printer that simulates the fully formed text characters produced by a high-quality office typewriter.

ligature   Two or more characters designed and cast as a distinct unit for aesthetic reasons.

Five letter combinations beginning with f (fi, ff, fl, ffi, and ffl) and two diphthongs (ae and oe) commonly are printed as ligatures.

line chart (or line graph)   A chart that uses lines to show the variations of data over time or to show the relationship between two numeric variables. In general, the x-axis is aligned horizontally and the y-axis is aligned vertically. A line chart, however, may have two y-axes. See *bar chart*, *column chart*, *x-axis*, and *y-axis*.

line spacing   See *leading.*

linked pie/column chart   A pie chart paired with a column graph so that the column chart displays the internal distribution of data items in one of the pie's slices.

Linotronic   Brand name of the best known PostScript compatible typesetting machines. The Linotronic typesetters print at 1,270 or 2,540 dots-per-inch resolution.

logarithmic chart   A chart displayed with a y-axis incremented exponentially in powers of 10.

logo   An identifying name or symbol, often designed for an artistic effect.

low resolution   In output devices, such as monitors or printers, the lack of sharpness produced by a display or printing technology that does not generate enough dots per inch to resolve an image fully. A low-resolution display, for example, displays characters and graphics with jagged edges.

Microsoft Windows   A windowing environment and application user interface (API) for DOS that brings to IBM-format computing some of the graphical user interface features of the Macintosh, such as pull-down menus, multiple typefaces, desk accessories (a clock, calculator, calendar, and notepad, for example), and the capability of moving text and graphics from one program to another via a clipboard.

mixed column/line chart   See *combination column/line chart*.

Moire distortion   An optional illusion, perceived as flickering, that sometimes occurs when you place high-contrast line patterns (such as cross-hatching in pie graphs) too close to one another.

monospace   A typeface such as Courier in which the width of all characters is the same, producing output that looks like typed characters. See *proportional spacing*.

multimedia   The presentation of information on a computer using graphics, sound, animation, and text.

nameplate   The name of an organization or publication that is set in a distinctive type that also can serve as a logo.

near-letter quality (NLQ)   A dot-matrix printing mode that prints typewriter-quality characters. As a result, printers using this mode print slower than other dot-matrix printers.

New Century Schoolbook   An easily read typeface developed for magazines and school textbooks (see fig. A.10).

ABCDEFGHIJKLMNOPQRSTUVWXYZ
abcdefghijklmnopqrstuvwxyz 1234567890

Fig. A.10   The New Century Schoolbook typeface.

newspaper columns   A page format in which two or more columns of text are printed vertically on the page so that the text flows down one column and continues at the top of the next.

numeric format   The way in which Excel displays numbers in a cell. You can choose from many options—including currency, percent, and date formats.

oblique   The italic form of a sans serif typeface. See *sans serif*.

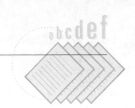

object (or object-oriented graphic)   A graphic image composed of discrete objects such as lines, circles, ellipses, and boxes, that you can move independently.

Object-oriented graphics often are called *vector graphics* because the program stores them as mathematical formulas for the vectors, or directional lines, that compose the image. Unlike bit-mapped graphics, you can resize object-oriented graphics without introducing distortions.

OCR (Optical Character Recognition) A hardware and software system that can scan printed text into the computer for editing.

one hundred percent (100%) column chart   A column chart that resembles a pie graph in that each column displays the relative percentage of the data item compared to the total.

organization chart   A text chart that you use to diagram the reporting structure of a multilevel organization, such as a corporation or club.

orientation   The way that text or graphics is placed on a page. In addition to being able to change the orientation of text on a page horizontally or vertically, with Excel you also can change the orientation of text within a cell. The normal orientation is horizontal; however, you also can orient the text vertically. See *landscape orientation* and *portrait orientation*.

orphan   A formatting flaw in which the first line of a paragraph appears alone at the bottom of a page.

Most word processing and page-layout programs suppress widows and orphans; the better programs enable you to turn on and off widow and orphan control and to choose the number of lines for which the suppression feature is effective. See *widow*.

outline font   A printer or screen font in which a mathematical formula generates each character, producing a graceful and undistorted outline of the character, which the printer then fills at its maximum resolution.

Because mathematical formulas produce the characters, you need only one font in the printer's memory to use any type size from 2 to 127 points. With bit-mapped fonts, you must download into the printer's memory a complete set of characters for each font size, and you cannot use a type size that you have not downloaded.

overhead (projector/transparency) A presentation device which is relatively portable and can project images from transparent sheets (transparencies, also called *foils*) onto a wall or portable screen. Some plotters and printers can print directly onto a transparency. Otherwise, you can copy a printed page onto a transparency.

overlay An image projected on top of another image. A series of transparencies can overlay each other to show change or progress. You may overlay an image of the muscles of the human body on top of the image of a skeleton, for example.

overstrike The way a printer produces a character not found in a printer's character set by printing one character, moving the print head back one space, and printing a second character on top of the first.

overtype mode An editing mode that enables you to enter and edit text; the characters you type erase existing characters, if any.

page layout program An application program that assembles text and graphics from various files, with which you can determine the precise placement, sizing, scaling, and cropping of material in accordance with the page design represented on-screen.

page orientation See *landscape orientation* and *portrait orientation*.

paint file format A bit-mapped graphics file format in graphic programs such as PC Paintbrush.

paired bar chart A bar graph with two y-axes.

Palatino A weighty, formal, serif typeface used for body type (see fig. A.11).

ABCDEFGHIJKLMNOPQRSTUVWXYZ
abcdefghijklmnopqrstuvwxyz 1234567890

Fig. A.11 The Palatino typeface.

palette A display containing a set of colors or patterns that you can use.

paste To insert text or graphics at the cursor's location.

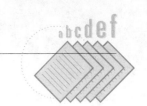

pattern The design of fill-in for cells and portions of charts (pie slices, bars, and columns). A pattern can be empty, solid, or a variation of dots and lines.

PCX PC Paintbrush file format.

PIC Lotus 1-2-3 PICT file format.

pica A unit of measure equal to approximately 1/6 inch, or 12 points. In typewriting and letter-quality printing, a 12-point monospace font that prints at a pitch of 10 characters per inch (cpi).

Picas usually describe horizontal and vertical measurements on the page, with the exception of type sizes, which are expressed in points.

pie chart (or pie graph) A chart that displays a data series as a circle to emphasize the relative contribution of each data item to the whole. Each slice of the pie appears in a distinctive pattern.

pitch A horizontal measurement of the number of characters per linear inch in a monospace font, such as those used with typewriters, dot-matrix printers, and daisywheel printers.

By convention, pica pitch (not to be confused with the printer's measurement of approximately 1/6 inch) equals 10 characters per inch, and elite pitch equals 12 characters per inch. See *monospace*, *pica*, and *point*.

pixel The smallest element (a picture element) that a device can display on-screen and out of which the displayed image is constructed. See *bit-mapped graphic*.

plot area The area of a chart where Excel plots data, usually inside the x-axis and y-axis.

plotter A printer that produces high-quality output by moving ink pens over the surface of the paper. The printer moves the pens under the direction of the computer, so that printing is automatic. Plotters commonly are used for computer-aided design and presentation graphics.

PNTG Macintosh Paint file format.

point The fundamental unit of measure in typography; 72 points equals one inch.

portrait orientation The default printing orientation for a page of text, with the longest measurement oriented vertically. See *landscape orientation*.

PostScript   A sophisticated page-description language for medium- to high-resolution printing devices.

PostScript, developed by Adobe Systems, Inc., is a programming language that describes how to print a page that blends text and graphics.

PostScript laser printer   A laser printer that includes the processing circuitry needed to decode and interpret printing instructions phrased in PostScript—a page description language (PDL) widely used in desktop publishing.

PPIC   PC Paint Plus file format.

presentation graphics   Text charts, bar charts, pie charts, and other charts and graphs, which you enhance so that they are visually appealing and easily understood by your audience. See *analytical graphics*.

presentation graphics program   An application program designed to create and enhance charts and graphs so that they are visually appealing and easily understood by an audience.

A full-featured presentation graphics package such as Harvard Graphics includes facilities for making text charts, bar graphs, pie graphs, high/low/close graphs, and organization charts.

The package also provides facilities for adding titles, legends, and explanatory text anywhere in the chart or graph. A presentation graphics program includes a library of clip art so that you can enliven charts and graphs by adding a picture related to the subject matter (for example, an airplane for a chart of earnings in the aerospace industry). You can print output, direct output to a film recorder, or display output in a computer slide show.

printer font   A font available for printing, unlike screen fonts available for displaying text on-screen.

process color   A standard color that does not require custom ink mixing.

proportional spacing   The allocation of character widths proportional to the character shape, so that a narrow character such as *i* receives less space than a wide character such as *m*. See *kerning* and *monospace*.

pull quote   A quotation printed in large letters to spark interest in an adjoining article.

radar chart   A chart that illustrates changes or frequencies of data relative to a center point and to each other. Each category has its own value axis extending from the center point. Lines connect all the data markers in the same series.

radio buttons   In a graphical user interface, the round option buttons that appear in dialog boxes. Unlike check boxes, radio buttons are mutually exclusive; you can pick only one of the radio button options.

ragged-left alignment   The alignment of each line of text so that the right margin is even, but the left remains ragged. Synonymous with *flush right*.

ragged-right alignment   The alignment of each line of text so that the left margin is even, but the right remains ragged. Synonymous with *flush left*.

raised cap   A large initial capital letter that extends above the first line of text. Raised and drop caps guide the reader's eye to the beginning of body text.

registration mark   A printer's guide mark that ensures that color separations used in four-color printing will print in perfect alignment.

resident font   A font built into printer hardware. Most PostScript printers, for example, have 35 resident fonts.

resolution   A measurement—usually expressed in linear dots per inch (dpi), horizontally and vertically—of the sharpness of an image generated by an output device such as a monitor or printer.

In monitors, resolution is expressed as the number of pixels on-screen. A CGA monitor, for example, displays fewer pixels than a VGA monitor; therefore, a CGA image appears more jagged than a VGA image.

Dot-matrix printers produce output with a lower resolution than laser printers.

right justification   The alignment of text along the right margin and the left margin, producing a superficial resemblance to professionally printed text. The results may be poor, however, if the printer is incapable of proportional spacing; in such cases, right justification can be achieved only by inserting unsightly gaps of two or more spaces between words. For readability, most graphics artists advise computer users to leave the right margin ragged.

Roman An upright serif typeface of medium weight (see fig. A.12).

```
ABCDEFGHIJKLMNOPQRSTUVWXYZ
abcdefghijklmnopqrstuvwxyz 1234567890
```

Fig. A.12 The Roman typeface.

roughs The preliminary page layouts created by a designer using pencil sketches to represent page design ideas. Synonymous with *thumbnails*.

rotated type In a graphics or desktop publishing program, text that has been rotated from its normal, horizontal position on the page. The best graphics programs, such as CorelDRAW!, enable you to edit the type even after it has been rotated.

rule A horizontal or vertical line used to separate text and images. Such lines often are used to separate a newsletter nameplate from the body text area.

sans serif A typeface that lacks *serifs*—the fine cross strokes across the ends of the main strokes of a character (see fig. A.13).

Sans serif typefaces, such as Helvetica (and Arial in Windows), are preferred for display type but are harder to read than serif typefaces, such as Times Roman, when used for body type. See *body type*, *display type*, *serif*, and *typeface*.

```
ABCDEFGHIJKLMNOPQRSTUVWXYZ
abcdefghijklmnopqrstuvwxyz 1234567890
```

Fig. A.13 A sans serif font.

scalable font See *outline font*.

scaling The adjustment of the y-axis chosen by the program so that differences in the data are highlighted.

scanned image A bit-mapped, or TIFF, image generated by an optical scanner. See *TIFF*.

scanner A peripheral device that digitizes artwork or photographs and stores the image as a file that can be merged with text.

scatter chart (or scatter diagram)   A chart in which data items are plotted as points on two numeric axes. Scatter diagrams show clustering relationships in numeric data.

screen   A shade of gray added to a box. Screens darker than 10% may interfere with the readability of black text; screens lighter than about 60% may interfere with the readability of reversed (white) text.

screen font   A bit-mapped font designed to mimic the appearance of printer fonts when displayed on medium-resolution monitors.

script   A typeface that resembles handwriting (see fig. A.14).

> *ABCDEFGHIJKLMNOPQRSTUVWXYZ*
> *abcdefghijklmnopqrstuvwxyz 1234567890*

Fig. A.14   The script typeface.

serif   The fine cross strokes across the ends of the main strokes of a character (see fig. A.15).

Serif fonts, such as Times Roman, are easier to read for body type, but most designers prefer to use sans serif typefaces for display type. See *sans serif*.

> ABCDEFGHIJKLMNOPQRSTUVWXYZ
> abcdefghijklmnopqrstuvwxyz 1234567890

Fig. A.15   The serif font.

shadow box   A box with a shadow that creates the illusion that the box is floating above the page. Synonymous with *drop shadow*.

sidebar   A short section of text accompanying a main article, usually set in a separate box.

simple list text chart   A text chart used to enumerate items in no particular order and with each item given equal emphasis.

sink   White space at the top of each page of a document that remains the same on each page.

slide show   A predetermined list of presentation charts and graphs displayed one after the other.

Some programs can produce interesting effects, such as fading out one screen before displaying another and enabling you to choose your path through the charts available for display. See *presentation graphics*.

soft font   See *downloadable font*.

spell checker   A procedure that checks for the correct spelling of words in a document or worksheet. Each word is compared against a file of correctly spelled words.

spot color   Color applied selectively to rules, boxes, headline text, and so on.

spread   Two facing pages.

stacked column chart   A column chart in which two or more data series are displayed, not adjacent to one another, but on top of one another.

standing head   A headline that introduces a regular feature, such as a department, in a newspaper, newsletter, or magazine.

stress   See *stroke consistency*.

strikeout   An attribute, such as type, struck through with a hyphen to mark text.

Strikeout often is used to mark text to be deleted from a coauthored document so that the other author can see changes easily.

stroke   The thickness of the letters of a font. Typeface stroke variations may include bold, narrow, and heavy.

stroke consistency   A design characteristic that refers to the variation in thickness of the marks that make up a letter. Synonymous with *stress*.

stroke width   A design characteristic of type that indicates the width of the marks that form the letter.

subscript   A number or letter printed slightly below the typing line. See *superscript*.

superscript   A number or letter printed slightly above the typing line. See *subscript*.

surface chart   A chart that illustrates the data as a sheet of cellophane stretched over a 3-D line chart. This chart can show interrelationships between large amounts of data that are otherwise difficult to see. The use of color indicates areas that are the same height but does not mark the data series.

Swiss   A sans serif typeface. See *sans serif*.

Symbol   A font provided with Excel and Windows which contains special characters, such as arrows and circled numbers (see fig. A.16). See *dingbats*.

ΑΒΧΔΕΦΓΗΙϑΚΛΜΝΟΠΘΡΣΤΥςΩΞΨΖ
ΑΒΧΔΕΦΓΗΙϑΚΛΜΝΟΠΘΡΣΤΥςΩΞΨΖ 1234567890

Fig. A.16   The Symbol typeface.

template   A file containing the basic formatting commands for a document, chart, or worksheet. A newsletter template, for example, may contain the nameplate, column formatting codes, headers and footers, and so on.

text box   A rectangular area of the Excel worksheet where you can type characters. As you type the text, it wraps within the box.

text chart   A chart designed for display to an audience using a slide or transparency. See *bulleted list chart*, *column chart*, *free-form text chart*, *organization chart*, and *simple list text chart*.

text efficiency   A design characteristic of type that refers to the shape of letters.

text file   A file consisting of nothing but the standard ASCII characters (with no control characters or higher order characters).

thumbnail   A small, hand-drawn or computer-generated sketch of one or more document pages. Some programs can print up to 16 thumbnails on an 8 1/2-by-11-inch page.

tick mark   Small vertical and horizontal marks on the x-axis and y-axis frame of a graph or chart indicating locations of the divisions of time, values, or other categories.

TIFF (Tagged Image File Format) A bit-mapped graphics format for scanned images with resolutions of up to 300 dpi. TIFF simulates gray-scale shading.

Times Roman A serif typeface frequently used for body type applications and occasionally for display type (see fig. A.17). In Excel and Windows, a variation of this typeface is called Times New Roman. See *serif*.

ABCDEFGHIJKLMNOPQRSTUVWXYZ
abcdefghijklmnopqrstuvwxyz 1234567890

Fig. A.17 The Times Roman typeface.

toolbar An area containing picture icons or tools that perform tasks. Excel contains a number of toolbars. The Standard, Formatting, Utility, Chart, and Drawing toolbars contain tools used for desktop publishing and graphics.

tools Icons (symbols) on the toolbar that represent computer functions or tasks.

trim size The final size of a document page after the pages have been physically trimmed to equal size by the printer.

TrueType A new feature of Windows 3.1 which enables fonts to be used on any printer. TrueType fonts are scalable; they can be changed to any height. TrueType fonts also appear on-screen as they will print on the printer.

typeface The distinctive design of a set of type, distinguished from its weight and size.

Typefaces are grouped into two categories: serif and sans serif. Serif typefaces frequently are chosen for body type because they are more legible. Sans serif typefaces are preferred for display type. See *sans serif* and *serif*.

type size The size of a font, measured in points (approximately 1/72 inch) from the top of the tallest ascender to the bottom of the lowest descender. See *pitch*.

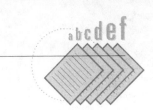

type style The weight (such as Roman or boldface) or posture (such as italic) of a font, distinguished from a font's typeface design and type size. See *attribute*.

VGA (Video Graphics Array) A color bit-mapped graphics display standard, introduced by IBM in 1987 with its PS/2 computers. VGA adapters and analog monitors display as many as 256 continuously variable colors simultaneously with a resolution of 640 pixels horizontally by 480 pixels vertically.

vertical justification Aligning the bottoms of adjacent columns by selectively adding or subtracting small amounts of leading to text or adding extra space between paragraphs, text and headings, and photographs and text.

volume/high-low-close chart A combined column and line chart in which a stock's (or other variable's) volume, high value, low value, and closing price are displayed.

weight The overall lightness or darkness of a typeface design, or the gradations of lightness to darkness within a font family.

A type style can be light or dark. Within a type style, you can see several gradations of weight (extra light, light, semilight, regular, medium, semibold, bold, extra bold, and ultrabold). See *typeface*.

white space The portion of the page not containing text or graphics. A good page design involves the use of white space to balance the areas that receive text and graphics.

widow A formatting flaw in which the last line of a paragraph appears alone at the top of a new column or page.

Most word processing and page layout programs suppress widows and orphans; better programs enable you to turn on and off widow/orphan control and to choose the number of lines. See *orphan*.

Windows See *Microsoft Windows*.

word wrap A feature of word processing programs (and other programs that include text-editing features) that wraps words down to the beginning of the next line if they go beyond the right margin. In Excel, text can be wrapped in a *text box* or within a cell.

workbook In Excel, a series of spreadsheet files that are saved together. A workbook file contains a table of contents which lists all the files. The workbook file facilitates working with related spreadsheets as in company divisions, time periods, or presentations.

WPG   WordPerfect Graphics file format.

wrap-around type   Type contoured so that it surrounds a graphic.

WYSIWYG (what you see is what you get)   A design philosophy in which formatting commands directly affect the text displayed, so that the screen shows the appearance of the printed text.

x-axis   In a business graph, the x-axis is usually the horizontal axis. See *bar graph*, *column graph*, and *y-axis*.

x-height   The height of a font's lowercase letters that do not have ascenders or descenders (such as x, a, and c).

xy chart (or xy graph)   See *scatter chart*.

y-axis   In a business graph, the y-axis is usually the vertical axis. See *bar chart*, *column chart*, and *x-axis*.

z-axis   In a three-dimensional graphics image, the third dimension of depth. See *x-axis* and *y-axis*.

Zapf Chancery   A graceful typeface developed by Herman Zapf (see fig. A.18). Use sparingly because of its poor legibility.

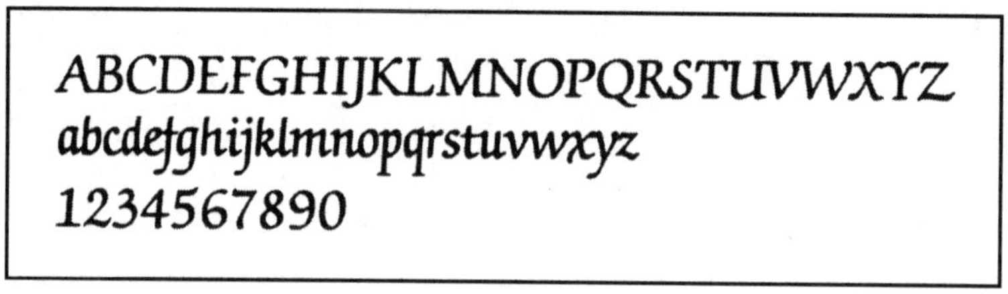

ABCDEFGHIJKLMNOPQRSTUVWXYZ
abcdefghijklmnopqrstuvwxyz
1234567890

Fig. A.18   The Zapf Chancery typeface.

B

Excel
Character Sets

While you are preparing presentations, there may be many cases when you need characters not present on the keyboard. Excel provides you with an extended character set that enables you to produce additional characters. These characters include mathematical, business, and editing symbols as well as foreign currency, foreign letters, and others.

ach font produces a unique set of characters. Although many fonts produce the same characters in different styles, some fonts produce a unique set of characters. The availability of characters depends on your version of Excel, your version of Windows or other operating system, and your printer. Table B.1 lists the characters available with three fonts. The first two sets of characters are from a sans serif font (Arial) and a serif font (Times New Roman). The characters are the same with the exception of the styling. Notice the difference between the A (number 65). The serif font has feet on the bottom, and the sans serif font does not.

The third font is the symbol font. Most of the characters here are different from the other two fonts. The symbol font includes characters for the Greek alphabet and math as well as other symbols.

You can produce a character in two ways. First, you can type the function =CHAR(*n*) in a cell. The number that appears in the parentheses is the number on the left column of the table. Second, you can press Alt while typing the number on the numeric keypad. For numbers greater than 126, include a zero before the number in the left column. Press Alt and type **0131** to get the guilder symbol, for example. You then can change the font by using the Forma**t** Font command.

If you use Windows 3.1, you can see each complete set of characters on-screen by selecting Accessories from the Program Manager and then selecting Character Map (see fig. B.1). You can use this accessory to see what the Alt-*character* combination is (see bottom right side of window). You also can copy characters from the map to the clipboard and then use **E**dit **P**aste when you return to Excel. If you want to draw special borders, look at the line draw and terminal fonts in the character map.

Table B.1   Characters Available with Sans Serif, Serif, and Symbol Fonts

CHARACTERS AVAILABLE					
CHAR()	SANS SERIF*	SERIF*	Description	SYMBOL	Description
33	!	!	Exclamation Point	!	Factorial
34	"	"	Double Quotes	∀	For all
35	#	#	Number sign, pounds	#	Number sign, pounds
36	$	$	Dollars	∃	For some
37	%	%	Percent	%	Percent
38	&	&	Ampersand (and)	&	Ampersand (and)
39	'	'	Single quote, apostrophe	∋	Epsilon, lowercase
40	(	(	Open parenthesis	(	Open parenthesis
41	)	)	Close parenthesis	)	Close parenthesis
42	*	*	Asterisk	*	Asterisk
43	+	+	Plus (addition)	+	Plus (addition)
44	,	,	Comma	,	Comma
45	-	-	Minus (subtraction)	−	Minus (subtraction)
46	.	.	Period	.	Period
47	/	/	Slash	/	Slash

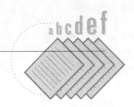

	CHARACTERS AVAILABLE				
CHAR()	SANS SERIF*	SERIF*	Description	SYMBOL	Description
48	0	0	Zero	0	Zero
49	1	1	One	1	One
50	2	2	Two	2	Two
51	3	3	Three	3	Three
52	4	4	Four	4	Four
53	5	5	Five	5	Five
54	6	6	Six	6	Six
55	7	7	Seven	7	Seven
56	8	8	Eight	8	Eight
57	9	9	Nine	9	Nine
58	:	:	Colon	:	Colon
59	;	;	Semicolon	;	Semicolon
60	<	<	Less than	<	Less than
61	=	=	Equal sign	=	Equal sign
62	>	>	Greater than	>	Greater than
63	?	?	Question mark	?	Question mark
64	@	@	At sign	≡	Congruent
65	A	A	A uppercase	A	Alpha uppercase
66	B	B	B uppercase	B	Beta uppercase
67	C	C	C uppercase	X	Chi uppercase
68	D	D	D uppercase	Δ	Delta uppercase (change)
69	E	E	E uppercase	E	Epsilon uppercase
70	F	F	F uppercase	Φ	Phi uppercase
71	G	G	G uppercase	Γ	Gamma uppercase
72	H	H	H uppercase	H	Eta uppercase
73	I	I	I uppercase	I	Iota uppercase
74	J	J	J uppercase	ϑ	Theta uppercase variant
75	K	K	K uppercase	K	Kappa uppercase
76	L	L	L uppercase	Λ	Lambda uppercase
77	M	M	M uppercase	M	Mu uppercase
78	N	N	N uppercase	N	Nu uppercase
79	O	O	O uppercase	O	Omikron uppercase
80	P	P	P uppercase	Π	Pi uppercase
81	Q	Q	Q uppercase	Θ	Theta uppercase
82	R	R	R uppercase	P	Rho uppercase
83	S	S	S uppercase	Σ	Sigma uppercase
84	T	T	T uppercase	T	Tau uppercase
85	U	U	U uppercase	Y	Ypsilon uppercase
86	V	V	V uppercase	ς	Sigma uppercase
87	W	W	W uppercase	Ω	Omega uppercase
88	X	X	X uppercase	Ξ	Xi uppercase
89	Y	Y	Y uppercase	Ψ	Psi uppercase
90	Z	Z	Z uppercase	Z	Zeta uppercase
91	[	[	Open bracket	[	Open bracket
92	\	\	Backslash	∴	Therefore
93	]	]	Close bracket	]	Close bracket
94	^	^	Caret (to power of)	⊥	Perpendicular
95	_	_	Underscore	_	Underscore
96	`	`	Grave accent		Overscore
97	a	a	a lowercase	γ	Gamma lowercase
98	b	b	b lowercase	η	Eta lowercase
99	c	c	c lowercase	ι	Iota lowercase
100	d	d	d lowercase	φ	Phi lowercase
101	e	e	e lowercase	κ	Kappa lowercase
102	f	f	f lowercase	λ	Lambda lowercase (wavelength)
103	g	g	g lowercase	μ	Mu lowercase (micro)
104	h	h	h lowercase	ν	Nu lowercase
105	i	i	i lowercase	o	Omicron lowercase
106	j	j	j lowercase	π	Pi lowercase (3.1419...)
107	k	k	k lowercase	θ	Theta lowercase
108	l	l	l lowercase	ρ	Rho lowercase

continues

CHARACTERS AVAILABLE					
CHAR()	SANS SERIF*	SERIF*	Description	SYMBOL	Description
109	m	m	m lowercase	σ	Sigma lowercase
110	n	n	n lowercase	τ	Tau lowercase
111	o	o	o lowercase	υ	Upsilon lowercase
112	p	p	p lowercase	ϖ	Pi lowercase variant
113	q	q	q lowercase	ω	Omega lowercase
114	r	r	r lowercase	ξ	Xi lowercase
115	s	s	s lowercase	ψ	Psi lowercase
116	t	t	t lowercase	ζ	Zeta lowercase
117	u	u	u lowercase	[	Open bracket
118	v	v	v lowercase	∴	Therefore
119	w	w	w lowercase	]	Close bracket
120	x	x	x lowercase	⊥	Perpendicular
121	y	y	y lowercase	_	Underscore
122	z	z	z lowercase		Overscore
123	{	{	Open brace	{	Open brace
124	|	|	Vertical Bar	|	Vertical Bar
125	}	}	Close Brace	}	Close Brace
126	~	~	Tilde (not)	~	Tilde (not)
127	□	□			
128	□	□			
129	□	□			
130	,	,	Comma		
131	ƒ	ƒ	Guilder		
132	„	„	Lower double quote close		
133	…	…	Ellipses (and so on)		
134	†	†	Single dagger, footnote		
135	‡	‡	Double dagger, footnote		
136	^	^	Circumflex accent		
137	‰	‰	Per thousand, Per mill		
138	Š	Š	Czech sh uppercase		
139	‹	‹	Left angle parenthesis		
140	Œ	Œ	OE ligature uppercase		
141	□	□			
142	□	□			
143	□	□			
144	□	□			
145	'	'	Open single quote		
146	'	'	Close single quote		
147	"	"	Open double quote		
148	"	"	Close double quote		
149	•	•	Bullet		
150	–	–	En mark		
151	—	—	Em mark		
152	~	~	Tilde		
153	TM	TM	Trademark symbol		
154	š	š	Czech sh lowercase		
155	›	›	Right angle parenthesis		
156	œ	œ	oe ligature lowercase		
157	□	□			
158	□	□			
159	Ÿ	Ÿ	Y umlaut uppercase		
160					
161	¡	¡	Inverted exclamation point	ϒ	Euler's constant
162	¢	¢	Cent sign	′	Apostrophe
163	£	£	British pound sterling	≤	Less than or equal
164	¤	¤	International currency sign	/	Slash
165	¥	¥	Yen sign	∞	Infinity
166	¦	¦	Broken vertical line	ƒ	Function of
167	§	§	Section symbol	♣	Clubs
168	¨	¨	Umlaut accent	♦	Diamonds
169	©	©	Copyright symbol	♥	Hearts
170	ª	ª	Superscript a (footnote)	♠	Spades

CHARACTERS AVAILABLE

CHAR()	SANS SERIF*	SERIF*	Description	SYMBOL	Description
171	«	«	Left angle quotes	↔	Left,right symbol (if and only if)
172	¬	¬	End of line symbol, logical NOT	←	Left arrow
173	-	-	Hyphenation	↑	Up arrow
174	®	®	Registered trademark symbol	→	Right arrow (if then)
175	‾	‾	Overline character	↓	Down arrow
176	°	°	Degree symbol	°	Degree symbol
177	±	±	Plus or minus sign	±	Plus or minus
178	²	²	Two superscript	"	Open double quotes
179	³	³	Three superscript	≥	Greater than or equal to
180	´	´	Acute Accent	×	Times (multiplication), Crossed with (hybrid)
181	µ	µ	Greek mu	∝	Is proportional to
182	¶	¶	Paragraph symbol	∂	Variation of
183	·	·	Center dot	•	Bullet
184	¸	¸	Cedilla accent	÷	Divide by
185	¹	¹	One superscript	≠	Not equal to
186	º	º	Ring accent	≡	Identical
187	»	»	Right angle quotes	≈	Approximately equal
188	¼	¼	One quarter	…	Ellipses (And so on)
189	½	½	One half	|	Long vertical line
190	¾	¾	Three quarters	—	Long horizontal line
191	¿	¿	Inverted question mark	↵	Enter symbol
192	À	À	A grave uppercase	ℵ	Aleph (Hebrew)
193	Á	Á	A acute uppercase	ℑ	Magnetomotive force
194	Â	Â	A circumflex uppercase	ℜ	German R, reluctance
195	Ã	Ã	A tilde uppercase	℘	Per
196	Ä	Ä	A umlaut uppercase	⊗	X in circle, tensor product
197	Å	Å	A ring uppercase	⊕	Cross in circle, sum of vectors, Earth
198	Æ	Æ	AE dipthong uppercase	∅	Empty set
199	Ç	Ç	C Cedilla uppercase	∩	Intersection
200	È	È	E grave uppercase	∪	Union
201	É	É	E acute uppercase	⊃	Implies
202	Ê	Ê	E circulflex uppercase	⊇	
203	Ë	Ë	E umlaut uppercase	⊄	Not proper subset
204	Ì	Ì	I grave uppercase	⊂	Proper subset
205	Í	Í	I acute uppercase	⊆	Subset of
206	Î	Î	I circulflex uppercase	∈	Element of
207	Ï	Ï	I umlaut uppercase	∉	Not element of
208	Ð	Ð	Icelandic eth uppercase	∠	Angle
209	Ñ	Ñ	N tilde uppercase	∇	Nabla operator
210	Ò	Ò	O grave uppercase	®	Registered
211	Ó	Ó	O acute uppercase	©	Copyright
212	Ô	Ô	O circulflex uppercase	™	Trademark
213	Õ	Õ	O tilde uppercase	∏	Product
214	Ö	Ö	O umlaut uppercase	√	Square root
215	×	×	Times (multiply)	·	Small bullet
216	Ø	Ø	O slash uppercase	¬	End of line, logical NOT
217	Ù	Ù	U grave uppercase	∧	And (conjunction)
218	Ú	Ú	U acute uppercase	∨	Or (disjunction)
219	Û	Û	U circulflex uppercase	⇔	Open left-right arrow
220	Ü	Ü	U umlaut uppercase	⇐	Open left arrow
221	Ý	Ý	Y acute uppercase	⇑	Open up arrow
222	Þ	Þ	Icelandic thorn uppercase	⇒	Open right arrow
223	ß	ß	German sharp lowercase	⇓	Open down arrow
224	à	à	a grave lowercase	◊	Open diamond
225	á	á	a acute lowercase	⟨	Left angle parenthesis
226	â	â	a circumflex lowercase	®	Registered
227	ã	ã	a tilde lowercase	©	Copyright
228	ä	ä	a umlaut lowercase	™	Trademark

continues

CHAR()	SANS SERIF*	SERIF*	Description	SYMBOL	Description
			CHARACTERS AVAILABLE		
229	å	å	a ring lowercase	Σ	Sum
230	æ	æ	ae dipthong lowercase	(	Large parenthesis left upper
231	ç	ç	cedilla lowercase		Large parenthesis left mid
232	è	è	e grave lowercase	(	Large parenthesis left lower
233	é	é	e acute lowercase	[	Large bracket left upper
234	ê	ê	e circumflex lowercase		Large bracket left mid
235	ë	ë	e umlaut lowercase	[	Large bracket left lower
236	ì	ì	i grave lowercase	{	Large brace left upper
237	í	í	i acute lowercase	{	Large brace left mid
238	î	î	i circumflex lowercase	{	Large brace left lower
239	ï	ï	i umlaut lowercase			Vertical line
240	ð	ð	"Th" (pronunciation)		
241	ñ	ñ	n tilde (Spanish) lowercase	)	Right angle parenthesis
242	ò	ò	o grave lowercase	∫	Integral
243	ó	ó	o acute lowercase	(	Large integral upper
244	ô	ô	o circumflex lowercase		Large integral mid
245	õ	õ	o tilde lowercase	)	Large integral lower
246	ö	ö	o umlaut lowercase	)	Large parenthesis right upper
247	÷	÷	divide		Large parenthesis right mid
248	ø	ø	o slash lowercase	)	Large parenthesis right lower
249	ù	ù	u grave lowercase	]	Large bracket right upper
250	ú	ú	u acute lowercase		Large bracket right mid
251	û	û	u circumflex lowercase	]	Large bracket right lower
252	ü	ü	u umlaut lowercase	}	Large brace right upper
253	ý	ý	y acute lowercase	}	Large brace right mid
254	þ	þ	Icelandic thorn lowercase	}	Large brace right lower
255	ÿ	ÿ	y umlaut lowercase		

Each code may have different descriptions shown depending on your application

* Sans Serif font shown is Arial (ANSI codes)

* Serif font shown is Times New Roman (ANSI codes)

Fig. B.1   A character map showing the Symbol font characters.

Excel Toolbars

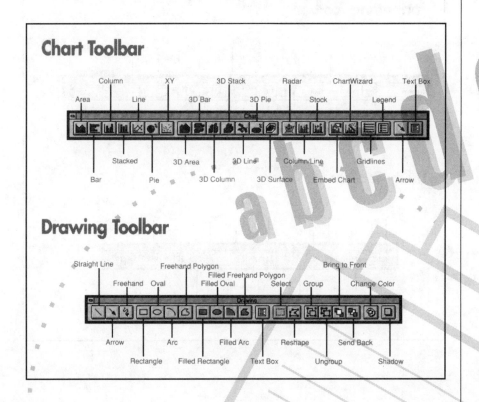

Chart Toolbar

Area, Column, Line, XY, 3D Bar, 3D Stack, 3D Pie, Radar, Stock, ChartWizard, Legend, Text Box, Chart, Bar, Stacked, Pie, 3D Area, 3D Column, 3D Line, 3D Surface, Column/Line, Embed Chart, Gridlines, Arrow

Drawing Toolbar

Straight Line, Freehand, Oval, Freehand Polygon, Filled Oval, Filled Freehand Polygon, Select, Group, Bring to Front, Change Color, Drawing, Arrow, Rectangle, Arc, Filled Rectangle, Filled Arc, Text Box, Reshape, Ungroup, Send Back, Shadow

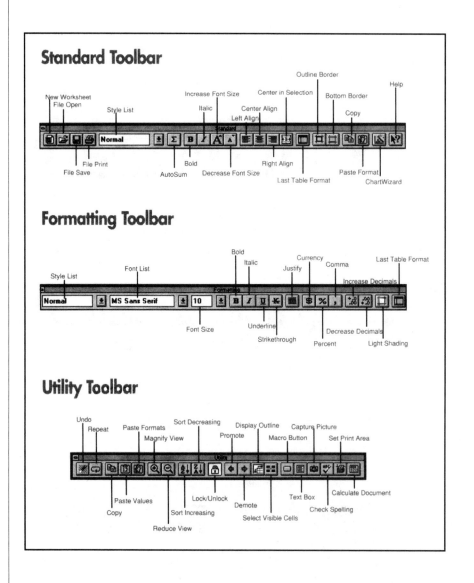

Standard Toolbar

Formatting Toolbar

Utility Toolbar

Excel Shortcut Menus

The Right Mouse Button

Clicking on the following items with the right mouse button displays the shortcut menus.

Cell

Cut	Ctrl+X
Copy	Ctrl+C
Paste	Ctrl+V
Clear...	Del
Delete...	
Insert...	
Number...	
Alignment...	
Font...	
Border...	
Patterns...	

Row

Cut	Ctrl+X
Copy	Ctrl+C
Paste	Ctrl+V
Clear...	Del
Delete	
Insert	
Number...	
Alignment...	
Font...	
Border...	
Patterns...	
Row Height...	

Column

Cut	Ctrl+X
Copy	Ctrl+C
Paste	Ctrl+V
Clear...	Del
Delete	
Insert	
Number...	
Alignment...	
Font...	
Border...	
Patterns...	
Column Width...	

Toolbar

✓Standard
Formatting
Utility
Chart
Drawing
Microsoft Excel 3.0
Macro
Toolbars..
Customize...

Object

Cut	Ctrl+X
Copy	Ctrl+C
Paste	Ctrl+V
Clear	Del
Edit Object	
Patterns...	
Bring to Front	
Send to Back	
Group	
Object Properties...	
Assign Macro to Object...	

**Chart
Data Series**

Clear...	Del
Gallery...	
Attach Text...	
Edit Series...	
Patterns...	
Main Chart...	
Overlay...	
3-D View...	

Chart Title

Clear	Del
Patterns...	
Font...	
Text...	

Chart Legend

Clear	Del
Patterns...	
Font...	
Legend...	

Chart Axis

Clear	Del
Attach Text...	
Axes...	
Gridlines...	
Patterns...	
Font...	
Scale...	
Text...	

Index

italics
   for emphasis, 202-203
   type style for
      presentations, 288
   typefaces in business
      forms, 264

J-K

Justify Align tool, 80
justifying text, 50-51

key points, using graphics
   for presentations, 294
keyboard shortcut keys,
   formatting text, 65-66
keyboards in worksheets,
   16-18
keys
   alphanumeric, 18-19
   editing, 63
   special character, 18-19
   see also keyboard shortcut
      keys

L

label headings, using
   different levels, 190-192
labels, consistency on charts,
   140
Landscape orientation, 55,
   89-90
layout
   of pages, 52-55

of promotional pieces
   guidelines, 332
layouts, 172
   designing worksheets,
      177-179
   duplicating with template
      files, 209-212
   for presentations, row-
      and-column structure,
      303-304
   for worksheets, 182-205
   of pages for business
      forms, 256
   promotional pieces,
      332-333
   white space
      in worksheets, 179-180
      with columns and rows,
         191-195
   using
      columns and rows, 190
      different levels of label
         headings, 190-192
leading, standard, 48-50
Left Align tool, 77, 81
left-justified text, 50
legends
   adding to charts, 155
   of charts, 127
letter templates
   creating, 226-228
   entering text, 234-235
   including company logo,
      228-234
letters, creating, 27, 220-246
Light Shading tool, 80
line charts, 115
Line tool, 81, 160

moire distortion, 152

monospaced fonts, 39-40

mouse

  right button, clicking to display shortcut menus, 397

  using in worksheets, 16-18

moving

  data, 73

  slides, 317-318

  while previewing, around and between pages 97-98

MS WordArt applet, 354

multicolumn layout, 52-54

multiple ranges, performing enhancements, 16-18

multiple shapes, selecting, 162

multiple-page reports, using workbooks, 242-243

N

named styles, using in spreadsheet publishing, 207-212

negative leading, 49

New Worksheet tool, 77

newsletters

  creating, 34

  designing guidelines, 325-326

  emphasizing important information, 328-331

  guidelines for developing layout, 332-338

headers or footers, 332

  one or multiple worksheets, 331-332

  organizing message, 326-328

notes, creating and printing, 102

numbered lists, creating, 193

numbers, formatting, 66

O

Object Linking and Embedding (OLE), 26, 346, 351-355

objects

  copying

    between Excel and other applications, 345-351

  embedded, 26

  embedding Microsoft Word for Windows in Excel worksheets, 352-353

  linked, 26

office correspondence, creating, 220-246

OLE, *see* Object Linking and Embedding

on-screen presentations

  modifying display, 304-307

one-fold brochure, 339-340

one-page flier 342

Open File tool, 77

Que—The Leader in Spreadsheet Information!

Teach Yourself
with QuickStarts from Que!

The ideal tutorials for beginners, Que's QuickStart Books use graphic illustrations and step-by-step instructions to get you up and running fast. Packed with examples, QuickStarts are the perfect beginner's guides to your favorite software applications.

MS-DOS 5 QuickStart

Que Development Group

This is the easy-to-use graphic approach to learning MS-DOS 5. The combination of step-by-step instruction, examples, and graphics make this book ideal for all DOS beginners.

DOS 5

$19.95 USA
0-88022-681-1, 420 pp., 7³/₈ x 9¹/₄

Windows 3.1 QuickStart

Ron Person & Karen Rose

This graphics-based text teaches Windows beginners how to use the feature-packed Windows environment. Emphasizes such software applications as Excel, Word, and PageMaker, and shows how to master Windows' mouse, menus, and screen elements.

Through Version 3.1

$21.95 USA
0-88022-730-3, 500 pp., 7³/₈ x 9¹/₄

1-2-3 for DOS Release 2.3 QuickStart

Release 2.3

$19.95
0-88022-716-8, 500 pp., 7³/₈ x 9¹/₄

1-2-3 for DOS Release 3.1+ QuickStart, Special Edition

Releases 3, 3.1, & 3.1+

$29.95 USA
0-88022-843-1, 975 pp., 7³/₈ x 9¹/₄

1-2-3 for Windows QuickStart

1-2-3 for Windows

$19.95 USA
0-88022-723-0, 500 pp., 7³/₈ x 9¹/₄

dBASE IV 1.1 QuickStart

Through Version 11

$19.95 USA
0-88022-614-5, 400 pp., 7³/₈ x 9¹/₄

Excel 3 for Windows QuickStart

Version 3 for Windows

$19.95 USA
0-88022-762-1, 500 pp., 7³/₈ x 9¹/₄

MS-DOS QuickStart, 2nd Edition

Version 3.X & 4.X

$19.95 USA
0-88022-611-0, 420 pp., 7³/₈ x 9¹/₄

Q&A 4 QuickStart

Versions 3 & 4

$19.95 USA
0-88022-653-6, 450 pp., 7³/₈ x 9¹/₄

Quattro Pro 3 QuickStart

Through Version 3.0

$19.95 USA
0-88022-693-5, 450 pp., 7³/₈ x 9¹/₄

Windows 3 QuickStart

Version 3

$19.95 USA
0-88022-610-2, 440 pp., 7³/₈ x 9¹/₄

WordPerfect 5.1 QuickStart

WordPerfect 5.1

$19.95 USA
0-88022-558-0, 427 pp., 7³/₈ x 9¹/₄

WordPerfect for Windows QuickStart

WordPerfect 5.1 for Windows

$19.95 USA
0-88022-712-5, 400 pp., 7³/₈ x 9¹/₄

To Order, Call:
(800) 428-5331
OR
(317) 573-2500

Personal computing is easy when you're using Que!

Using 1-2-3 for DOS Release 2.3, Special Edition
$29.95 USA
0-88022-727-8, 584 pp., 7³/₈ x 9¹/₄

Using 1-2-3 for DOS Release 3.1+, Special Edition
$29.95 USA
0-88022-843-1, 584 pp., 7³/₈ x 9¹/₄

Using 1-2-3 for Windows
$29.95 USA
0-88022-724-9, 584 pp., 7³/₈ x 9¹/₄

Using 1-2-3/G
$29.95 USA
0-88022-549-7, 584 pp., 7³/₈ x 9¹/₄

Using AlphaFOUR
$24.95 USA
0-88022-890-3, 500 pp., 7³/₈ x 9¹/₄

Using AmiPro
$24.95 USA
0-88022-738-9, 584 pp., 7³/₈ x 9¹/₄

Using Assembly Language, 3rd Edition
$29.95 USA
0-88022-884-9, 900 pp., 7³/₈ x 9¹/₄

Using BASIC
$24.95 USA
0-88022-537-8, 584 pp., 7³/₈ x 9¹/₄

Using Borland C++, 2nd Edition
$29.95 USA
0-88022-901-2, 1,300 pp., 7³/₈ x 9¹/₄

Using C
$29.95 USA
0-88022-571-8, 950 pp., 7³/₈ x 9¹/₄

Using Clipper, 3rd Edition
$29.95 USA
0-88022-885-7, 750 pp., 7³/₈ x 9¹/₄

Using DacEasy, 2nd Edition
$24.95 USA
0-88022-510-6, 584 pp., 7³/₈ x 9¹/₄

Using DataEase
$24.95 USA
0-88022-465-7, 584 pp., 7³/₈ x 9¹/₄

Using dBASE IV
$24.95 USA
0-88022-551-3, 584 pp., 7³/₈ x 9¹/₄

Using Excel 3 for Windows, Special Edition
$24.95 USA
0-88022-685-4, 584 pp., 7³/₈ x 9¹/₄

Using FoxPro 2
$24.95 USA
0-88022-703-6, 584 pp., 7³/₈ x 9¹/₄

Using Freelance Plus
$24.95 USA
0-88022-528-9, 584 pp., 7³/₈ x 9¹/₄

Using GeoWorks Ensemble
$24.95 USA
0-88022-748-6, 584 pp., 7³/₈ x 9¹/₄

Using Harvard Graphics 3
$24.95 USA
0-88022-735-4, 584 pp., 7³/₈ x 9¹/₄

Using Harvard Graphics for Windows
$24.95 USA
0-88022-755-9, 700 pp., 7³/₈ x 9¹/₄

Using LetterPoerfect
$24.95 USA
0-88022-667-6, 584 pp., 7³/₈ x 9¹/₄

Using Microsoft C
$24.95 USA
0-88022-809-1, 584 pp., 7³/₈ x 9¹/₄

Using Microsoft Money
$19.95 USA
0-88022-914-4, 400 pp., 7³/₈ x 9¹/₄

Using Microsoft Publisher
$22.95 USA
0-88022-915-2, 450 pp., 7³/₈ x 9¹/₄

Using Microsoft Windows 3, 2nd Edition
$24.95 USA
0-88022-509-2, 584 pp., 7³/₈ x 9¹/₄

Using Microsoft Word 5.5: IBM Version, 2nd Edition
$24.95 USA
0-88022-642-0, 584 pp., 7³/₈ x 9¹/₄

Using Microsoft Works for Windows, Special Edition
$24.95 USA
0-88022-757-5, 584 pp., 7³/₈ x 9¹/₄

Using Microsoft Works: IBM Version
$24.95 USA
0-88022-467-3, 584 pp., 7³/₈ x 9¹/₄

Using MoneyCounts
$24.95 USA
0-88022-696-X, 584 pp., 7³/₈ x 9¹/₄

Using MS-DOS 5
$24.95 USA
0-88022-668-4, 584 pp., 7³/₈ x 9¹/₄

Using Norton Utilities 6
$24.95 USA
0-88022-861-X, 584 pp., 7³/₈ x 9¹/₄

Using Novell NetWare, 2nd Edition
$24.95 USA
0-88022-756-7, 584 pp., 7³/₈ x 9¹/₄

Using ORACLE
$24.95 USA
0-88022-506-8, 584 pp., 7³/₈ x 9¹/₄

Using OS/2 2.0
$24.95 USA
0-88022-863-6, 584 pp., 7³/₈ x 9¹/₄

Using Pacioli 2000
$24.95 USA
0-88022-780-X, 584 pp., 7³/₈ x 9¹/₄

Using PageMaker 4 for Windows
$24.95 USA
0-88022-607-2, 584 pp., 7³/₈ x 9¹/₄

Using Paradox 4, Special Edition
$29.95 USA
0-88022-822-9, 900 pp., 7³/₈ x 9¹/₄

Using Paradox for Windows, Special Edition
$29.95 USA
0-88022-823-7, 750 pp., 7³/₈ x 9¹/₄

Using PC DOS, 3rd Edition
$24.95 USA
0-88022-409-3, 584 pp., 7³/₈ x 9¹/₄

Using PC Tools 7
$24.95 USA
0-88022-733-8, 584 pp., 7³/₈ x 9¹/₄

Using PC-File
$24.95 USA
0-88022-695-1, 584 pp., 7³/₈ x 9¹/₄

Using PC-Write
$24.95 USA
0-88022-654-4, 584 pp., 7³/₈ x 9¹/₄

Using PFS: First Choice
$24.95 USA
0-88022-454-1, 584 pp., 7³/₈ x 9¹/₄

Using PFS: First Publisher, 2nd Edition
$24.95 USA
0-88022-591-2, 584 pp., 7³/₈ x 9¹/₄

Using PFS: WindowWorks
$24.95 USA
0-88022-751-6, 584 pp., 7³/₈ x 9¹/₄

Using PowerPoint
$24.95 USA
0-88022-698-6, 584 pp., 7³/₈ x 9¹/₄

Using Prodigy
$24.95 USA
0-88022-658-7, 584 pp., 7³/₈ x 9¹/₄

Using Professional Write
$24.95 USA
0-88022-490-8, 584 pp., 7³/₈ x 9¹/₄

Using Professional Write Plus for Windows
$24.95 USA
0-88022-754-0, 584 pp., 7³/₈ x 9¹/₄

Using Publish It!
$24.95 USA
0-88022-660-9, 584 pp., 7³/₈ x 9¹/₄

Using Q&A 4
$24.95 USA
0-88022-643-9, 584 pp., 7³/₈ x 9¹/₄

Using QBasic
$24.95 USA
0-88022-713-3, 584 pp., 7³/₈ x 9¹/₄

Using Quattro Pro 3, Special Edition
$24.95 USA
0-88022-721-4, 584 pp., 7³/₈ x 9¹/₄

Using Quattro Pro for Windows, Special Edition
$27.95 USA
0-88022-889-X, 900 pp., 7³/₈ x 9¹/₄

Using Quick BASIC 4
$24.95 USA
0-88022-378-2, 713 pp., 7³/₈ x 9¹/₄

Using QuickC for Windows
$29.95 USA
0-88022-810-5, 584 pp., 7³/₈ x 9¹/₄

Using Quicken 5
$19.95 USA
0-88022-888-1, 550 pp., 7³/₈ x 9¹/₄

Using Quicken for Windows
$19.95 USA
0-88022-907-1, 550 pp., 7³/₈ x 9¹/₄

Using R:BASE
$24.95 USA
0-88022-603-X, 584 pp., 7³/₈ x 9¹/₄

Using Smart
$24.95 USA
0-88022-229-8, 584 pp., 7³/₈ x 9¹/₄

Using SuperCalc5, 2nd Edition
$24.95 USA
0-88022-404-5, 584 pp., 7³/₈ x 9¹/₄

Using TimeLine
$24.95 USA
0-88022-602-1, 584 pp., 7³/₈ x 9¹/₄

Using Turbo Pascal 6, 2nd Edition
$29.95 USA
0-88022-700-1, 800 pp., 7³/₈ x 9¹/₄

Using Turbo Pascal for Windows
$29.95 USA
0-88022-806-7, 584 pp., 7³/₈ x 9¹/₄

Using Turbo Tax: 1992 Edition Tax Advice & Planning
$24.95 USA
0-88022-839-3, 584 pp., 7³/₈ x 9¹/₄

Using UNIX
$29.95 USA
0-88022-519-X, 584 pp., 7³/₈ x 9¹/₄

Using Visual Basic
$29.95 USA
0-88022-763-X, 584 pp., 7³/₈ x 9¹/₄

Using Windows 3.1
$27.95 USA
0-88022-731-1, 584 pp., 7³/₈ x 9¹/₄

Using Word for Windows 2, Special Edition
$27.95 USA
0-88022-832-6, 584 pp., 7³/₈ x 9¹/₄

Using WordPerfect 5
$27.95 USA
0-88022-351-0, 584 pp., 7³/₈ x 9¹/₄

Using WordPerfect 5.1, Special Edition
$27.95 USA
0-88022-554-8, 584 pp., 7³/₈ x 9¹/₄

Using WordStar 7
$19.95 USA
0-88022-909-8, 550 pp., 7³/₈ x 9¹/₄

Using Your Hard Disk
$29.95 USA
0-88022-583-1, 584 pp., 7³/₈ x 9¹/₄

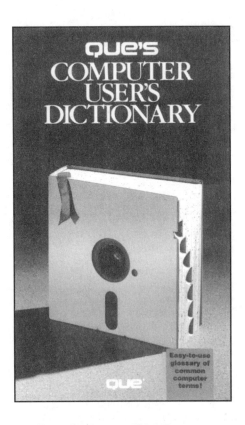